# Gabriel Orozco

DIRECTORIO

CAMBIAR
TEXTURA
BARANDAL

MONEDERO ABIERTO
AL FONDO

PICANDO
ALGO

RELOJES

# Gabriel Orozco

## Ann Temkin

**WITH ESSAYS BY**
**Ann Temkin**
**Briony Fer**
**Benjamin H. D. Buchloh**
**Paulina Pobocha**
**Anne Byrd**

**Tate Publishing**

First published in the United Kingdom 2011
  by order of the Tate Trustees
by Tate Publishing, a division of Tate Enterprises Ltd,
Millbank, London SW1P 4RG
www.tate.org.uk/publishing

on the occasion of the exhibition *Gabriel Orozco*

The Museum of Modern Art, New York
13 December 2009–1 March 2010

Kunstmuseum Basel
18 April–10 August 2010

Musée national d'art moderne, Centre Georges
Pompidou, Paris
15 September 2010–3 January 2011

Tate Modern, London
19 January–2 May 2011

Major support for the exhibition is provided by
the National Council for Culture and the Arts
(CONACULTA), and Fundación Televisa, Mexico.

A catalogue record for this book is available from the
British Library

ISBN 978-1-85437-921-4

FRONT COVER: Notebook 6 (July 21, 1994–November 5,
1994), p. 184. Cut-and-pasted printed paper (original
photographic images by Robb Kendrick and
Alberto Garcia) glued into notebook, 9 15/16 × 19"
(25.3 × 48.3 cm). Collection of the artist

BACK COVER: *La DS*. 1993. Modified Citroën DS,
55 3/16" × 15' 9 15/16" × 45 5/16" (140.1 × 482.5 × 115.1 cm).
Fonds national d'art contemporain (Cnap), Ministère
de la Culture et de la Communication, Paris, Fnac
94003

FRONT ENDPAPERS: Notebook 2 (July 17, 1992–
March 23, 1993), pp. 145–46. Ballpoint pen and cut-and-
taped printed paper on notebook pages, 10 3/4 × 8 1/16"
(27.3 × 20.5 cm). Collection of the artist

OPPOSITE HALF-TITLE PAGE: Notebook 2 (July 17, 1992–
March 23, 1993), p. 56. Ballpoint pen, graphite, and
sticker on notebook page, 10 3/4 × 8 1/16" (27.3 × 20.5 cm).
Collection of the artist

FRONTISPIECE: Notebook 2 (July 17, 1992–March 23,
1993), p. 95. Ballpoint pen, graphite, and photographs
on notebook page, 10 3/4 × 8 1/16" (27.3 × 20.5 cm).
Collection of the artist

OPPOSITE P. 256: Notebook 3 (March 1–July 24, 1993),
p. 43. Cut-and-taped printed paper and graphite on
notebook page, 10 3/4 × 8 1/16" (27.3 × 20.5 cm). Collection
of the artist

BACK ENDPAPERS: LEFT Notebook 2 (July 17, 1992–
March 23, 1993), p. 30. Cut-and-taped printed paper and
leaves on notebook page, 10 3/4 × 8 1/16" (27.3 × 20.5 cm).
Collection of the artist; RIGHT p. 29. Ballpoint pen, cut-
and-taped printed paper, and board on notebook page,
10 3/4 × 8 1/16" (27.3 × 20.5 cm). Collection of the artist

Measurements of artworks are given in inches, height
before width before depth, followed by centimetres in
parentheses.

Produced by the Department of Publications
  The Museum of Modern Art, New York
Edited by Libby Hruska
Designed by Pure+Applied (Paul Carlos and
  Urshula Barbour) with Gabriel Orozco
Production by Christina Grillo
This book is typeset in Swift, designed by Gerard Unger
Printed and bound by CS Graphics, Singapore

# Contents

8    Foreword

9    Acknowledgments

10    **Open Studio**
Ann Temkin

22    **Constellations in Dust: Notes on the Notebooks**
Briony Fer

34    **Sculpture between Nation-State and Global Commodity Production**
Benjamin H. D. Buchloh

**Chronology**
Paulina Pobocha and Anne Byrd

| | | |
|---|---|---|
| 44 | **1981–1991** | Early Years |
| 60 | **1992** | Migrations |
| 72 | **1993** | First Was the Spitting |
| 90 | **1994** | Portable Puddle |
| 104 | **1995** | Bubble Maker |
| 112 | **1996** | Player for an Empty Club |
| 122 | **1997** | Emptying the Mind |
| 134 | **1998** | Free Market Is Anti-Democratic |
| 146 | **1999** | Photogravity |
| 156 | **2000** | The Prodigal Sun |
| 162 | **2001** | Fear Not |
| 170 | **2002** | Down to Earth |
| 180 | **2003** | Everyday Altered |
| 192 | **2004** | Prototypes |
| 198 | **2005** | Planting Seeds |
| 210 | **2006** | The Whale and the House |
| 222 | **2007** | Imprints |
| 230 | **2008** | The Obituary Collector |
| 236 | **2009** | Reconstructing Cacti |

242    Endnotes

244    List of Illustrations

250    Selected Exhibition History

253    Selected Bibliography

The National Council for Culture and the Arts (CONACULTA) and Fundación Televisa are proud to support this mid-career retrospective of Gabriel Orozco.

Gabriel Orozco is considered a leading conceptual and installation artist of his generation. His exploration of the creative associations among everyday objects allows for an unusual interaction between the artwork and the audience. A master of diverse mediums and subject matters, he has created a substantial body of work that, at each stage of his career, comprises multiple contexts and readings.

This publication, as well as the exhibition it accompanies, presents a careful selection of his most outstanding works from the past two decades, including drawings, sets of small objects, photographs, and paintings, as well as many of his large-scale installations, many of them seen in London for the first time.

The National Council for Culture and the Arts and Fundacion Televisa are delighted to join Tate Modern in bringing this collection of works together in one of the most exceptional retrospectives ever dedicated to a contemporary Mexican artist. This shared admiration presents an unique opportunity to share the work of one of Mexico's most outstanding contemporary artists with the world.

Emilio Azcárraga      Consuelo Sáizar
C.E.O      President
Televisa      National Council for Culture and the Arts

# Foreword

SINCE THE EARLY 1990S, when Gabriel Orozco began exhibiting widely, he has developed a career of continuing innovation and revelation, creating installations, sculptures, paintings, drawings, and photographs unique in formal power and intellectual rigor. His body of work is variously cerebral and spontaneous, convivial and hushed, the result of painstaking planning and fortuitous accident. From the now iconic *Yogurt Caps* (1994) to the tempera and gold leaf *Samurai Tree* paintings, the heterogeneous group of objects that constitutes Orozco's oeuvre resists categorization and yet is thoroughly cohesive. A spirit of constant invention makes his production one of the most intriguing and original of his generation, the final generation to come of age in the twentieth century. Tate Modern is honoured to present this exhibition devoted to two decades of his work.

Orozco's practice has always been informed by his surroundings. Central to his working method is a penchant for travel that has allowed him to make and exhibit in an extraordinary number and variety of places. In keeping with this approach, Orozco has conceived this exhibition as a unique collaboration with the curator at each venue on the tour. Jessica Morgan, Curator of Contemporary Art, has been the organiser of the London presentation, working closely with Assistant Curator Ben Borthwick to develop and shape the presentation at Tate Modern. We join The Museum of Modern Art, Kunstmuseum Basel, and Musée national d'art moderne, Centre Georges Pompidou, in presenting an exhibition that will transform from one venue to the next, responding to the distinctive architectures of our four institutions while reflecting the context of each city as only Orozco's work can.

During the course of the twenty years surveyed by this exhibition, our institutions have each strongly supported the work of Orozco. Included in the opening exhibition at Tate Modern in 2000, Orozco was also featured prominently in the exhibition *Common Wealth* (2003), and his work is represented in the Tate Collection by the seminal pieces *Until You Find Another Yellow Schwalbe* (1995) and *Carambole with Pendulum* (1996), as well as *Polvo Impreso* (2002). Orozco also has strong ties to London itself, where he realised such significant projects as *Empty Club* (1996) and has held solo exhibitions at the Institute of Contemporary Arts (1996) and the Serpentine Gallery (2004). The Museum of Modern Art, Kunstmuseum Basel, and Musée national d'art moderne, Centre Georges Pompidou, have similarly championed this artist's efforts. This exhibition provides us with the opportunity to build upon our individual histories with this artist in order to present his work, many pieces for the first time, to the broad range of visitors to our museums.

I gratefully acknowledge the support of the lenders to the exhibition, both public institutions and private collectors in Mexico, Europe, and the United States. Their eager willingness to participate and in many cases to lend fragile works for an unusually long period of time is a testament to the high regard in which they hold this artist. This travelling exhibition would not be possible without generous financial sponsorship. Major support for the exhibition is provided by the National Council for Culture and the Arts (CONACULTA), and Fundación Televisa, Mexico. With profound appreciation, I thank our sponsors for their magnanimous support.

I am indebted most of all to Gabriel Orozco. From the moment of the exhibition's inception, he has been an amiable and audacious collaborator, demanding from himself far more than from all of us. His work has been an ongoing source of pleasure, inspiration and surprise.

Vicente Todolí
Director
Tate Modern

# Acknowledgments

AN EXHIBITION OF THIS SCOPE can only be realised with the support and vision of many individuals and institutions. I would like to thank all those who not only agreed to lend important works from their collections, but also shared with us a commitment to Gabriel Orozco's work. It would not have been possible to create such an exhibition without the generosity of the institutions and individuals who have lent works form their collections and heartfelt thanks goes to them for making this unique exhibition possible.

I would like to thank Tate Modern Director, Vicente Todolí, for his early commitment and guidance on the exhibition, and Ben Borthwick, Assistant Curator, for his careful attention to the organisation of the exhibition. Thanks are also due to other colleagues at Tate Modern, whose input has been vital: Stephen Mellor, Exhibitions Coordinator, Phil Monk, Art Installation Manager, and the art handling and conservation teams.

I am delighted to have collaborated with Ann Temkin at The Museum of Modern Art, New York, who has led on the selection of works and direction of the exhibition, Bernhard Mendes Bürgi at Kunstmuseum Basel, and Christine Macel at the Musée national d'art moderne, Centre Georges Pompidou, all of whom have pooled their expertise in Orozco's work for this retrospective; I thank each of them for their insight and consideration. I would also like to extend my thanks to Glenn D. Lowry, Director, and Jennifer Russell, Senior Deputy Director, Exhibitions, Collections and Programs, at MoMA for their support and realization of this exhibition. Paulina Pobocha, Curatorial Assistant at MoMA, has been invaluable for her work on the catalogue and coordination of this exhibition. While each venue is different in form they collectively gather together important bodies of work, highlighting key moments in an exceptional career. Tate Modern is delighted to be able present such a comprehensive retrospective, and in doing so reveal the extraordinarily rich and abundant oeuvre of this artist to a wider audience.

The catalogue has been expertly produced by MoMA's Department of Publications and thoughtfully designed by Paul Carlos of Pure+Applied in tandem with the artist. At Tate Publishing I would like to thank James Attlee and Beth Thomas for their work on the coordination of the UK version. The essays by Benjamin Buchloh and Briony Fer add to their already important observations and critical understanding of the artist's work, and Ann Temkin's essay offers new avenues for insight into Orozco's work. With Anne Byrd, Paulina Pobocha also undertook the demanding task of writing the nineteen Chronology sections.

Marian Goodman and her staff in New York, including Andrew Richards, have followed every stage of this exhibition's development and facilitated numerous loans, for which we are very grateful. José Kuri and Mónica Manzutto of kurimanzutto in Mexico City have similarly been generous with their time and enthusiasm as well as their in-depth knowledge of the artist's work, as have Chantal Crousel in Paris and Jay Jopling in London. I am most appreciative of their help in developing the exhibition and additional loans for Tate Modern. I would also like to acknowledge the sponsors of the exhibition, the National Council for Culture and the Arts (CONACULTA) and Fundación Televisa. Their support for this exhibition has been considerable and thanks are due to them for their commitment to Tate and Gabriel Orozco.

This exhibition would not have been possible without the vital support and enthusiasm of Gabriel Orozco, whose unique sensibility for selecting and installing his own works has been a pleasure to witness and participate in as well as an opportunity to learn from. I am profoundly indebted to him for his passion and for his enormous contribution to contemporary art.

Jessica Morgan
Curator, Contemporary Art
Tate Modern

# Open Studio

## Ann Temkin

I N 1971 FRENCH ARTIST DANIEL BUREN DESCRIBED the studio as one of the "ossifying customs of art."[1] In a remarkable text published in English in 1979, he clearly and simply pointed out that whereas many artists of the late 1960s had rejected or redefined the exhibition spaces of the commercial gallery or museum, it was equally imperative to abandon the studio. Without that refusal, there would be no hope of overturning the artistic traditions Buren and his peers had inherited—traditions that valorized the genius at the expense of the community, and celebrated the object at the expense of the idea. The studio bore as much culpability as the museum for nourishing such a culture, Buren argued. "To question one while leaving the other intact accomplishes nothing."[2]

Almost forty years have passed since that bold declaration, and the artist's studio has been abolished no more than has the commercial gallery or the museum. Yet for Gabriel Orozco, and for many artists of his generation, the convictions reflected in Buren's words were of signal importance to the work they would do. The goals articulated at the end of the 1960s marked a rupture with inherited values that resonated mightily with artists who came of age during the mid-1980s. For members of the final generation that would be making twentieth-century art, the path to the future was one paved by artists who—in the late 1960s and at various points before—were challenging the problematic legacy of a modernism whose ideals no longer seemed wholly compelling.

This affinity was by no means a matter of seamless continuity. To the contrary, Orozco's generation entered art school during a moment in which the radical aspirations of the 1960s and the Conceptual art of the 1970s were nearly invisible. As if the dematerialization of the object witnessed in the late 1960s were an ignorable aberration, the booming economy of the 1980s brought with it a resurgence of large, handcrafted, expensive paintings. They were sold in the white box of the commercial gallery, and sanctioned in large museum exhibitions. And they were painted in spacious, well-appointed studios, places widely celebrated in magazines and documentaries.

In reaction, as the 1980s turned into the 1990s, Orozco and others rejected the lure of the studio. Whether as a matter of principle or circumstantial happenstance, many artists whose work would come to define the '90s would do without the fully outfitted base that for so long had signified setting up shop, the passage to adulthood of which art students dreamed. In most cases these artists chose not to make paintings, immediately obviating the automatic need for space and equipment. It was no coincidence that the art market had crashed and the prospects for selling conventional works of art were slim. A way of life that could be called post-studio—a term coined by Lawrence Alloway in writing about Robert

OPPOSITE:
Gabriel Orozco. Notebook 2 (1992–93), p. 65. Graphite and cut-and-taped printed paper on notebook page, 10 3/4 × 8 1/16" (27.3 × 20.5 cm)
Collection of the artist

RIGHT:
Photograph of bicycle, New York, c. 1992

Smithson—was concomitant with the production of a kind of art that was generally created in situ, was often ephemeral, and might involve no objects at all.[3] This way of life presupposed a decentered activity. Like Orozco, many of this generation were emigrants from one nation to another, and rather than settling in one place (as so many earlier twentieth-century artists had done in cities like Paris or New York) they reinforced this status by remaining firmly unattached to one specific locale.

Orozco's first art-making removed from a studio occurred when he was studying in Madrid in 1986–87. For the previous five years he had, with four friends, rented a building in Tlalpan, a southern section of Mexico City. There he had made paintings and drawings in a rich variety of abstract manners. But in Madrid a different practice emerged. Orozco rented a small studio, but he did not use it, in part because the room was unheated and intolerably cold. As Orozco has described it, he made his work walking to and from classes at the Círculo de Bellas Artes with whatever he found along the way, including scraps from a conveniently nearby lumberyard. The sculptures he made were temporary, as ephemeral as the countless unremarkable human tableaux constantly forming and unforming on the streets and sidewalks.

Nothing could be further in ambition or assumption from the typical nineteenth- or twentieth-century sculptor's studio. Such a studio was confirmed by long tradition as a sanctuary in which the artist constructed a personal universe all his (rarely her) own. Its four walls kept the outside world at bay, and its doorway offered the privilege of entry only to those so invited. It was a fictional world in which an artist could immerse himself in his own fantasies. Pygmalion could turn an ivory statue into a beautiful lover. Short of that god-given gift, a sculptor could turn living women into creatures never before seen on this planet: for example, in the case of Constantin Brancusi, elegantly curved forms with gleaming surfaces, or, later, in Alberto Giacometti's studio, attenuated figures of jagged linearity.

A century-long tradition of photographs of the sculptor's studio verifies the status of this space as the artist's all-encompassing universe. For example, Brancusi's hundreds of photographs of his studio insist upon the definitive unity of the artist's vision. The sculptures are cast as alluring vedettes, adored by a camera in poses that highlight such attributes as the works' reflectivity or textural contrasts. It is precisely in this tradition that we must seek the context for Orozco's photographs, which he began to make in Mexico in the mid-1980s. The first such works were made simply to record his ephemeral outdoor sculptures. As with Brancusi's photographs, these are a sculptor's records of his creations, but here the studio has become the street or the landscape. Orozco's photographs depict two types of situations. On the one hand, they capture the readymade sculptures the artist noted as a passerby, such as *River of Trash* (1990). Alternatively, they record the quiet interventions Orozco would make by means of a few deft moves, as in *Chair with Cane* (1990), a photograph made with the cooperation of a roadside vendor who repaired caned chairs. Orozco brought a chair, inserted the vendor's tall bundle of caning through its broken seat, and then documented the statuesque form against a shadowed wall.

These images implicitly deny the separate realm of a studio, so essential to the vision of earlier artists. Instead, Orozco positions his work in a place where art and life intermingle haphazardly. Robert Rauschenberg is perhaps the most important precursor of this viewpoint, and indeed it is in his early photographs that one finds a striking antecedent to Orozco's own. In 1953, for example, Rauschenberg photographed his *Personal Fetishes* arranged in the Pincio Gardens in Rome. These assemblages had been made during Rauschenberg's and Cy Twombly's travels in North Africa the year before, a time during which Rauschenberg had neither a studio nor any way to carry much with him. Although the photographs portray independent sculptures, and their ritualistic spirit sets them apart from Orozco's, they share the warm wit that eyes the everyday world as a ready platform for art.

Orozco's peripatetic way of life began full force in 1991, when he set off for a trip to Brazil and sublet the house where he lived and worked in Tlalpan, guessing that it would be an extended bout of travel. In fact he would not have a studio in Mexico for the rest of the decade. His new base would become New York City, where in 1992 he and his future wife, Maria Gutierrez, rented a small apartment on East Twelfth Street. There was no means of separating art and life in this compressed space (which in the lingo of New York real estate curiously enough is called a studio apartment). The table in the apartment served as Orozco's workplace, and it is here that he "cut oranges, played with plasticine, and worked on the notebooks."[4] The arrangement was in part an economic decision: Orozco could not understand why artists would give up their freedom, taking day jobs as waiters or assistants, in order to pay the rent on large loft studios they would then have little time to occupy. Instead, he developed a practice accepting of limitations. For instance, Orozco pinned a clear plastic Dannon yogurt cap to the apartment wall; after looking at it for many months he decided that since it had not bored him he might as well try it out on the public (*Yogurt Caps*, 1994). He made a plasticine ball and rolled it around on his building's tar roof to test its capacity for

ABOVE AND RIGHT:
Tabletop, artist's house, Tlalpan, Mexico City, c. 1991–92

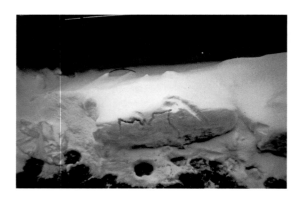

imprints (*Yielding Stone*, 1992). He packed all his little experiments in shoe boxes and then decided that it was worth displaying an empty one (*Empty Shoe Box*, 1993). Orozco's habits in New York also echoed those of his year in Madrid. There he spent many hours walking and bicycling around the city, composing and photographing, whether it be his own arrangement of debris to mimic the skyline with the Twin Towers in the distance (*Island Within an Island*, 1993) or the found stain of a dog's urine on newly fallen snow (*Dog Urine in Snow*, 1993).

As much as Orozco's tactics were a matter of financial necessity, they were also a matter of principle. In a dialogue with Benjamin Buchloh in 1998, Orozco asserts that even the modifications applied to the concept of the studio in the 1960s and '70s, variously adopting metaphors such as the laboratory, the office, and the factory, were thin disguises for an idealizing vision he could not accept. When Buchloh asks him to name his social model as an artist, he says that he would like it to be "my apartment." And when the conversation drifts elsewhere, he directs it back to this point:

> Just to finish something: the idea of the apartment is important; the idea of avoiding to have a studio or a factory, and just doing anything we can from here, from a common place; then going outside, having situations that produce this or that. The idea of making something more is an (*sic*) utopia in the end: the utopia of the office, the utopia of the factory, the utopia of the explorer, the utopia of the studio like a laboratory, for a genius. . . .[5]

Time in and around the New York apartment, however, was matched or exceeded by time away from it, time that allowed productive "situations." In either case, Orozco wished to be empty-handed. The essence of the light traveler is he who carries just a toothbrush, and Orozco was able to make art as such: several drawings from 1993 are made with toothpaste that has been swished around in the artist's mouth and spat upon the waiting graph paper, then completed with ink and pencil. As many critics have noted, other works from the 1990s alert the viewer to an artist in perpetual motion. Drawings made on train tickets and the now extinct carbon-paper pages of airline tickets imply work made in transit, and trace the artist's travels to and from Mexico City, New York, Paris, Calcutta, and so on. For his contribution, in 1995, to the exhibition series Migrateurs at the Musée d'Art Moderne de la Ville de Paris (the series' title an apt descriptor of this generation), Orozco could well have relied on the proverbial change of socks in one's backpack. He showed the papier-mâché sculpture *Two Socks*, the molds for which are indicated by the work's title. And the recurrence of vehicles—bicycles, cars, motorcycles—in his sculptures of the mid-1990s all invoke an artist on the move. The archetypal photograph of the sculptor in his studio needed to be replaced,

JUNIO 1993

Artist's apartment on East Twelfth Street, New York, c. 1992

Artist's apartment on Washington Place, New York, c. 2001

for Orozco and many of his peers, by one of the artist buckled into his or her economy-class seat on an airplane.

The newfound strength with which the biennial exhibition culture took hold of the international art world in the early 1990s had much to do with this new state of affairs. The efflorescence of places for showing art paralleled the decentralization of a place for working. Cities throughout Europe, Asia, Africa, Australia, and South and North America hosted events that bypassed the standard venue of the art museum and instead borrowed from the model of the music or theater festival. For the most part, these occasions replaced the white walls of the museum or the commercial gallery with spaces that felt more provisional, in exact parallel to the non-studio aspects of the artists' workplaces. Organizers adopted locations like abandoned buildings and outdoor parks and pavilions as well as art museums. While many artists shipped a selection of preexisting works to the exhibitions, often the work was made for the occasion and, in Orozco's case, even created on the spot. His work for the 1st Kwangju Bienniale in South Korea, in 1995, exemplifies this approach: he arrived only with notebooks filled with drawings of circular motifs. In a city where light-box advertisements are ubiquitous, he found a fabricator to translate his drawings into ten light boxes. Produced in an ordinary sign shop rather than a studio, the boxes married a cheap form of mass marketing with the most intimate and noncommercial aspect of an artist's work.

Similarly improvisational positions could be taken even when the setting was a conventional museum. Following Buren's equation, the rejection of the studio implied that of the museum gallery, too. Thus in Orozco's first solo museum show, a Projects exhibition at The Museum of Modern Art in the fall of 1993, he bypassed the isolated white space of the customary Projects gallery and instead chose to display his works in public areas usually devoid of art: the long space between the up and down escalators (*Dial Tone*, 1992), the freestanding structural columns (photographs), and the passages near the escalators and elevators (*Recaptured Nature*, 1990, and *Yielding Stone*, 1992). The two works newly made for the show occupied space outside the building: *Hammock Hanging Between Two Skyscrapers* was placed in the Abby Aldrich Rockefeller Sculpture Garden, and *Home Run* featured the display of single oranges in the windows of the offices and residential apartments across Fifty-fourth Street. Adopting the baseball lingo of the American setting, the title recognized that the work of art "ball" had indeed been hit right out of the museum "park."

Much as *Home Run* relied on the participation of the Museum's neighbors, Orozco's approach generally has required collaboration with workmen and workshops that are not art-related. The diversity of the mediums of the sculpture reflected a diversity of fabrication sites. A French automobile garage, a South Korean sign shop, and a British billiard table factory certainly have nothing in common other than their role as sites for making work by Gabriel Orozco. This is very different from the fabrication done for artists such as Donald Judd or Richard Serra. Even when these older artists engaged workers who were not, strictly speaking, art workers, they trained them in the making of their works, annexing the factory as an extension of their studios. The works all come from one or a set of fabricators who make them to the specifications of the artist, and together they build up to a coherent set of materials and forms. In a sense the studio is relocated but not dispersed, as it would be with Orozco.

For him, the decentralization of the manufacturing practice mirrors a rich heterogeneity of object and material. There is no way to identify a work by Orozco in terms of physical product. Instead, it must be discerned through leitmotifs and strategies that constantly recur, but in always mutating forms and configurations. Whereas for the previous generation post-studio work still involved a signature material or format—the branding effect of a Buren stripe is not so far removed from the classic Newman "zip" or Pollock "drip"—in the 1990s it seemed necessary to avoid repeating oneself, to always be unexpected. Rirkrit Tiravanija, a friend of Orozco's, could have gone on cooking Thai food on the occasions of his exhibitions, but instead he deliberately moved beyond the work that had made his reputation. The work of Maurizio Cattelan depends precisely on a sense of unpredictability, sustaining a pattern begun when all visitors to an early exhibition were greeted by a "Torno Subito" (I'll be right back) sign on the closed gallery door.[6] For the artists associated with the term "relational aesthetics," work could take the form of guerilla actions, more spontaneous than studied in nature.[7] Every occasion was an opportunity for surprise.

Particular to Orozco's work is an ongoing engagement with the city, first initiated while he was studying in Madrid. His methodology involves close listening to the urban landscape, which requires spending more time outdoors than in. Even when made available to him, studios have incited claustrophobia. In Berlin, for example, a DAAD grant in 1995 brought with it a spacious studio, but after a few weeks of discomfort Orozco converted it to a bedroom and devoted the majority of his time to riding around the city on a yellow Schwalbe scooter. He looked for matching scooters he would then photograph next to his own, ultimately producing a set of forty images collectively presented as *Until You Find Another Yellow Schwalbe.* Just as Orozco could reject a studio, he could effectively do away with a gallery space. Also in 1995 he converted Galerie Micheline Szwajcer in Antwerp into a literal *Parking Lot*, which he realized would be of far more appeal to a neighborhood overcrowded with traffic than would be a few new works of art for sale.

Back in New York in 1996, Orozco rented a new, larger apartment off of Washington Square. But its character was still far more that of a home office than a studio, its artistic function mostly limited to the making of the artist's notebooks and drawings. Exceptionally, the apartment was the site of creation for

*Penske Work Project* (1998) in progress, New York, 1998

*Black Kites*, the "skullpture" he sent to Documenta 10 in Kassel, Germany, in June 1997. But the apartment's unusual role as sculpture studio had explicit cause: a collapsed lung that kept Orozco indoors for several months. Following this, the outdoors once again became his foremost workplace, as demonstrated in his *Penske Work Project* in 1998. Trolling for inspiration on the streets of Manhattan, aloft in the driver's seat of a Penske rental truck, Orozco would pull over to make sculptures in situ, usually at construction-site Dumpsters that were treasure troves of materials. The street was the studio and the truck a mobile storage unit, ultimately unloaded at 24 West Fifty-seventh Street for final setup in Marian Goodman Gallery.

If Orozco's body of work is explicit about the way in which it evades the studio, it also presents directly the studio practice that does exist for him. This occurs in the *Working Tables*, of which three sets are now in museum collections.[8] These works feature large assemblies of the small found and handmade objects that Orozco accumulates in the course of testing various ideas and materials. Initially he kept such objects stored in shoe boxes in a closet; working with Bernhard Bürgi for his show at the Kunsthalle Zürich in 1996, Orozco decided that they could have a public life. He specifically chose a table, rather than a vitrine or case, for its implicit role as an active social space, a literal platform for all sorts of work, or, perhaps even better, for the playing of games.

Transferred directly into the museum or the gallery, the *Working Tables* offer the insights that one would normally gain only by visiting the artist's workplace. Although these fragments are made at home or on the road rather than in a conventional studio, they carry the perfume of the studio into the public realm. They present the artist's hand and brain in action, the sculptural equivalent to the notebooks that also are compiled and kept at home. The intimacy they allow is one generally kept at safe remove from the finished work of art. Orozco likens the experience of them to his pleasure at walking into an auto mechanic's garage and seeing all the small car parts and tools and equipment laid out on big tables.

Despite Orozco's mention of the garage, the *Working Tables* are important indications that his work operates along a pole more feminine than masculine in spirit. Indeed, masculinity is one of the codes for the modernism against which this work positions itself. In the history of modern art it has generally been the male artist who was entitled to the studio, as the businessman his office. Jackson Pollock took over the barn next to the farmhouse he shared with Lee Krasner, while she painted in an upstairs bedroom. Such a history often resulted in an aversion to the tradition of the studio and all that it implied, even upon the arrival of the era when women could claim its privileges for themselves. Eva Hesse rented a loft studio on the Bowery in New York, but she preferred to work in her living space below: "I work only downstairs. In my corner. . . . Feels less lost and lonely that way. Upstairs is unknown unfamiliar to me."[9] Orozco's *Working Tables* are, as Briony Fer has described them, "the art of kitchen tables."[10] They have their parallels in compilations of small-scale objects by artists such as Hesse, Louise Bourgeois, and Kiki Smith. While the approach is not limited to women artists—Joseph Beuys collected and displayed similar bits and pieces in his vitrines—they advertise their unmonumental, unheroic nature as modest works that are neither clearly finished nor unfinished. Provisional in tone, this is work of the sort that could be interrupted by the cooking of meals or fetching of children. Equally, it could be continued while getting on a plane or moving to another city for several weeks or months.

Over the past five years, Orozco has begun to make paintings—scores of them—a development that initially shocked his admirers and still causes considerable misunderstanding. After a few initial experiments, Orozco made a painting, *The Samurai's Tree* (2004), that he decided to use as a template for a large series. Manipulating its design by computer, he applied a set of rules that yielded 672 different permutations in gold, white, red, and blue, collectively titled *Samurai Tree Invariants*.[11] In 2005 Orozco strayed from the predetermined design schemes and began creating paintings that are composed individually, a practice that continues today alongside the making of the *Invariants*. His return to this traditional

Artist's apartment in San José, Costa Rica, c. 2001

medium appeared to repudiate much that his work was thought to have stood for. Orozco's renunciation of the culture of the studio is paramount among the basic principles called into question by this new activity. Surely one cannot make paintings without a studio.

Indeed one cannot, yet the subject of the studio turns out to be a valuable key to understanding the place of the paintings in Orozco's thinking. When Orozco left Mexico at the beginning of the 1990s, his disinterest in a studio perfectly expressed the new way by which he wanted to define being an artist. But in 2004, after a fifteen-year-long hiatus from creating paintings, a desire to make them resurfaced, and Orozco decided to accommodate it. An opportune site for this project was the studio occupied by Philippe Picoli, with whom he had first collaborated in 1993 on the making of *La DS*—the sculptural transformation of a Citroën DS automobile—and with whom he since then had shared a few other projects as well. Picoli lived and worked in the studio that Le Corbusier had built for Jacques Lipchitz in 1924, located near the Bois de Boulogne on the outskirts of Paris.[12] Rich in history and handsome in design, the studio lent itself to an experimental venture into the territory of early-twentieth-century abstraction.

For a year, from late summer 2004 through early fall 2005, Orozco worked "shoulder to shoulder" with Picoli, who had not been trained as a painter.[13] But once Picoli's skills were finely honed, and the project of turning the *Invariant* diagrams into paintings had been firmly established, Orozco departed. The work of painting is now one that he delegates to Picoli in Paris and Christian Macia in Mexico City. Macia had first assisted Orozco with *Mobile Matrix* (2006), drawing in graphite on the skeleton of a whale. He now works in a nineteenth-century house lent to him by Manuel Sevrano, an eminent restorer who first showed Orozco how to paint in tempera on wood panel, in the manner of medieval icons. Sevrano also has a large shop that serves as a site of production—it is here that the canvas and wood supports are prepared before being sent to Macia for painting. (An atelier in Bonn provides the supports for the French paintings.) Picoli and Macia work with a few assistants, all trained artists or art students, who are paid per project.

All the genius mythology that once went together with the studio—isolation, inspiration, struggle, ecstasy, despair—is absent in the making of Orozco's paintings. The process

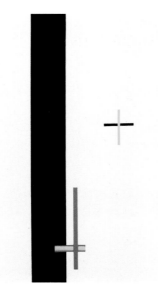

DERRIDA

SIMÓN

CAPITALIST ARTIST.
KAPITAL KUNSTLER
KAPITAL KUNST
EMPRESA EN LUGAR DE TALLER
FÁBRICA EN LUGAR DE COMUNIDAD
→ RELACIÓN PERVERTIDA A PRODUCCIÓN.

EMPLEADO EN LUGAR A DISCÍPULO
SUBORDINADO EN LUGAR A COLEGA.

POLÍTICA ECONÓMICA EN LA
PRODUCCIÓN A LA OBRA.

REPRODUCCIÓN DE LA CULTURA
DE CAPITAL

POP ART CONVERTIDO EN CAP ART

| POPULAR | | CAPITAL |
|---|---|---|
| PRIVATE PUBLIC | | PUBLIC INTO PRIVATE |
| UNDERGROUND | | STATUS |
| CHEAP TO PRODUCE | | EXPENSIVE TO PRODUCE |

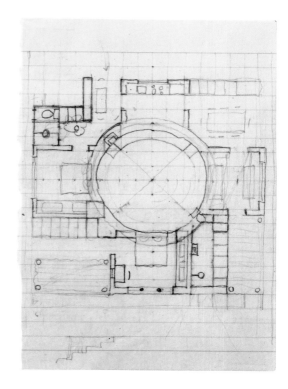

has more in common with that of László Moholy-Nagy's three *Telephone Pictures* (1922), which he proudly described as having been called in to a sign-making factory, ordered as identical compositions in small, medium, and large sizes.[14] Eighty-five years later Orozco's telephone is an iPhone, and he uses his laptop to chat in real time with Grazia Cattaneo, Picoli's wife, using software that allows two users to share a screen and discuss what they see. The technology enables a process more collaborative than that of Moholy-Nagy. As Orozco makes decisions about the paintings' structures and colors, Cattaneo clicks the mouse to make the changes on the screen. When he pronounces satisfaction with a design, she will hand it to Picoli in the Paris studio or e-mail it to Macia in Mexico City. The paintings will be made while Orozco is busy doing something else, perhaps a country or a continent away.

Orozco sees the two studios as temporary sites for a project that has an end, and the assistants who make the paintings understand that their role is a finite one. In Orozco's mind, he has not become a painter; on the contrary, his interest resides in the building of the compositions, not the craft of their execution. The whole operation has nevertheless prompted skepticism from some quarters because it comes unnervingly close to the traditional enterprise of a painter's studio, with its paint boxes and brushes, its vistas and aromas. Yet one should not mistake Orozco for a modern-day Peter Paul Rubens, supervising a workshop of painters who will in large part make the paintings sold under his name.[15] For Orozco, even the role of on-site general or coach overstates the case. Rather, the artist is an occasional visitor to the studios, one who freely admits that he wishes not to interfere in the daily practice of painting.

What is at stake here? Is there a way to bring back the making of paintings and the display of paintings that is not complicit with discredited values, with art's role as a luxury enjoyed only by an elite? Is there a way in which looking at a *Samurai Tree* painting on the wall can function on the same level as looking at the cap of a yogurt container? In the early 1990s the extreme statement of the latter was necessary to explain everything that Orozco's art was not about. With his paintings, begun a decade later, the artist made a wager that his previous activity had carved out a viable place for painting. The wariness that greeted the work proved that he was overly optimistic. Despite, or because of, the eventual commercial popularity of the paintings, this wariness has not entirely evaporated. Misplaced assumptions obscure the fact that the paintings up the ante on Orozco's original dare: with these works on canvas and on wood, he investigates if and how one can meld a practice forged under the sign of Marcel Duchamp and John Cage with one that also incorporates the legacy of Brancusi and Piet Mondrian.

Over the years, Orozco has not felt the need or the desire to build a workplace that fulfills the potential traditionally ascribed to an artist's studio: to create a universe, wholly defined and shaped by the vision of its occupant. He has, however, conceived and designed Observatory House, completed in 2006. Located on a breathtaking promontory over the sea on Mexico's Pacific coast, the house centers on a circular swimming pool open to the sky above. The design was inspired by the Jantar Mantar observatory, an eighteenth-century building in New Delhi, India, which Orozco first discovered on a visit in 1996. Like its source, Orozco considers the structure an instrument, a vehicle for concentration. Largely open to the elements, it is a place through which air, light, and sounds constantly circulate.

The model of the observatory is stunningly apt for this artist. The house underscores that Orozco, while ostensibly relaxing, is exactly who he is while working in countless cities and countries: an observer, with camera and compass and other tools at hand. Perched between sea and sky, the house translates into architecture the formal universe of Orozco's work. And at the same time it recognizes as Orozco's true concern *the* universe, which cannot be entered through a doorway or contained by four walls, nor reserved for one individual or those he invites. For Orozco, it is the role of the artist to work within that cosmos, and to honor and illuminate it through an oeuvre assembling rhymes and accidents with no apparent association but with an inarguably compelling sense of order.

PROYECTO BIBLIOTECA: ACCIÓN COTIDIANA. RECORRIDO PROVOCANDO CASUALIDADES, GENERANDO CONEX-
CIONES. PALABRAS = HECHOS. (FACTS). IMÁGENES. LIBROS DE ENCUENTOS. ACUMULACIÓN Y ORDENA-
MIENTO DEL CAOS. RUTINA, COSTUMBRE COMO FUERZA ORGANIZADORA. VOLUNTAD = GRAVEDAD.
IMÁGENES, PALABRAS Y OBJETOS. DIBUJO, FOTO, TEXTO, COLLAGE, INTERVENCIONES, APRO-
PIACIONES. DIARIO. DOCUMENTACIÓN Y REGISTRO DE LOS RECORRIDOS POR EL LA-
BERINTO.
OFICINA EN ESPACIO PÚBLICO.— PORTAFOLIO, WALKMAN, CORBATA, LENTES.
APROPIACIÓN DE IMÁGENES Y TEXTOS EN LA BIBLIOTECA. RECOLECTOR. ASTRONAUTA EN
OTRO PLANETA. PROPÓSITO CAMINANDO. CONSTRUIR EL UNIVERSO. ORDEN-CAOS-ORDEN.
PREFERENCIA.
SISTEMA DE PREFERENCIAS, VOLUNTAD Y AZAR. CASUALIDAD. HILO CONDUCTOR: VOLUNTAD.
ELECCIÓN. LA ELECCIÓN DÍA A DÍA ES EL HILO CONDUCTOR DE LOS POEMAS. NO NOVELA.
NO CAUSA. NOVELA = CAUSALIDAD. POEMA = ¿CASUALIDAD?
APARENTE CAOS EN LA COLECCIÓN DE DATOS.
EL PRIMER DÍA LO MOTIVÓ LA VOLUNTAD Y LA PALABRA REALIA. (LA VOLUNTAD IMPORTA POCO).
·BIBLIOTECA·SUPERMERCADO·CALLES·MUSEOS. TALLER.
TRABAJAR EN UN ESPACIO DESDE LA PERSPECTIVA Y LAS POSIBILIDADES DE UN INDIVIDUO, POR UNOS
INSTANTES Y CON LOS MATERIALES Y HERRAMIENTAS QUE ENCUENTRA AHÍ MISMO.
LA CASUALIDAD Y EL CAOS SIEMPRE HAN TENIDO MEJOR "GUSTO" QUE EL HOMBRE. ORDENALOTODO.
HABITAR UNA BIBLIOTECA.
OBJETOS POSIBLES EN UNA BIBLIOTECA: (OBJETOS GENERADOS POR LA LECTURA Y LA RECOLECCIÓN EN LA
                                                                                                        BIBLIOTECA).
•LIBRO CIRCULAR DE LOMO CONTINUO.
•DIRECTORIO RÍO.                                                                    R E A L I A
•CORAZÓN DEL RÍO.
•LIBRO HOJAS DE PLÁTANO. DOCUMENTO FOTOGRÁFICO.
•PLASTILINA EN REVISTAS.
•HOJA PAPEL BLANCO EN EL SUELO.
•FOTOGRAFÍAS HOJAS PAPEL BLANCO.
•DIARIO.

        18 VII 92

"HEAP OF LANGUAGE" DE R. SMITHSON.
PRONUNCIAR TODAS LAS PALABRAS EN TODOS LOS IDIOMAS AL MISMO TIEMPO, SUCESIVAMENTE, HASTA OIR EL
SONIDO DE AGUA CORRIENDO, CONVERTIDAS EN UN RÍO.
SMITHSON: ACUMULACIÓN, MONTAÑA. PERMANECE. SÓLIDO.
PÁJARO: SUCESIÓN Y ACUMULACIÓN, RÍO. FLUIDO. LÍQUIDO.
INCANTORY: PRONUNCIACIÓN SIN SIGNIFICACIÓN.

CONCIERTO DE J. CAGE EN EL MOMA. 7:30 P.M.
MÚSICA ACOPLADA A LA REALIDAD. SONIDO DE PÁJAROS Y COCHES Y VIENTO Y RUIDOS PRESENTES EN
LAS NOTAS EXTENDIDAS DEL CELLO. ORDEN-ACCIDENTES-ORDEN-ACCIDENTE.
LA MÚSICA ES EL MARCO DE LO QUE SUCEDE. ES LA BASE DE LA OBRA QUE ES LO QUE
SUCEDE. LO QUE SE OYE EN EL ENTORNO. SEÑALA LO QUE ESTÁ SONANDO. TODOS
LOS SONIDOS DEL ENTORNO SE REVELAN. NOS INVITA A DISTRAERNOS Y ESCUCHAR
LO OTRO, LO QUE NO ES "MÚSICA". LA MÚSICA SE ADAPTA A LAS LEYES RÍTMICAS
SONORAS DE LA REALIDAD. LAS SEÑALA. LAS ENMARCA.
CON UN LIGERO TOQUE LA AVISPA SE ASUSTA Y VUELA. AL TOCAR Y AL OBSERVAR
ACTIVAMOS LA NATURALEZA DE LO QUE NOS RODEA. TOCAR LA AVISPA Y SEGUIR SU
VUELO. NO MATARLA, NO APREHENDERLA. SEÑALARLA ACTIVANDO SU EXISTENCIA.
DISFRUTAR Y EXPRESAR ESE GOZO. EXPRESAR LO QUE ESTÁ ALLÁ AFUERA. REVE-
LARLO, HACERLO AUDIBLE O VISIBLE. PRESENTARLO.
MARCO = TESTIGO   EL ARTE COMO MARCO DE LA REALIDAD.
ENTRE EL INSTRUMENTO Y EL ESPECTADOR ¿QUÉ SUCEDE? EN ESE ESPACIO ENTRE LA
OBRA Y EL ESPECTADOR SUCEDE LO QUE SUCEDE. LO QUE SEA ES LO QUE SEA ES
LA REALIDAD ESTÁ EN MEDIO. LA ILUSIÓN LA EMPAÑA. EL SILENCIO LA ILUMINA.

PLASTILINA:

MATERIAL VULNERABLE. TRANSFORM
MATERIAL TRANSITORIO. CÁLIDO Y LI
INTERMEDIARIO PARA HACER ALGO
TIVO Y LA PLASTILINA CONTIENE
TODO SE LE PEGA (EL AGUA NO). P
REVOLVERLA EN ARENA, GRAVA,
MATERIA ORGÁNICA Y CON BASI
HACER UNA PIEDRA. ESCULPIR I
OBJETO DE SUCIEDAD, NO BIOD
LA PLASTILINA NO HA TENIDO VI
JUGUETE.
MATERIAL DESECHABLE. INTEF
EL GESTO Y SU DURABILIDAD (
GRAN RESIDUO. RECIPIENTE.
PLANETA. WANDERING STAR.
ORGANISMO. NUNCA ES ESCULT
CADA MANO QUE LA TOQUE DEJA
DENTADA. RECOLECTORA. A

ES
LA
PO
2
M
M
VI
ES
Fi

FEA. HORRIBLE. CACA. BOLO ALIM
(¿CON RAMAS?) (¿HIERBA?) ¿DE
EN QUE YO PUEDA CARGARLA.
MONUMENTO A LA PLASTILINA. I
ARTE. ES UNA BOLA DE PLASTILI
    PUEDE SER BLANCA PARA Q
O AMARILLA. PUEDO HACERLA I
DAÑOS NO DRAMA). POLVO. PAPE
EDIFICIO Y SE APLASTARÁ CON
IMPORTANTE EN LA ESCULTURA
NA (QUE ES UN PLANETA O UN A
SERÁ EL CHOQUE DE DOS FUN
FUERZAS.
    PRE-ESCULTURA. ANTES DE C

20 VII 92
    ESCRIBIR TODAS LAS PALABRAS
HASTA FORMAR UNA MANCHA DENS
HACIA EL FENÓMENO. PARENTE
FÍSICO).

    SUBSTITUCIÓN IMPLICA UNA F
NOS INDICA ALGO QUE ESTÁ ALLI
PLA YA NO EXISTE, HASTA QUE LO
Y LO SUEÑA Y CASI TODO ES UNO
SUEÑO SI NO SE PRONUNCIA I
MA PORQUE TODO LO QUE SU

# Constellations in Dust:
# Notes on the Notebooks

**Briony Fer**

GABRIEL OROZCO'S NOTEBOOKS ARE BOTH at the very heart of his activity as an artist and slightly to one side of it. They are only notebooks, after all, and it is usual to see notebooks and sketchbooks as much less important, to say the least, than an artist's main work. And yet I think Orozco's notebooks are different, or at least I want to suggest here that they beg at least as many questions about what they *are* as they do about what they contain. I'll start by picking a single word from one of the earliest of them that he wrote out in neat capitals: REALIA. It heads an entry made on July 17, 1992, and is followed not by a definition but by a series of examples: ". . . include such items as objects, specimens, samples, relics, artefacts, souvenirs and even models and dioramas. And realia which one used in construction of exhibition and bulletin boards. Real things, actual facts."[1] The word is used by librarians to describe all those everyday artifacts that are not books but that can serve as teaching aids or demonstrational tools of one kind or another. As Orozco notes, realia cannot be learned in books. As visual supports or props, they are set apart from the idea of a library solely as a repository of the word. They are physical things, which makes them sound more like the contents of older cabinets of curiosity. And as in those earlier collections, there is often something immense and mysterious to be observed in the kind of small and mundane objects that interest Orozco.

Realia is a specialist term that is not in general use and looks outdated: a dusty word. The fact that it could now apply to things like video aids or digital media or other modern equivalents seems a bit absurd. Orozco came upon this odd word and breathed his own life into it. By picking it out he holds it up for inspection as if it is a material thing, or an actual bit of the (English) language that got caught in the net of his thought. This and other small, handwritten words, printed in black or blue ink, often in capital letters to mark their significance, however temporary, gather in his notebooks, but they are only a part of what is collected there. The notebooks themselves are made up of numerous and disparate elements, including writing, photographs, drawings, found images, collage scraps, diagrams, plans, lists, and other ephemera.

It is telling that the term realia has an indirect connection to the idea of a library. For whatever else they are, Orozco's notebooks are first and foremost books, to date seventeen of them, each the same standard format bound in plain gray linen. The notation "Biblioteca. DIA UNO: REALIA" appeared at the very beginning of the second volume. The word realia lingers for a page or two, then disappears almost as fast as it appeared. But still, if the word gets set aside, its associations do not. For example, in 2002, Orozco made a folio of twelve etchings, which he called *Polvo Impreso* (Pressed dust), and then in 2006 he installed a huge public project in the Biblioteca Vasconcelos in Mexico City: a whale skeleton overdrawn in graphite with intricate circular patterns that is suspended in a vast space between the hanging structures of open bookshelves. The result is that the whole building has become a vast skeletal body housing another. Even more than the enormous size of the whale, it is the huge differential of scale between the different kinds of things Orozco makes that is striking—and which, of course, the notebooks themselves, as small repositories of not only a vast number but also a huge network of connecting works and projects, also act out.

Orozco dates the first of his notebooks to January 1992. Though he had made many conventional sketchbooks before then, filled with drawing rather than writing, 1992 is established (retrospectively) as a fictional starting point for these works. The notebooks follow a strict sequence: each entry dated, each page numbered by hand. The first notebooks are denser than the later ones, and filled with more words. The notebooks are all a standard size, but the time each takes to fill varies greatly: some earlier volumes contain only a few months of work, while the later ones may contain up to two years' worth. After having been built up slowly over many years they now sit consecutively on the bookshelves in the room where Orozco works in his apartment in New York. It is not so surprising that prominently represented in that extensive library is Jorge Luis Borges, the greatest keeper of libraries in the literary universe.

In 1939 Borges wrote an essay titled "The Total Library," the bare bones of which would become the short story "The Library of Babel," published two years later. To call one nonfiction and the other fiction suggests a border where there is none (it is more like one is inside the other). The story is annotated with footnotes, which creates the illusion of a certain kind of factual document, but in the supposedly nonfictional piece Borges imagines a library or utopia that was "of astronomical size," that would be all-encompassing: "Everything" he wrote, "would be in its blind volumes. Everything: the detailed history of the future."[2] Even future time does not escape the unimaginable scale of it. What Borges does in the story is take the impossibility of describing the infinitely vast and overwhelming totality and make that problem—the problem of writing—the motor that drives the words onto the page. The narrator is in an impossible position, as are we. It is well known that Borges's texts are themselves intricate labyrinths of words, which invite readers in only to make them more lost. The author might tempt you with the promise of finding a way through it, but this path is always thwarted in the end. This is a bit like being inside Orozco's notebooks, which are also like mazes. Words pile up. Drawings pile up. Words take shape, and they also make shapes. And though the pages are sequential, little else is. Like Borges's library, they are "unlimited and cyclical."[3]

Orozco's notebooks are full of the beginnings of things, of plans for work in the making or yet to be done and hypothetical projects. They are a history of the future in Borges's sense, but of course they are also full of residues from work already made and of the ideas that have gotten lost in translation as others have evolved. Although often densely packed with writing, the blocks of text are also shaped around drawings, photographs, and other bits and pieces that have been pasted into them. Orozco is careful to call these books notebooks and not sketchbooks, their status indeterminate. The artist's large retrospective at the Museo del Palacio de Bellas Artes in Mexico City in 2006 was the first time that he exhibited a selection of them alongside other plans and diagrams of his exhibition installations.[4] For Orozco the exhibition is not just where work ends up but a medium through which it continues to transform itself in each new architectural setting. Demonstrating something about those shifting conditions and contingencies is not external to the work but a part of it.

Although artists' sketchbooks and jottings, like writers' notebooks and manuscripts, are generally thought of as secondary to the work proper, they also are the subject of intense fascination. They invite elaborate footnoting and explanatory marginalia from scholars sitting in archives and libraries, who like to identify the most arcane detail or the least likely connection to make a vast map of the inner workings of the creative mind. Sketchbooks, often undated, offer the art historical detective the opportunity to try to resolve conundrums—the blind alleys, the frankly obscure—and to identify every (usually) iconographical source for the artist's proper "work," betraying a deep-seated desire to make out of them the totality of an "oeuvre." Of course, this is a two-way street, and for all the attempts to order disorder, sketchbooks are disobedient—they tend to resist the urge to tidy them up and pull instead toward some kind of fugue state. I am not denying that a sketchbook, however chaotic it may look, obeys certain conventions. It is not so provisional an artifact as to escape the constraints of the time in which it was made. Part of what interests me is how these conventions have changed radically over the twentieth century, and certainly irrevocably since the 1960s. In some ways these changes have been fueled by the precarious status that sketchbooks have had as the underside of art practice. One need only to look at the role of the fragment in books of artists' drawings, or the collage effect of the page, or the remarkable freedom to rotate one fragment against another to see how a peculiar and complex order runs counter to regimes of representation at work elsewhere in the culture (a Cézanne drawing, for instance, with an intricate rendering of a

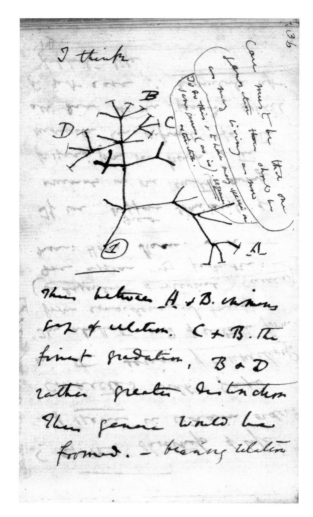

P. 22:
Gabriel Orozco. Notebook 2 (1992–93), p. 2. Ballpoint pen, graphite, and cut-and-taped printed paper on notebook page, 10 3/4 × 8 1/16" (27.3 × 20.5 cm)
Collection of the artist

P. 23:
Gabriel Orozco. Notebook 2 (1992–93), p. 3. Ballpoint pen, graphite, and cut-and-taped printed paper on notebook page, 10 3/4 × 8 1/16" (27.3 × 20.5 cm)
Collection of the artist

ABOVE:
Charles Darwin. *Tree of Life.* c. 1837. Ink on paper, 6 9/16 × 3 11/16" (16.6 × 9.3 cm)
Charles Darwin Papers, Notebook 'B,' p. 36, MS.DAR 121. Cambridge University Library

OPPOSITE:
Gabriel Orozco. Notebook 2 (1992–93), p. 106. Ballpoint pen, graphite, and cut-and-taped printed paper on notebook page, 10 3/4 × 8 1/16" (27.3 × 20.5 cm)
Collection of the artist

spoon at a right angle to the incomplete, fleeting sketch of the head of his small son, marooned on an empty page, quite out of proportion one to another).

It is also worth remembering that we are all in the impossible position of Borges's narrator in relation to so compact an object that nevertheless seems to contain *everything*. The world opened onto is at once concrete and as vertiginous as any fictional one. It is an equally dizzying prospect to try to say something about the sketchbook's history, even its modern variants, ranging from Antonin Artaud's "*dessins-écrits*" to Marcel Duchamp's vast note-world to Hannah Höch's scrapbooks to Pablo Picasso's prodigious cahiers to Jasper Johns's elegant reductions to Ellsworth Kelly's panoramic "tablets" to Mel Bochner's working drawings.[5] Even that list barely scrapes the surface. It is a history that is reasonably uncharted, and that Orozco's notebooks not only act within but upon—that is, they demonstrate not only something about his own work but about how we might think about the *work* that is art. After all, as I said at the outset, notebooks and sketchbooks are at the center of art as an activity but also at its edge, both the main work and the marginalia to the main work. As a direct consequence of this ambiguous position, they have been the site of some seismic shifts in the conceptual status of the artwork. Most famously, Duchamp made his notes his art in his Green and White Boxes, in which tiny scraps of his writings and diagrams and drawings from the period preceding World War I were reproduced exactly (as torn and scrawled) in facsimile editions. Then Bochner's show *Working Drawings and Other Visible Things on Paper Not Necessarily Meant to Be Viewed as Art*, of 1966, exhibited as his own work photocopies of drawings by a number of other artists as well as anonymous technical drawings. This was never about making something that was pure idea at the expense of the physical object of art but rather about reimagining the kind of work that drawing can do.

It would be neat enough to situate Orozco's notebooks at the end of this conceptual lineage, but they defy such straight lines. And though Conceptual art's attacks on the object can never be "unthought," it is clear that Orozco's notebooks gravitate elsewhere. Partly this is because they are so militantly handmade rather than mechanically reproduced in multiple copies. In this respect, they are more reminiscent of Picasso's sketchbooks of the 1920s, with their hybrid collections of drawings—especially his abstract line drawings that plot out a page at the same time as they reference his sculpture. These graphic constellations coexisted with drawings *of* his collages, as well as the occasional collaged element literally stuck into the back of a book. Even the powerful idea that drawing is the materialization of thought deviates from a Duchampian model in favor of other kinds of artifact, like travel notes or *carnets de voyages* or the famous page from Darwin's notebook that he kept on his travels to the Galápagos Islands that comprised a schematic diagram of a few lines pointing downward and then dividing into smaller lines, like a basic root system, above which is written simply "I think." Few ideas could be bigger than Darwin's theory of evolution, yet even a schema like Darwin's, which has come to represent the first "eureka" moment of an idea taking shape, can only be seen as such after the fact. And seen from a graphic rather than a scientific perspective, it is a drawing that delineates the paradigmatic shape of a thought at a given time as it is caught in the act of self-recognition.

Orozco's notebooks demonstrate how a page can plot out, in its shape as much as by the content of what is actually written, an intricate pattern of thought. Definitions of words fix a thought for a moment by taking it out of circulation and noting it down. In one notebook from 1992, for example, Orozco writes, "Methonymy [*sic*]": "Things that are contiguous, related only by proximity or juxtaposition."[6] The word not only creates a space on a page but also describes a spatial way of thinking (linking by adjacence or nearness). Metonymy names a powerful drive in Orozco's work, but it is also a term that gets caught up in the larger drift of a lexicon in the making. Collecting the word is not the origin of the idea, but a moment of recognition of a process that has been at work all along. Working something through is not about finding an answer but of making a space for new questions. Naming or finding words for things is a part of figuring

LA BASE BLANCA. ENTRE
HORMIGUERO. ¿QUÉ HAY
O. ESCONDERSE DEBAJO
EL ESPACIO ENTRE

POLVO

LINA SE AMURALLA CON
IEMPRE PIEDRA. UNA
SIGO MISMA SU BASE:
LO OTRO, CON EL
IR, SUERO. CAPA PRO-
INVULNERABLE.
NTERMEDIO, INVISIBLE,
NO SABEMOS) Y ESE
1 ESTÁ OSCURO. (LA
N ELLO).
MÁS BASES. BASE SOBRE
ESCULTURAS PARA BASES.
ETURA Y LA BASE.
AS UNA FRANJA. HORMIGUERO.
TRE AGUA Y
RA DE PLASTILINA.
ESPACIO INTERMEDIO
1 ESA COSA. ENTRE
EDE Y LO QUE PERCIBI-

BOLA PLASTILINA

EL NOMBRE.

PIFAR, COMER, LA PALA
S POSIBILIDADES DEL
E SUCEDIÓ INFINITA-
TO CONTENIDO. DEB

SE PIENSA
SE HACE
SE ARTE

1 QUEREMOS DECIR. NUES-
TEMA. EL SECRETO DE
S NAVES ESPACIALES
1 QUE SEA. NUESTRA
1OS FLODEARLO. NOSO-
TEMA, PRESENTE ES
SISTEMATIZA EL CAOS
IR UN SISTEMA POSI-
2O. SISTEMA DE
1—SOLTURA. CAMI-
R Y NUESTRO EXTE-
R. RECORRER. VER
NBO. SIN PENSAR
REMOLINO Y ESPIRAL.
QUINA. TERMINATOR.
PLANETAS. MOLECU-
PENSAMIENTO.

CORCHOLATAS EN TIRA
PAVIMENTO

137

30 XI 92

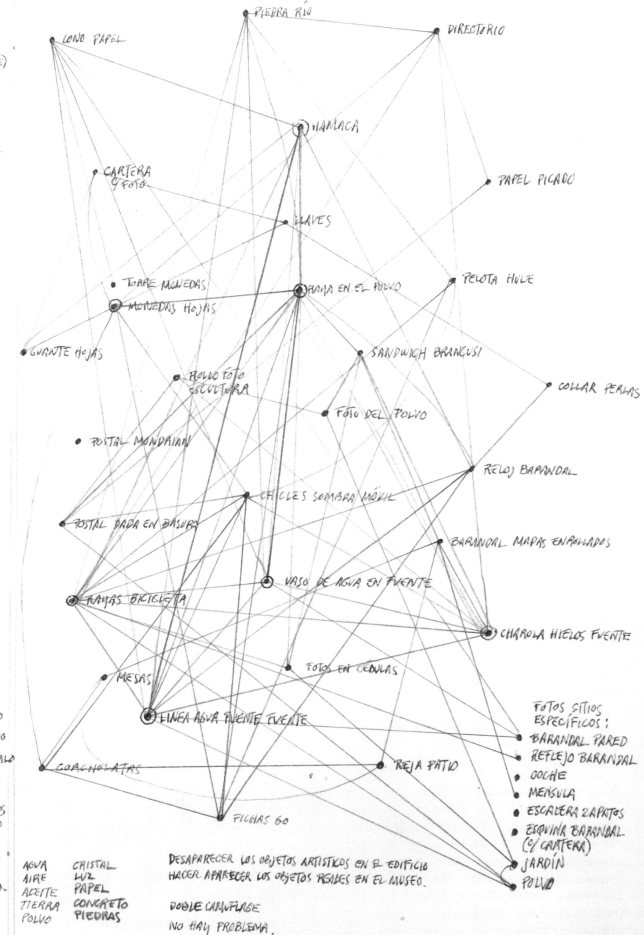

HAMACA (LINEA
VASO AGUA AGUA
FUENTE)
RAYAS BICICLETA
RAYIN POLVO

PIEDRA RÍO
DIRECTORIO
RELOJ BARANDAL

MONEDAS HOJAS
CHAROLA HIELOS
CHICLES SOMBRA

CORCHOLATAS
GO

O. ARTE:
CORAZÓN BARRO
PLASTILINA
DIRECTORIO.
CORAZÓN RÍO
DIBUJO MANO
TELA ALBÓNDIGA

O. REALES:
RELOJ
CARTERA
COLLAR
LENTES
CASSETTE
ZAPATO

SENTIDO LIMITADO
SINSENTIDO LIMITADO

ACEPTAR EL SENTIDO
ENCUBIERTO. NO
SABERLO. DISFRUTARLO

TODAS ESAS COSAS
QUE POR ESTAR
CONTIGUAS SOLEMOS
LLAMAR UNIVERSO

TODAS ESAS COSAS,
QUE POR EL HECHO
DE ESTAR JUNTAS,
LLAMAMOS UNIVERSO.

¿QUÉ ES ESO?

AGUA      CRISTAL
AIRE      LUZ
ACEITE    PAPEL
TIERRA    CONCRETO
POLVO     PIEDRAS

DESAPARECER LOS OBJETOS ARTÍSTICOS EN EL EDIFICIO
HACER APARECER LOS OBJETOS REALES EN EL MUSEO.

DOBLE CAMUFLAGE

NO HAY PROBLEMA.

PIEDRA RÍO
DIRECTORIO
LONO PAPEL
HAMACA
CARTERA
Y FOTO
PAPEL PICADO
LLAVES
TORRE MONEDAS
RAYA EN EL POLVO
PELOTA HULE
MONEDAS HOJAS
GUANTE HOJAS
SANDWICH BRANCUSI
ROLLO FOTO
ESCULTURA
COLLAR PERLAS
FOTO DEL POLVO
POSTAL MONDRIAN
RELOJ BARANDAL
CHICLES SOMBRA MÓVIL
POSTAL DADA EN BASURA
BARANDAL MAPAS ENROLLADOS
VASO DE AGUA EN FUENTE
RAYAS BICICLETA
CHAROLA HIELOS FUENTE
FOTOS EN CÉDULAS
MESAS
LÍNEA AGUA FUENTE FUENTE
FOTOS SITIOS
ESPECÍFICOS:
BARANDAL PARED
REFLEJO BARANDAL
NOCHE
MÉNSULA
ESCALERA ZAPATOS
ESQUINA BARANDAL
(C/ CRÁTERA)
JARDÍN
POLVO
CORCHOLATAS
REJA PATIO
FICHAS GO

out what the artist is doing as he is doing it, or making sense to himself of things that he has done. The process can be surprisingly concrete or barely graspable. And what in retrospect have come to seem like pivotal points in his work are often accompanied by a sudden flurry of extensive and expansive working notes on a particular project.

At times these disturbances are particularly turbulent: in late 1992, for instance, in preparation for his exhibition in Kortrijk in Belgium, the proliferation of possibilities includes a page of drawings of irregular stones—graphite forms that resemble prehistoric flint arrows—alongside the term "resting sculptures."7 Elsewhere, we find words like "by-product" or "waiting sculpture." Often they point not to active processes of making but to the way objects can *do nothing*, giving the sense of something that is lying in wait or dormant, temporarily out of circulation but far from quiescent. This is, incidentally, in striking contrast to the active doing of Richard Serra's famous *Verb List* (1967–68), where the handwritten descriptions of his activities—"to roll to crease to fold to store to bend" and so on—accumulate over the space of two pages. In Orozco's notebooks it is, of course, only retroactively that the full force of what has erupted onto the page becomes apparent, just as a language evolves amid any number of false starts and other words and phrases that seem, equally only in retrospect, to have since fallen by the wayside. Ideas come and go, but it is often that which seems to have drifted completely out of sight that returns with the greatest force, even many years later.

Words are as much visual elements on a page as anything else, just as drawings extend through a seemingly never-ending metonymic chain of associative connections and slippages. Words and images are carried over from one page to another, or one book to another. As ideas unfold, they leave a trail. Threads of thought interweave, just as texts and images are interleaved. In the second volume of Orozco's notebooks, for instance, the Spanish word "*polvo*," or dust, is written at the top of the right-hand margin of a page of notes on *Yielding Stone* (1992), and just below it is a tiny sketch of the Plasticine ball that would collect all kinds of dust and debris when rolled through the street. And then almost ten years later, in the twelfth notebook, from 2002, those dust particles have drifted again. At the time, Orozco was working on both *Polvo Impreso*, made from the fibrous residue from industrial drying machines, and *Cazuelas (Beginnings)*, the terracotta pots he has described as "starting pots." He calls this drift of thought the "perspective of dust/*la perspectiva del polvo*."8 This is a way of describing (in two languages) a direction and a movement that are not only spatial but also temporal, revolving around beginnings and endings, where there is a precise correspondence between coming into being and being leftover. Seen from that point of view, the photograph of his handprint on the inside front cover of the notebook registers not only the primordial mark but also the fact that it is already a residual trace. In the end, being between languages is only one possible act of translation among many (this to that, now to then, and so on).

The notebooks not only bear witness to the process of making the work but are themselves a part of the work. Then gradually, over time, as well as being a part of the work, they seem to have become something more like *a* work, albeit a permanently incomplete one whose status is permanently unresolved. It is inconceivable to think this without Conceptualist precedents, such as Bochner's working drawings, and yet the notebooks operate entirely differently, as if the handmade and the artisanal form of the book could be the most risky way to reimagine what the work of art might be now. They are not strictly speaking "working books"—as opposed to simply workbooks—or at least Orozco does not call them by that name. But still there seems, at least in the operation they perform, a striking and profound link to his *Working Tables*. The first of these was made in 1996 at an exhibition in Zurich. There are Polaroids of it in the making in the notebook from March of that year, annotated with the words "*como basura tirada*/by-products/*modellon y maquetas*/*reciventes*."9 All these terms have previously appeared in the notebooks at various intervals, and they gather again here. It is not just the fact that there are containers on the table, but that the table itself becomes

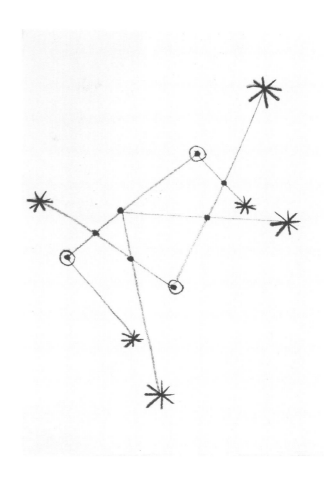

OPPOSITE:
Gabriel Orozco. Notebook 2 (1992–93), p. 137. Ballpoint pen and graphite on notebook page, 10 3/4 × 8 1/16" (27.3 × 20.5 cm)
Collection of the artist

ABOVE:
Pablo Picasso. *Sketchbook No. 92.* 1926. Cardboard-covered notebook; p. 14, colored pencil on paper, 19 5/16 × 12 3/16" (49 × 32.5 cm)
Private collection

a container or receptacle. Books are containers too, of course, and inserted into the notebooks is a variety of things, from leaves to seedpods to a barcode to any number of leaflets or cutouts. This sense of the notebooks as containers is made particularly palpable by Orozco's decision to insert the pages of the first notebook in the series into the larger standard gray notebook that he subsequently used. Each page—whether stained with coffee or barely marked—was meticulously cut out of the original and slotted into the new book.

Although the book is perhaps the most conventional format in which Orozco works, he treats it the same way as any other: as a living thing. It is worth remembering that we talk about the pages of books as leaves, and about books having spines. A book has a symmetry that can be worked as much as it is worked in the artist's paintings, which also often rotate around a central spine. And although books are sequential, we know that narrative is not. When Orozco has, over the last few years, come to fill his notebooks with photographs of work already done, maybe the phenomenon is not so different from the way sketchbooks traditionally often served as inventories. He frequently arranges the images two on a page, so that each spread consists of four photographs, which, as he has remarked, creates a rotation. A spread of photographs demonstrates the circularity of time, as the rotation tracks, for example, the melting of ink-filled ice cubes that look like dirty gem stones lying on the window sill of his apartment.[10] This layout has its origin in the notebooks but has become one way to show his photographs as well.

There is something archaic about the notebooks. They are bound books in a computer age, reminiscent of a library or archive. It is easy to get lost in them, and yet at the same time they function as some kind of mnemonic tool or prosthetic memory. Increasingly, they have become a means to inventory the work through

ABOVE:
Pablo Picasso. *Sketchbook No. 92.* 1926. Cardboard-covered notebook; p. 17, leaf collage, 19 5/16 × 12 3/16" (49 × 32.5 cm)
Private collection

BELOW:
Gabriel Orozco. Notebook 13 (2002–03), p. 180. Ballpoint pen and photographs on notebook page, 10 3/4 × 8 1/16" (27.3 × 20.5 cm)
Collection of the artist

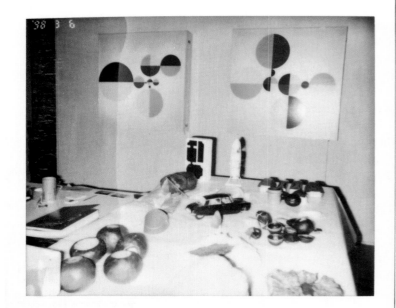 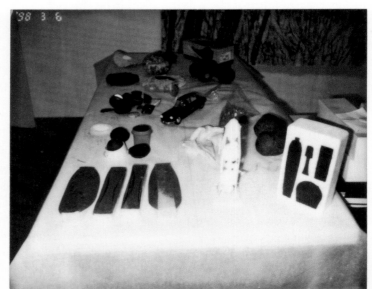

CAJA TENIS CONVERS
ESCUPIDA EN TORTILLA
MASA QUE CRECE
LIMONES U NARANJAS
NIDO INCOMPLETO. ROTO.
PUNTOS NEGROS EN TELA.

CEBOLLA CORONA
D.S.
TAZAS DE TÉ
SEMILLAS - HOJAS
TAPA DETERGENTE
CUATRO CAJAS

LUNAR LANDER
DOS PIEDRAS
RECIPIENTE Y
NEGRO.

COMO BASURA TIRADA.
BY PRODUCTS.
MODELOS Y MAQUETAS
RECIENTES.

Gabriel Orozco. Notebook 8
(1995–96), p. 51. Ballpoint pen
and graphite on Polaroids on
notebook page, 10 3/4 × 8 1/16"
(27.3 × 20.5 cm)
Collection of the artist

photographs. And yet Orozco's sense of realia as "real things, actual facts" transforms this demonstrational model into a radically different realm. I admit the notebook is an unlikely critical weapon. But precisely because it occupies such an unexpected and indeterminate place it becomes possible to think of a handmade notebook as a means to reflect on the conditions of art production now—and as a way of resisting the high-scale production values that have become dominant. After all, Orozco is an artist who uses computer programs to generate the variations within the geometric patterns of his paintings, and he has long made drawings out of paper printed with digital templates filled in with patterns by hand. But it was just when he found himself increasingly working with the computer that he decided to exhibit his notebooks, as he did in 2006. This bears on his own practice by making even more volatile the distinctions between the handmade and the machine-made, which so much of his work blurs.

Orozco reflected on this in a note from 2005, saying, "If the artist does not make, it means there is no process (no research) there is just production. And the artist's brain dries out, because it is in the mistakes and accidents of the process that we get the ideas for the work to follow."[11] The act of making things by hand is not some nostalgic throwback to a more authentic form of creativity, but a strategic way of demonstrating the radical efficacy of the opacity of making art. The notebooks contain the work *in* the work: the thinking it, the writing it, the drawing it. Loose ends, even dead ends get you closer to what is at stake, not because they dramatize or inflate the creative process but because they ground it at a micro level. Plans for exhibitions and diagrams of installations plotting out an arrangement of interconnecting points are both works in progress and what is remaindered after the projects have been completed. Projects that work often get made out of others that are abandoned or long delayed. A case in point would be the circuitous route by which Orozco came to build his house, which he calls Observatory House, on the Pacific coast of Mexico in 2006—a winding path that

BELOW:
Gabriel Orozco. Notebook 4 (1993–94), p. 94. Ballpoint pen and electrostatic print on notebook page, 10¾ × 8¹⁄₁₆" (27.3 × 20.5 cm) Collection of the artist

OPPOSITE:
Gabriel Orozco. Notebook 4 (1993–94), p. 95. Graphite, gouache, and wood veneer on notebook page, 10¾ × 8¹⁄₁₆" (27.3 × 20.5 cm) Collection of the artist

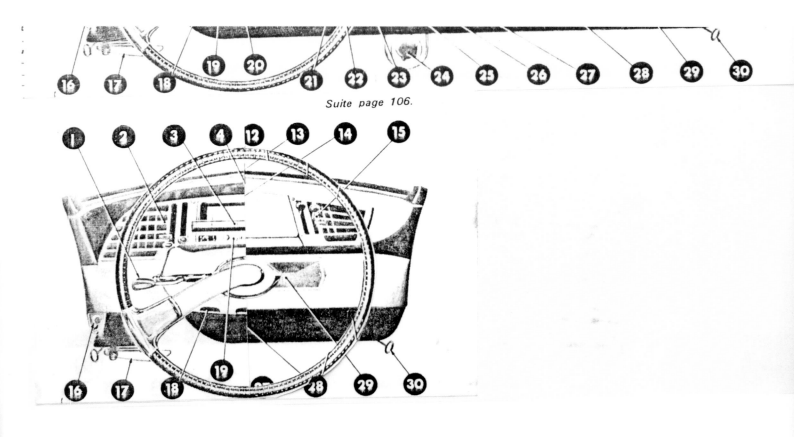

Suite page 106.

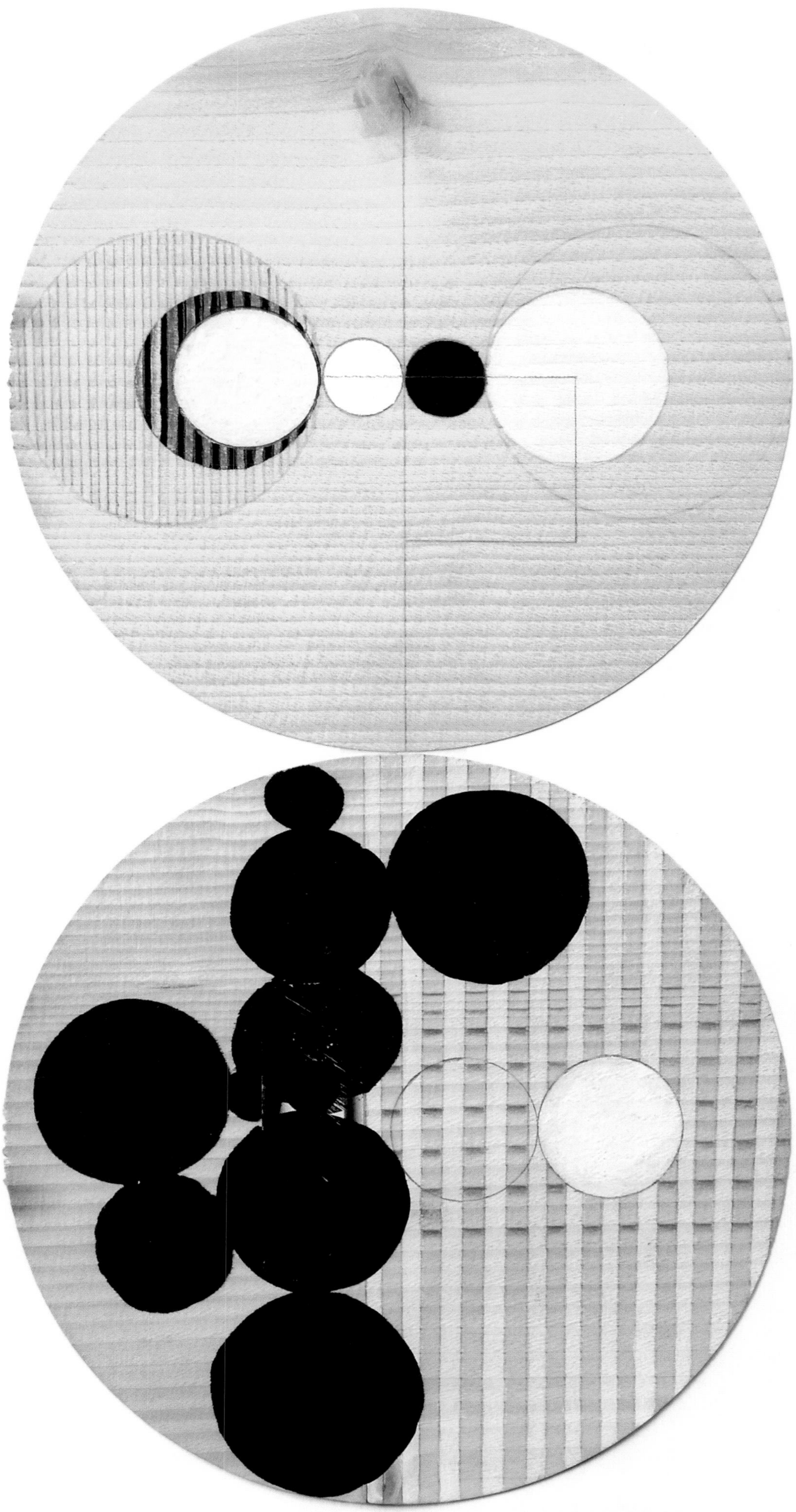

10 · 14 · 94

Gabriel Orozco. Notebook 6
(1994), p. 66. Ballpoint
pen and photographs on
notebook page, 10 ¾ × 8 ¹⁄₁₆"
(27.3 × 20.5 cm)
Collection of the artist

OPPOSITE:
Gabriel Orozco. Notebook 2
(1992–93), p. 138. Ballpoint
pen, graphite, and coffee
stains on notebook page,
10 ¾ × 8 ¹⁄₁₆" (27.3 × 20.5 cm)
Collection of the artist

OPPOSITE, TOP RIGHT:
Stéphane Mallarmé. *Jamais un
coup de dés n'abolira le hasard:
poème.* Paris: A. Vollard, 1897.
Proofs with corrections and
annotations by the author,
pp. 6–7
Bibliothèque nationale de France,
Paris

30 XI 92

○ CAFÉ.   ⊙ CAFÉ CON AZÚCAR   ○

○   CAFÉ CON LECHE   ○ C

1 XII 92

QUISIERA CORREGIR, LIMPIAR, SOMETE
LOS TEXTOS QUE HE ESCRITO. QUITAR
REITERACIONES. BORRAR LO QUE
TO A QUERIDO CONFIRMARME.
    PERO NO PUEDO DETENERM
RELEERME. ENCUENTRO TANTOS
CRIBIRLOS MEJOR. COMETER OT
QUISIERA SER BORGES Y DETE
DISTRAERME TANTO CON EL F.
ESTA HOJA. ESTE CUADERNO
QUIEN) Y DESEARÍA QUE F
ESTÁ TAN LLENO DE INEXA
DESTRUIRLO. EL DÍA QUE L
AQUÍ ESTÁ ESCRITO, ESTE C
ÉL, YO MISMO, CON MIS M.
RÁN PALABRAS DE IMPREN
IMAGEN DE ALGUIEN QUE NO
QUE YO FUERA. Y POR ES
TEXTOS SOBRAN, COMO S
    HOY NO PUEDO CORREGI
IDEAS Y HACER A UN LAD
NCARME A REFLEXIONAR
CUALQUIER PERSONA LO HA
LEÍDO PORQUE SERÁ LEÍD
CORREGIRSE SI LO G
QUE YO NO SÉ?
    ALGÚN DÍA DEJARÉ D
ALGÚN DÍA TOMARÉ MI CAF
DO TODO LO QUE SOÑÉ Y
VOY A SOÑAR. ALGÚN D
NO SIEMPRE SE PUEDE COG
(LAS PLUMAS VUELAN MIENT
SU PESO)

3:45 UN LADRILLO ES UNA CAJ
FALSAS, (QUE SON CAJAS), UN
PIEZA EN BARRO EN FORMA
VEO COMO UNA CAJA SIN T
SIMULAR LA TAPA Y EL OR
PIEDRA QUE CONTIENE PIEDRA
SU VACÍO, LA PLENITUD.

VACÍO PLENO. VACÍO PLENO

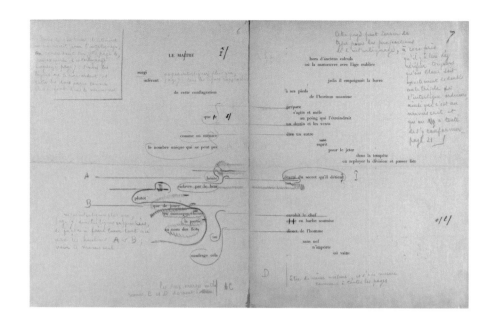

takes us from his first visit to India and his earliest notebook entry, in early 1996, recording the great Jantar Mantar observatory in New Delhi, on which the house is based, through to a quick sketch on a paper napkin stuck into the fourteenth book, in December 2003. It is entirely characteristic that a giant instrument created to measure the movement of the stars should lead to a throwaway doodle on a napkin.

It may have been because I had been looking at the notebooks for too long and for days on end: with several of them open and placed at random on the desk before me, the end of one spine almost touching another, the notebooks came to look as if they were themselves splayed open like vertebrae. And in the end I don't think it is too implausible to see them as working parts within the body of Orozco's work as a whole. The notebooks might be inanimate objects, but they also continue to grow as if they are living things. They may not take up much shelf space, but they open onto the astronomical capabilities of the imagination. The layouts for installations show how the work is brought together, but also how the work disperses on the page—gathering in only temporary constellations, not so different from the way exhibitions collect works for just a short time. When Paul Valéry was confronted with the proofs of poet Stéphane Mallarmé's great word experiment "Jamais un coup de dés jamais n'abolira le hasard," he commented, "[Mallarmé] has undertaken . . . finally to raise the printed page to the power of the midnight sky."[12] In the poem a little galaxy of words like "*C'ÉTAIT/ issu stellaire*" (IT WAS/born of the stars) are suspended at the top of a page full of blanks. The constellation *is* the page. The empty spaces between the words are full of frenetic activity, just as they are for Orozco in the intervals between his works. His notebooks only serve to highlight this impulse to constellate and reconstellate that is the overwhelming direction of the work. It is not an infinite vastness, let alone the cosmos, that is at stake here. Rather, it is the sense of the notebooks as an impossible object, which in turn reflects upon our own impossible position as subjects in relation to them.

# Sculpture Between Nation-State and Global Commodity Production

**Benjamin H. D. Buchloh**

**T**HROUGHOUT THE TWENTIETH CENTURY we have witnessed the most intense oppositions in sculptural production (confronting, for example, each in their respective decades, Constantin Brancusi and Marcel Duchamp, Joseph Beuys and Arman, Richard Serra and Eva Hesse). Historians have, for the most part, preferred to engage only with the work of individual artists or identifiable formations (such as Minimalism or Arte Povera), and with the most productive phases at that, since it seems far less rewarding to contemplate those periods when the production of sculpture has been arrested for mostly unknown or incomprehensible reasons (as, for example, in France since the 1960s, a time when sculpture — in spite of its former grandeur from Auguste Rodin to Henri

Matisse, from Brancusi to Alberto Giacometti — has reached a paradigmatic fatigue, the threshold of seemingly disappearing altogether from visual culture).

A similar, more general waning appears to have occurred in the beginning of the twenty-first century with the onset of globalized cultural production. This might be partially explained by the fact that the major discourses of sculpture that had originated in the 1960s in the United States and in Europe (Minimalism, Post-Minimalism, and Arte Povera)

had come to full fruition and had left — as in the universal presence of Serra and Donald Judd for example — an apparently incommensurable and insurmountable legacy. All the more astonishing, then, that an artist from Mexico, Gabriel Orozco, has redefined the parameters of sculpture in the present and has thus contributed to salvaging the category from extinction.[1] Coming from a country and a cultural context not generally known for its contributions to sculptural modernity, Orozco's situation is perhaps comparable to the moment when the Romanian Brancusi arrived in Paris to redeem sculpture from the crisis in which it found itself after Rodin, Aristide Maillol, and Matisse. Brancusi's work would evolve to perform all the possible permutations of sculpture to emerge in the twentieth century: from the most differentiated artisanal devotion to primitive forms of manual execution to a modernist credulity in the specificity of materials;

from the conception of the sculptural object as a fetish and totem to sculpture's mimetic emulation of the industrial commodity. This capacity to synthesize the rapidly changing formations of collectively given object relations — and their correlative materialization of desire — made Brancusi the most important sculptor of the first half of the twentieth century. In a similar manner, Orozco's work with common and uncommon materials, with made and found objects, and with photographs promises a synthesis of artisanal perfection (as seen in his terracotta pieces) and technology (the deployment of computer technology to display all the possible permutations inherent in one of his recent abstract paintings from the *Samurai*

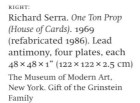

RIGHT:
Richard Serra. *One Ton Prop (House of Cards)*. 1969 (refabricated 1986). Lead antimony, four plates, each 48 × 48 × 1" (122 × 122 × 2.5 cm)
The Museum of Modern Art, New York. Gift of the Grinstein Family

ABOVE:
Gabriel Orozco. *Recaptured Nature*. 1990. Vulcanized rubber, approx.
29 1/2 × 41 5/16 × 33 7/16"
(75 × 105 × 85 cm).
One of three versions
Alma Colectiva, Guadalajara, Mexico

RIGHT:
Constantin Brancusi. *Princess X.* 1915–16. Polished bronze and limestone block, bronze, 24 5/16 × 15 15/16 × 8 3/4" (61.7 × 40.5 × 22.2 cm); block, 7 1/4 × 7 1/4 × 7 1/4" (18.4 × 18.4 × 18.4 cm)
The Louise and Walter Arensberg Collection, 1950. Philadelphia Museum of Art

*Tree* series, *Dandelion Animation*, 2008) as it hovers between taking recourse to primitivizing practices and mythical resources and the most advanced forms of a technological contemporaneity. While it suspends itself within perpetual global movement, transience, and ephemerality, at the same time it embraces, if not insists on, an almost paradoxical regionalist specificity of materials, morphologies, and iconographies.

Thus one could begin by asking whether—and to what extent—nation-state identities such as "Romanian" or "Mexican" actually affect sculptural production, since asychronicity of production, materials, and procedures due to national or generational divides could easily account for some of the stranger disjunctions

in the history of sculpture. And we would have to clarify whether the hiatus between obsolete procedures and materials and the newly emerging morphologies of form results from the culturally specific registers of the nation-state, or whether we are in fact confronted with a situation of asynchronicity in which the paradigms of a supposedly anchored tradition are suddenly confronted with radical technical and material innovations (in the manner that Brancusi recognized the aesthetic equality if not superiority of a machinic part to an

artisanally crafted sculptural object, or in the manner that Duchamp insisted on making the manufactured object the epistemic standard of all artistic object production in the readymade). After all, the fundamental epistemological changes that determine the production of sculpture occur first of all in the collective experience of the restructuring of objects themselves. For example, as late as the 1920s French mainstream sculpture attempted to reassert an archaic, geopolitically defined identity (as seen in the desperate claims for a Mediterranean Frenchness in Maillol's work) in order to sustain and seduce industrially produced yet nationally sutured subjectivities. The contradictions of such claims could be exemplified by pointing to the simultaneous appearance of Maillol's *Monument à Paul Cézanne* (1912–20), Brancusi's *Princess X* (1915–16), and Duchamp's

*Belle haleine—Eau de voilette* (1921)—if we are at all willing to accept an assisted readymade with a photographic complement within the canonical definitions of sculpture in the twentieth century. While Brancusi's work was perceived at the time by the traditional public as an act of obscene rebellion and subjected to censorship, the work would eventually advance our understanding that all sculptural desire (the one that motivates authorial as much as spectatorial behavior) originates in demands for experiential echoes of the

part object.[2] The Duchampian object went even further by fusing the desire for the part object directly with the shell of the commodity, and by inscribing the photographic construction of the androgynous authorial subject within the display functions of the object's container itself. Thus as sculpture—even more subversively than Brancusi—it dismantled the foundational patriarchal claims of the sculptor to have control over and access to the libidinal conception and representation of the (female) body, publically handing the claims of bodily representation over to the production of objects and the regimes of fashion and consumption, the sites where bodily representation in fact resided in any case by the 1920s.

Orozco has learned all the crucial lessons from Duchamp (and from John Cage and Piero Manzoni), and he has taken them perhaps more seriously than most of his peers. By frequently alternating found and artisanally manufactured objects, by hybridizing the body, the processes, and the matter of sculpture (from

terracotta to lint, from bronze to cactus leaves, from chance imprints to photographs), he has forfeited the centrality of the sculptor's intentionality and skills. He has given up traditional mastery and control over hierarchical orders that had isolated if not privileged particular experiential forms as specifically sculptural (still governing the work of artists such as Serra or Carl Andre all the way into the present). By liberating the category of sculpture from the constraints of its proper conventions, Orozco has uncovered a sheer infinity of new facets of what could constitute the current condition of the sculptural. Accordingly, his interventions reveal that the sculptural object's traditional facets of mass and matter, of volume and gravity, of texture, surface, and place have now been dispersed within these very registers—rather than, as in the context of Conceptual art, having been transferred into the registers of the performative, the photographic, the somatic, or the linguistic—and as a consequence the perception of the sculptural has been inevitably shifted into the disseminated registers of his spectators' distracted and destroyed relationships to the material world. Not surprisingly, the artist deploys the photographic image—in the manner of a Conceptualist—as a record to trace these discoveries and destructions, activities and disappearances of the sculptural from the subject's spheres of experience.

More precisely, Orozco's work teaches us that the active and the passive principles of sculptural perception are heterogeneous—lodged in the collective

conditions of object relations at large, in the subject's access to touch, to breath, and to vision (in, for example, *Recaptured Nature*, 1990)—but that they are equally controlled by the subject's breathless submission to the commodity's coercion. We learn from the contemplation of his work that sculptural tactility can be found in the increasingly precarious surfaces of water (as seen in *Pinched Ball*, 1993, or *From Roof to Roof*, 1993) or the fragile textures of plants (*Mixiotes*, 1999). Or we suddenly comprehend that sculptural experience in the present will more likely originate in the furtive accident, or that it will be found in the aleatory and indexical imprint (*Yielding Stone*, 1992). Most convincingly, Orozco seems to argue that the defining form of a sculptural body can equally be found in random accumulations of dispersed or dysfunctional, natural, or utilitarian objects (the oranges in *Crazy Tourist*, 1991, and *Home Run*, 1993, or Schwalbe scooters in *Until You Find Another Yellow Schwalbe,* 1995) as much as it can reside in an anthropocentric cranium (*Black Kites*, 1997) or the skeleton of a whale (*Mobile Matrix*, 2006). Orozco defines sculpture as a perpetual exchange between the myriad visible or invisible registrations of the subject's imprints on the world, its shadows and stains (as in *Dog Urine in Snow*, 1993, or in *Waiting Chairs*, 1998), as much as the myriad pressures the material world imprints on the subject. That exchange can take the form of an autochthonous agglomeration of dust particles *(Lintels,* 2001) or of the ultimate category of an unconscious, collective sculptural intentionality, declaring objects as "matter out of place," the nonobjects and voided materials of garbage itself (*Penske Work Project,* 1998).

Even in the most radical forms of sculpture of the 1960s, from Claes Oldenburg to Hans Haacke, the increasing diversification of sculptural processes and materials had still been quarantined within the specificity of a "sculptural" object. By contrast, Orozco has transferred these materials and processes into the sphere of the most common sites and structures. This is evident, for example, in a comparison between Haacke's *Condensation Cube* (1963–65) and Orozco's *Wet Watch* (1993) or *Breath on Piano* (1993), where the process of condensation is one of an infinite number of possible sculptural events occurring within a found object—rather than, as had been the case with Haacke, in a particular sculptural container—that

ABOVE:
Gabriel Orozco. *Breath on Piano.* 1993. Chromogenic color print, 16 × 20" (40.6 × 50.8 cm). Edition of 5
Courtesy of Marian Goodman Gallery, New York

BELOW:
Gabriel Orozco. *Wet Watch.* 1993. Silver dye bleach print, 20 × 16" (50.8 × 40.6 cm). Edition of 5
Courtesy of Marian Goodman Gallery, New York

RIGHT:
Hans Haacke. *Condensation Cube.* 1963–65. Clear plexiglass and distilled water, 30 × 30 × 30" (76.2 × 76.2 × 76.2 cm). Edition of 5

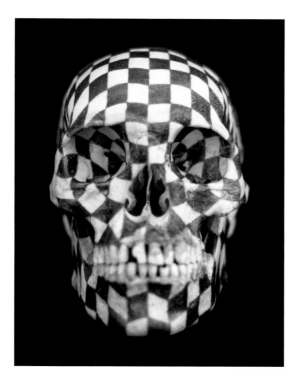

Gabriel Orozco. *Black Kites.*
1997. Graphite on skull,
8 1/2 × 5 × 6 1/4 (21.6 × 12.7 ×
15.9 cm)
Philadelphia Museum of Art.
Gift (by exchange) of Mr. and Mrs.
James P. Magill, 1997

Arman. *La vie à pleines dents.*
1960. Resin, metal, and
wood, 7 1/16 × 13 3/4 × 2 3/8"
(18 × 35 × 6 cm)
Musée national d'art moderne,
Centre Georges Pompidou, Paris.
Museum purchase from Daniel
Cordier (Juan-les-Pins) in 1968

is as valid as any other material or spatiotemporal definition. But we should not forget that the historically formed catalogue and categories of emerging and disappearing object relations, those lost and those still accessible to the subject, have dramatically changed in the past twenty years, the time frame of Orozco's rise as the sculptor of his generation. Therefore, it is not surprising to find a range of unheard-of materials and objects (for example, oranges and skulls, truck tires and whalebones) and unseen procedures and techniques (combining found objects with staged accumulations, as in *Until You Find Another Yellow Schwalbe* or *Home Run*, or registering given or aleatory processes as sculptural interventions, as in the *Lintels* or *Penske Work Project*) in Orozco's oeuvre that extend far beyond the dialectics that had been set up between Brancusi and Duchamp, between Beuys and Arman, or between Serra and Hesse. And in spite of initial appearances, Orozco's work is also fundamentally different from the legacies of Arte Povera, to which it has been too often compared. After all, Arte Povera, while situated at a similar transitional moment between artisanally based nation-state culture and the international corporatization of object production, was still driven by the desire to pursue the residual identity of a truly Italian art—through implicit or explicit references to the grand materials and traditions of the sculptural as a separate discipline—as evident, for example, in the work of Luciano Fabro or Jannis Kounellis, or in its ultimate acceptance of sculpture as a closed form and discrete object, as opposed to the post-Cagean concept of sculpture as an event or an infinitely extendable process or performance.

How, then, could we possibly identify and describe the national and historical specificity of Orozco's sculpture, the work's supposed Mexican identity—at times

persistent, at others fully unfathomable? One could argue, for example, that the historical and geopolitical specificity of the sculptures of Beuys and Hesse originated in the fact that both (on the opposite political grounds of victimizer and victim) had witnessed the annihilation of the human subject and had recorded the destruction of the human body on an industrial scale. Furthermore, one could argue that those experiences and forms of knowledge—while hardly, if ever, explicitly stated—constituted the foundational latency of these sculptors' relations to materials, morphologies, and surfaces. Obviously, the specificity of Orozco's historical and geopolitical condition is fundamentally different. He is an artist who emerged from a nation-state culture where, despite a continuously expanding industrialization, everyday culture seems to both suffer and benefit from a permeation of residual forms of mythical experience (manifestations of a population permeated by myth might include illiteracy or poverty, or relative proximity to preindustrial forms of production). All of these conditions in tandem, as a presumed proximity to the mythical, could offer the artist access to different types of subjectivity and object relations.[3]

What is the function of the "mythical" in sculptural formations? Examples might range from, once again, Brancusi's invocation of a supposedly unalienated preindustrial identity in the architectural peasant carvings of his Romanian home region to Orozco's particular devotion to surviving fragments of Mexican artisanal practices (the usage of terracotta or local plants, for example) or objects representative of Aztec and Maya ritualistic culture (the insistence on the circular, the spherical, or the ball as a valid sculptural form), or his penchant to mobilize so-called primitive procedures of manufacture and archaic object types (skulls, skeletons). First of all, Orozco knows full well that any sculptural object taking recourse to the outdated would inevitably partake in the Surrealist claims of a parasitical access to a dysfunctional and uninstrumentalized object experience that no other object is permitted to offer any longer. He also understands that any sculptural object claiming a recovery of the "natural" seduces one into a fraudulent deception, namely the belief that the collective structuring of object experience could still facilitate access to an uncontaminated nature when in fact it will only tolerate that experience as a spectacularized and commodified exception. Thirdly, and possibly most importantly, sculptural regressions into mythical primitivity, obsolescence, and the semblance of the natural also promise the spatial and material figurations of an experience of the mnemonic if not the uncanny, the certainty of having been in the maternal space beforehand, as Freud defined that dimension of spatial and object memory. Memories of that which has been, and which is now recollected in sculpture, can be found in Joseph Cornell's box assemblages, or, in a very different way, in Arman's accumulations, or even in sculptures devoted to the memory of the body: once this had been destroyed and had become irretrievable, it became representable only as the traumatized body in the fictions of the sculptural object (as, for example, in work by Eva Hesse).[4]

From the most archaic memory of bodily experiences to the most urgent response to a representational crisis in the present, Orozco's sculpture has answered these individual and collective demands. The chasm occurs precisely in the spaces between desirable transgressions and the available conventions of relating to objects and materials, between the conception of radically different sets of object relations and the existing practices of control and contamination of the subject within the ruling commodity regimes. In many ways, then, the "mexicanismo" of Orozco's work that seduces his Western European and American audiences originates in our own forms of recollection, in our own desire for a new myth of having access to the natural world, and in our own indubitable sense of actively participating in the destruction of the remote "natural" and "mythical" world. Orozco's sculpture articulates that at every moment of the day we are subjected to and promulgate the acceleration of obsolescence, that we witness traditional objects and materialities vanish underneath our own hands, and that we see them being replaced against our will, or outside of our control, by heretofore unknown textures and structures.

ABOVE:
Gabriel Orozco. Detail of Notebook 12 (2002), p. 34. Photograph, 2 7/16 × 3 1/8" (6.2 × 8 cm)
Collection of the artist

RIGHT:
Eva Hesse. *Repetition Nineteen III.* 1968. Fiberglass and polyester resin, nineteen units, each 19 to 20 1/4 × 11 to 12 3/4" (48 to 51 × 27.8 to 32.2 cm) diam.
The Museum of Modern Art, New York. Gift of Charles and Anita Blatt

Thus the conception of the mythical in Orozco—the regressive resuscitation of the specificities of myth and memory, lodged in the conventions of nation-state culture—always attains a dialectical reversal in the artist's projects: that which appears as a redemption of the object and the experience of the natural signals at the same time that the experience of the object is suspended in a condition of neglect, of obliteration or obsolescence. The object permeated by myth is here instantly recognizable as one that is always already afflicted by impoverishment and abandon. What appears as the stability of myth assaults us as a cliché deeply resonant with the condition of history as a nightmare. Orozco's mobilization of the mnemonic dimension of the object—as it must appear to the outside world—is more often an articulation of the object's forlorn and desolate condition, and a desire for its future emancipation, than one of a celebratory regression to a desirable state of identity, once attained but now lost.

These conditions of a universally destroyed relationship to the material world of object experience—the experience that could still consider objects as the result of labor, that retained the dimensions of their own making, that embodied the functions of use value and the temporality of memory—are probably the most strident motivations to become a sculptor in the present, and it seems that Orozco is the first to have made them the principle of his production. However, unlike some other artists, from Isa Genzken and Jason Rhoades to Rachel Harrison—sculptors who have yielded without resistance to the universal destruction of object experience and who have handed over the construction of sculpture to the merely haphazard accumulation of the grotesque, comical agglomeration of trash—Orozco insists on inscribing a dialectics of nature and culture within the structure of his work. It is a dialectics in which affluence is not equated with satisfaction but with suffocation, one in which the ceaseless availability of objects is not correlative to gratification but to endless destruction and the disappearance of resources, and one in which the regime and control of desire by strategies of consumption is not celebrated as the triumph of successful substitutions but as an infinite repetition of acts of loss: the tragic destruction of object experience in the present is at the origin of Orozco's sculptural intensity. Thus when, in 2006, Orozco installed *Mobile Matrix*—the immense skeleton of a whale—in the Biblioteca Vasconcelos in Mexico City, the spectator was confronted with an intense dialectical experience: on the one hand it was impossible not to see Orozco's insistence on the dimension of death and the disappearance of the natural, a condition clearly called forth by the sculpture's resurrection of a buried whale skeleton from the sands of Baja California. At the same time, when contemplating the whale in a library, it was impossible not to see it as a programmatic statement on the negation of sculptural utopian thought in the present, as though it were a reflection upon the history of Constructivist modernist sculpture (as, for example, in Aleksandr Rodchenko's *Oval Hanging Construction*, c. 1920, or the ludic optimism of Alexander Calder's mobiles of the 1930s) and its proud or playful insistence on transparency and modernist self-reflexivity, its declamatory and pedagogical ethos of structural evidence, teaching the spectator to see how texture and structure, mass and gravity, weight and matter all interrelate to not only define the body of a sculpture but also to constitute a self-conscious, perceiving, phenomenological subject in the spectatorial act. Thus the archaism and primitivity of the skeleton, deployed here as a primary model

ABOVE:
Gabriel Orozco. *Mobile Matrix*. 2006. Graphite on gray whale skeleton, 6' 5 3/16" × 35' 8 3/4" × 8' 8 3/4" (196 × 1,089 × 266 cm)
Biblioteca Vasconcelos, Mexico City

RIGHT:
Aleksandr Rodchenko. *Spatial Construction no. 12.* c. 1920. Plywood, open construction partially painted with aluminum paint, and wire, 23 × 33 × 18 1/2" (61 × 83.7 × 47 cm)
The Museum of Modern Art, New York. Acquisition made possible through the extraordinary efforts of George and Zinaida Costakis, and through the Nate B. and Frances Spingold, Matthew H. and Erna Futter, and Enid A. Haupt Funds

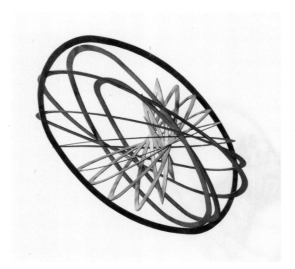

for corporeal order and structural support, signal the historical disappearance of utopian hope as it had been formerly embodied in the projects of modernist sculpture, from Rodchenko and Calder to Serra.

One of the questions that might emerge would be to what extent sculptural

production at this moment in history would have to mobilize the resources and the fictions of the mythical grounds of subjectivity in order to resist the total dissolution of the subject and of collective object experience within a system of universal technocratic control. Another question might ask for the registers in which such recourses to seemingly more deeply inscribed or more hardened features of a fictitious or authentic identity might occur. Would these recourses have to be partially lodged in the legacies of the nation-state, to simulate attitudes to make the spectator consider the possibility of an alternate object experience, different from the given one of total administration and instrumentalization? Or would these recourses work on the order of the unconscious (as in the Surrealist legacies) or historical memory (as in Beuys and Hesse)? Or would sculpture have to take recourse to a newly discovered dimension of an industrially formed spatiality? This could range from the sculptural work of Bernd and Hilla Becher, where the extreme specificity of their nation-state identity as postwar German artists could never be separated from the universality of their conception of the sculptural as the industrial, to Serra's recent large-scale works, where the immensity of the structures suddenly acquires an unexpected status of the sublime within the sphere of the technological itself, and thus acquires an equally unexpected, specifically American trait. Furthermore, to what extent would this mobilization of a mythical unity between subject and subject (as in ethnically, religiously, or nationally defined identitarian claims), between subject

RIGHT:
Alberto Giacometti. *Bust of Diego*. 1954. Bronze, 15 3/4 × 13 1/4 × 7 1/2" (40 × 33.7 × 19 cm)
Musée national d'art moderne, Centre Georges Pompidou, Paris. Museum purchase from the artist in 1961

ABOVE:
Gabriel Orozco. *La DS*. 1993. Modified Citroën DS, 55 3/16" × 15' 9 15/16" × 45 5/16" (140.1 × 482.5 × 115.1 cm)
Fonds national d'art contemporain (Cnap), Ministère de la Culture et de la Communication, Paris, Fnac 94003

RIGHT:
Joseph Beuys. *Eurasia Siberian Symphony 1963*. 1966. Panel with chalk drawing, felt, fat, hare, and painted poles, 6" × 7' 6 3/4" × 20" (183 × 230 × 50 cm)
The Museum of Modern Art, New York. Gift of Frederic Clay Bartlett (by exchange)

and object (as in the fiction of unalienated forms of pre-industrial existence and artisanal production), and between nature and culture merely take recourse to a fiction that no longer bears even a trace of any historical reality? And to what degree would it be necessary to recognize that the deep structures of cultural-identity formation are intrinsically inscribed with the deceptions and the inflictions according to which a subject had originally become an integral element in the process and pressures of political subjection, once called the formation of national identity?

In his by now classic text on the formation of the nation-state and its ideological functions, Benedict Anderson traced the determining links between disappearing religious identities and emerging national identities, serving supposedly as substitutions for the loss of subjective experience in cultic practices.[5] Not surprisingly, since Anderson's perspective is that of the historian, the function of aesthetic experience as one of dis-identification from the ethnic, the religious, and the nationalistic in a larger process of secularization are never addressed. Yet, inevitably, the aesthetic would have to occupy a major place in any such consideration since it is eternally subservient and subversive, suspended between cult and political rule, conflicted between loyalty and disobedience to the religious, the mythical, the historical, and the national processes of identity formation. Aesthetic practices have always insisted on an essential extraterritoriality, and on the utopian notion of a universal subject. Or they have insisted on the territoriality of their proper laws and conventions, as much as on the standards of their historical instantiations as the solely valuable normative or comparative legitimations. This is where yet another paradox opens up: the very conventionality of artistic language usages and aesthetic standards would be intricately bound up with the subject's formation within the coordinates of nation-state culture.

This fundamental duality—of simultaneously corroborating and dislodging the conventions of identity formation—originating in cult and state applies all the more to the moment in which emerging economic and technological orders provide the primary parameters of the subject's current constitution, offering a compelling yet mythical and ideological deception of the subject's presumed transcendence of the nation's traditional parameters. Just as the emerging economic and technological regimes promise a truly globalized culture and a final dissolution of the nation's fatal bonds, when the concept of nation-state identity itself is being displaced by economic and technological orders of globalization, the question concerning the functions of the aesthetic within the dialectics of identification becomes all the more urgent. The new orders seem to imbue the ideology of the nation-state with mythical regressive powers, similar to those that religion might have had at the moment of its dissolution. When it comes to cultural production, nation-state identities now have to be acknowledged as a system of determination—as a precondition for any construction of a mnemonic dimension in the work of art—that has to be overcome in order to articulate the necessity of an aesthetic transgression of all external conditions of overdetermination.

What makes the aesthetic an integral element within these debates is mainly its dis-identificatory functions within the force field of identitarian claims. As religious commissions since the Renaissance had always been surpassed by their painterly conception and execution as primarily serving the parameters of aesthetic ambition, so were the benevolent or imperious boundaries of nation-state culture always trespassed by artistic practices in pursuit of their primary aesthetic challenges (for example, the construction of a perspectival system, the application of a scientific theory of color in painting, or the programmatic revelation of the unconscious at work, to name but three major instances from the immense scope of Western painting), even if these challenges were at all times retroactively honored and officially claimed by the political powers of the nation-state as their proper progeny (as Italian Renaissance painting, as French Impressionism or French Surrealism). The same principle might well be at work in the present situation, when the global reorganization of identities has made the principles of exchange value and surplus value maximization the rule according to which subjects are collectively constructed. Perpetually oscillating between a mobilization

Gabriel Orozco. *My Hands Are My Heart*. 1991. Two silver dye bleach prints, each 9 1/8 × 12 1/2" (23.2 × 31.8 cm). Edition of 5
Courtesy of Marian Goodman Gallery, New York

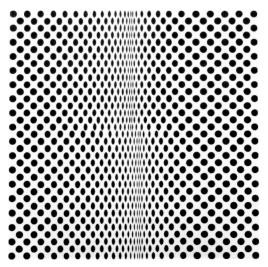

ABOVE:
Gabriel Orozco. *Black Kites*.
1997. Graphite on skull,
8 ½ × 5 × 6 ¼ (21.6 × 12.7 ×
15.9 cm)
Philadelphia Museum of Art.
Gift (by exchange) of Mr. and Mrs.
James P. Magill, 1997

RIGHT:
José Guadalupe Posada.
*Calavera huertista (Death of the
Dictator Huerta)*. 1911. Engraving,
8 ¹¹/₁₆ × 8 ¹¹/₁₆" (22 × 22 cm)

of the obsolescence of earlier formations and manifest diffidence of, if not outright opposition to, the newly emerging principles of enforced identification, Orozco's work plays out its references to myth and national identity against the delusions of the globalized subject, performing the necessary queries and contestations of the ideological constructions of a new global subjectivity.

An example of a work in which both Orozco's iconography and his material procedures of execution make these historical oppositions most evident is *Black Kites*, from 1997, a human skull covered in an intricate graphite checkerboard. The work's structural opposition between nature and culture finds its correlative in the opposition between the seemingly immutable Mexican iconography of the skull (and death-devoted imagery as an apparently foundational element of Mexican culture from archaic rites to the works of José Guadalupe Posada) and the very specific, almost technological inscriptions on the skull's surface by a carefully applied graphite drawing whose compositional order signals the scientific dimensions of cognitive and perceptual mapping in recent painterly practices of abstraction (such as the legacies of Bridget Riley). Historic irony has it that ten years later British artist Damien Hirst would pick up on Orozco's uncanny selection of a human skull as a sculpture with his work *For the Love of God* (2007)—a skull swathed in diamonds—though it is in the differentiation between the two works that the historical and theoretical divergences become most apparent. Orozco's return to one of the "foundational" icons of his national identity establishes the full scope of the contradictions that the formation of any identity innately demands, including the confrontation with systems of unconscious determination and control, and schemes of political, ideological, and economic interest disguised as the "natural" foundations of subjectivity. These "natural" foundations of the subject are transcended in the subject's acts of linguistic and communicative articulations within specific operative practices, such as the abstract stereometric drawing as a cognitive mapping of the skull. Thus the specificity of the local, regional, and national iconography operates as a mnemonic register in Orozco's work to articulate the complex process of subject formation as one of inevitably originating, yet necessarily being emancipated from, all forms of mythical subjection. By contrast, Hirst's model, particularly in its false claim to have a legitimate basis to cite the Aztec tradition of encrusting skulls with precious stones, delivers the striking evidence of a universal fraudulence (aesthetically called "kitsch"

302. Calavera of Huerta

in traditional parlance) in pretending that subjectivity would now in fact be exclusively constituted in the registers of symbolic sign exchange value and surplus value maximization.

Orozco's dialectical method of simultaneously negating a nation-state–based mythical identity and a mythical global universality has become obvious once again in a recent series of sculptures, exhibited in Mexico in the spring of 2009, made from natural varia

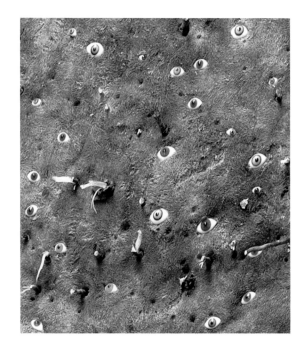

(desiccated tree trunks, mango trees and branches, and cacti that the artist had collected in the desert landscapes of Mexico). These works are titled *Rings in Thorns* (2009), *Stellar Tree* (2009), and, perhaps most strikingly, *Eyes Under Elephant Foot* (2009) and *Nopal Skin with Crystal Eyes* (2009). In the latter two works, found wooden reliefs and volumes were infused with what at first seems a rather incomprehensible onslaught of accumulated artificial eyes. While initially vaguely reminiscent of one of the icons of Mexican modernist photography, Manuel Álvarez Bravo's *Optical Parable* (1931), Orozco's insertion of innumerable glass eyes that stare back at us from the perforations and cells of the weathered wooden fragments neither rejoices in the Surrealist chance encounter of numerous images of eyes in the window of an optician's shop nor in the British power tantrum inflicting on us the mythical universality of death. Rather, these staring eyes induce an uncanny encounter with the spectator's own scopic compulsion, the very foundation and center of the contemporary consumption of cultural production. Thus the spectatorial gaze, the very reduction of the complexities of desire to the mere act of watching, the enforced withering of utopian aspirations, which had once been at the center of the artistic project, to the passive and consumptive greed of mere contemplative circumspection of that which is given, is returned here in the intense stare of the manufactured eyes.

ABOVE:

Gabriel Orozco. *Eyes Under Elephant Foot* (detail). 2009. Beaucarnea trunk and glass eyes, 57 7/8 × 56 7/8 × 55 1/8" (147 × 144.5 × 140 cm)
Charpenel Collection, Guadalajara, Mexico

RIGHT:

Manuel Álvarez Bravo. *Optical Parable*. 1931. Gelatin silver print, 9 1/2 × 7 3/16" (24.1 × 18.2 cm)
The Museum of Modern Art, New York. The Photography Council Fund

# Chronology

**Paulina Pobocha and Anne Byrd**

# 1981–1991: Early Years

**G**ABRIEL OROZCO WAS BORN IN 1962 in Jalapa, in the state of Veracruz, Mexico, to Cristina Félix Romandía, a student of classical piano, and Mario Orozco Rivera, a mural painter and art professor at the Universidad Veracruzana. When Orozco was six, the family relocated to the San Ángel neighborhood of Mexico City so that his father could work with artist David Alfaro Siqueiros on various mural commissions. These included Siqueiros's final and largest mural, *The March of Humanity on Earth toward the Cosmos* (1964–71), housed in the Polyforum Cultural Siqueiros in Mexico City. A third-generation muralist (Escuela Mexicana de Pintura), the elder Orozco belonged to the grand tradition of Siqueiros, José Clemente Orozco, and Diego Rivera.

This was the milieu in which Orozco and his younger sister, Alejandra, were raised. Their father was an outspoken communist who, like most of his colleagues, did not hide his anti-Americanism. Orozco and his sister attended Mexico City's progressive schools and belonged to the Young Pioneers, a communist scout organization. As artist Gabriel Kuri, a longtime friend of Orozco's, remembers, "Speaking English at home was practically forbidden by his father. In those latter days of the Cold War, this rejection of the culture and language of our northern neighbors was a quasi-compulsory political stance for many."[1] Orozco was constantly surrounded by artists and overheard countless conversations on art and politics. His father would take Gabriel to museum exhibitions and to work with him. In one way or another, art was always in the background—and often in the foreground—of Orozco's childhood.

OPPOSITE:
*Lattice.* 1990. Mixed mediums, including vulcanized rubber, catcher's mask, and ball, 15 3/4 × 11 13/16 × 3 15/16" (40 × 30 × 10 cm)

ABOVE:
*Broken Landscape.* 1985. Color slide

In 1981 Orozco enrolled at the Escuela Nacional de Artes Plásticas (ENAP), a division of the Universidad Nacional Autónoma de México (UNAM), from which he graduated in 1984. The academy provided its students a classical fine arts education. Orozco practiced such standards as life drawing, painting in various mediums (oil, watercolor, egg tempera), etching, and printmaking. And, while the school offered its students courses in sculpture and photography, both were disciplines he avoided. He dismissed them on the basis of the traditional parameters of the ENAP program; both would, however, become central to his mature aesthetic. Though few examples of Orozco's work from his student years survive, those that do reveal an interest in both abstract geometry and natural forms. A series of drawings made between 1982 and 1983, titled *Organic Composition*, features animal- and insect-like shapes submerged beneath intricate and loosely geometric armatures.

These years coincided with the beginnings of Orozco's earnest interest in photography. In 1985 an earthquake destroyed entire sections of Mexico City and took the lives of thousands. Soon after, as the city lay in ruins, Orozco would take long walks through the damaged areas. He has recalled, "The city was devastated, dusty and smelly. There was no electricity and not much traffic circulation. Many streets were blocked by rubbish."[2] In the quake's aftermath he was helping in a relief shelter, which housed some of the city's inhabitants whose homes had been demolished. "Walking around the city to help, I began also to take some pictures of the debris. The earthquake gave me an immediate awareness of the city in a different way. It was more exposed, vulnerable. I was uninterested in taking portraits of the suffering people. I would focus on the debris or the constructions in ruins and the street deformed by the shake of the earth. I honestly felt more identified with that, and my feelings about the tragedy were better expressed focusing the lens onto those views, many times not so spectacular at all."

While still in school Orozco lamented what seemed to him to be an overly conservative program of study, a conservatism that corresponded to the dearth of information on art being made outside of Mexico. As he has explained, "Mexico was very nationalistic and very enclosed. It followed from the powerful state apparatus: to create a self-sufficient environment not interested in the outside. And you can see that in the art that was being made at the time in Mexico." In 1986, to broaden his knowledge of contemporary art practice, Orozco left Mexico City for Madrid. There he enrolled in two courses at the Círculo de Bellas Artes.

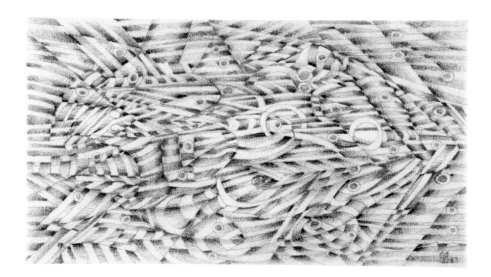

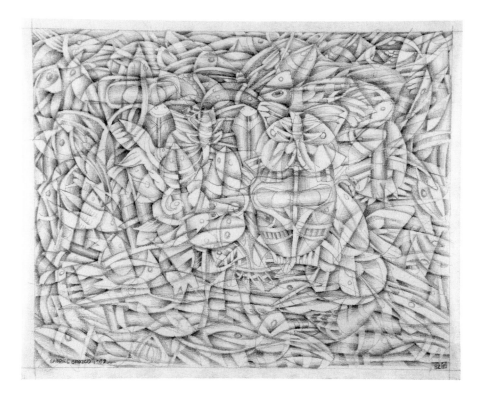

TOP:
Study for *Organic Composition*.
1983. Graphite on paper,
3 ¹⁵/₁₆ × 6 ¹¹/₁₆" (10 × 17 cm)

ABOVE:
*Organic Composition II*.
1982. Graphite on paper,
6 ¹¹/₁₆ × 7 ⁷/₈" (17 × 20 cm)

It was during this year that he first became acquainted with a broad range of postwar art not related to painting or classical sculpture. Particularly important was Orozco's introduction to the work of Robert Smithson, Gordon Matta-Clark, Piero Manzoni, and John Cage. Although much of this information came from his instructors, a significant portion he learned while perusing various bookshops. Orozco has recalled, "It was an exciting time to be in Spain. Spain was very open to new things for the first time. Previously it, too, was quite enclosed, but after the death of Franco it just opened up: there were many books from all over, translated. There was art coming from other parts of Europe. Joseph Beuys was a big deal, there was a big show of his work." This yearlong introduction to the history of Conceptual art markedly changed the artist's approach to his own work. While he did not abandon painting that year in Spain, he saw sculptural possibilities where previously there were none.

The three-dimensional work Orozco created in Spain was largely improvisational. Having no money with which to purchase materials, he made do with what

SISTEMA MASKING TAPE: TOMAR UN MADERO. APLICAR MAS-
KING TAPE FORMANDO RETÍCULA. AMARRANDO COSAS. AÑADIR
UN OBJETO MÁS. DIUREX TRANSPARENTE. CAPTURAR POLVO.
AÑADIR AL MADERO. + SENCILLO. PIENSA. ESCRIBIR POR ESCRIBIR
PORQUE TE GUSTA ESTA TINTA. ACTUAR POR ACTUAR PORQUE
TIENES QUE ACTUAR. SIN SIGNIFICADO. SIN PROPÓSITO FIJO.
CONTAZAR: UN DÍA DESCUBRÍ QUE ~~VAGAR ES MI DESTINO~~ YO
SOY DE LOS QUE SALE DE NOCHE SIN PRO-
PÓSITO FIJO. PLANETA — WANDER — DIVA-
GAR. UBICAR PLANETAS EN TODOS LA-
DOS. PLANETA-OBJETO—COSA DIVAGANDO
SIN SIGNIFICADO, SIN PROPÓSITO APARENTE
¿QUÉ SIGNIFICA? ¿QUE REPRESENTA?
¿POR QUÉ? ¿QUÉ IMPORTA?
COLOCA, INSTALA. HAS QUE LAS COSAS
DIVAGUEN COMO HASTA AHORA LO HAN HECHO. SI
LA TIERRA ESTÁ DIVAGANDO. ¿PORQUÉ TÚ NO
¿HACIA DÓNDE QUIERES DIRIGIRTE? ¿A QUIÉN QUIERES
ENSEÑARLE QUE? PLANETA = DIVAGADOR.
TOMA TUS PLANETAS Y DIVÁGALOS POR LA CIUDAD.
* BUSCAR ERA MI SIGNO. DIVAGA Y ENCUENTRA.
ACTÚA Y ENCUENTRA. NO CAZAR, SINO ENCONTRAR ¿NO
ES LO MISMO? YO NO CREO, NO HAGO MÁS QUE RECOR-
DAR (BORGES). NO GENERAR MÁS BASURA. SÓLO
ORDENARLA SIN SIGNIFICADO. SÍ CERTEZA. CUAN-
DO ESO QUE MANIPULAMOS NOS ACOMODA. ¿POR
QUÉ? ¿QUIÉN LO SABE? NO PIENSES QUE ACTÚAS.
OLVIDO OLVIDO OLVIDO. SISTEMA. CONTROL.
TEOLOGÍA Y GEOMETRÍA = CAOS.
DONDE QUIERA QUE ESTÉS, RECUERDA QUE LO MÁS IMPORTANTE
ES QUE AHÍ ESTÁS.

LEFT:
Detail of Notebook 1, p. 83.
Felt-tip pen and cut-and-
taped printed paper on
notebook page, 5 7/8 × 4 1/8"
(15 × 10.5 cm)

BELOW:
*Storm*. 1989. Synthetic
polymer paint on wood,
15 3/4 × 11 13/16 × 5 7/8"
(40 × 30 × 15 cm)

he found: pieces of discarded wood, branches, or bricks. And although he sometimes brought the materials into his small and unheated studio space, he just as
often created sculptural assemblages in situ, then abandoned them immediately
upon construction. Orozco later recalled, "On my way to the Bellas Artes from
Atocha, I created a lot of things. There was a timber yard nearby where I found
bits of planks, which I arranged on the pavement to see how they looked . . . . My
walk to the Bellas Artes was a process itself, finding things, making and undoing
. . . [I] was concentrating on the phenomenon, on the found objects and how to
assemble them."[3] It was in Madrid that Orozco embraced the impermanence of
the sculptural gesture while dissociating it from its monumental implications. Of
all the books, stories, and experiences Orozco brought back with him to Mexico,
this was the most consequential.

In 1987 Orozco returned to Mexico City. Soon his newly ignited enthusiasm
for sculpture made itself apparent even in painting. The paintings of this period,
while still loosely geometric and abstract, evidence a new attention to materiality.
Rather than use canvas or board, hefty chunks of wood now served as the support.

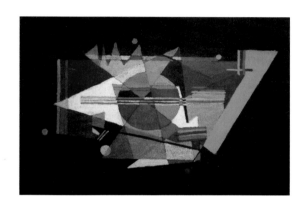

TOP:
*Salome's Dress*. 1989. Synthetic polymer paint on wood, 12 3/16 × 17 15/16 × 1 9/16" (31 × 45.5 × 4 cm)

ABOVE:
*Saturn*. 1975. Pastel on paper, 13 3/16 × 18 11/16" (33.5 × 47.5 cm)

* Unless otherwise noted, full bibliographic citations for accompanying quotations throughout these texts may be found in the Selected Bibliography on pp. 253–254 in this volume.

In a work like *Salome's Dress* (1989) the painted elements, though still the primary point of interest, compete for attention with the heavy, sculptural support. This effect is magnified in *Storm* (1989), a painting on a splintered piece of wood, that can best be described as a hybrid between painting and sculpture. These works also betray the unlikely influence of Byzantine and Russian icon painting. Orozco first encountered icon painting during a trip to the Soviet Union he took with his Young Pioneers troop. In 1986, traveling in Europe using Madrid as a base, he became reacquainted with the technique on a visit to the Alexander Nevsky Cathedral in Sofia, Bulgaria. What appealed to him most was the material nature of those paintings rather than their religious function.

Shortly after his return to Mexico City, Orozco was approached by a group of slightly younger art students who asked to work with him in his studio. They too were dissatisfied by the narrow education they were receiving in Mexico and by the limited information on non-Mexican art available at the time. The meetings evolved into a workshop rather than anything resembling a formal seminar. Soon Orozco and the others—Damián Ortega, Gabriel Kuri, Abraham Cruzvillegas, and Dr. Lakra (Jerónimo López Ramírez)—dubbed their weekly meetings Taller de los Viernes, or Friday Workshop. As Cruzvillegas has recalled:

> When our get-togethers at Gabriel's house came to be defined as "workshops," we probably had the teacher-apprentice relationship in mind; but the odd thing was that, in this case, there was no trade or craft to learn, no secret knowledge, no philosopher's stone; we were not in pursuit of a mystical state or extraordinary manual dexterity. . . . Our activities were quite different from those of an artist's studio or a class offered by ENAP; in fact, Gabriel himself always made very different things and never told us explicitly "this is how it's done," or "make it this way," nor did he ever say "don't do that." Once there we'd talk about common concerns and then, individually, spend our time doing other stuff, each person focusing on his own work, be it reading, drawing, painting, or watching someone else.[4]

The group met once a week for nearly five years. Other artists, curators, and writers occasionally began to visit the Workshop. Over time Orozco's home in Mexico City became a center for the exchange of ideas and a place where many artistic and curatorial projects took shape.

Gabriel Orozco, Mauricio
Maillé, and Mauricio
Rocha. *Scaffolding for Our
Modern Ruins*. 1987. Wood,
dimensions variable

*Chapel*. 1989. Taxidermied
elephant head and tree
trunks, dimensions variable.
Installation view of *A propósito*,
Museo del Ex-Convento
del Desierto de los Leones,
Mexico City

52:
*Heart of the River*. 1991. Silver
dye bleach print, 16 × 20"
(40.6 × 50.8 cm). Edition of 5

*The Hero of the Earthquake*. 1985
(printed 2005). Chromogenic
color print, 16 × 20" (40.6 × 50.8
cm). Edition of 6

P. 53:
*Stones in the Fence*. 1989. Silver
dye bleach print, 16 × 20"
(40.6 × 50.8 cm). Edition of 5

*River of Trash*. 1990. Silver
dye bleach print, 16 × 20"
(40.6 × 50.8 cm). Edition of 5

The work Orozco was making in the late 1980s was not figurative, and had
nothing to do with either Surrealism or with Neo-Mexicanism, the commercially
popular style of painting produced in Mexico in the late 1980s. In general, it did
not attract notice. One exception was Orozco's 1987 contribution to the salon
Alternative Spaces (Espacios Alternativos). First held in 1985, the salon was a state-
sponsored art competition that showcased work by younger artists. It was the
only government-sanctioned exhibition that recognized art under the broader
designations of installation art, ephemeral art, readymade art, and so on. In 1987
Orozco, together with artist Mauricio Maillé and architect Mauricio Rocha, created *Scaffolding for Our Modern Ruins* for the competition. *Scaffolding for Our Modern
Ruins* was just what its title indicated: wooden beams hammered together to form
an ostensibly supportive structure that was then positioned at the entrance to
Mexico City's Museum of Modern Art, as if to prop up the walls and doorways of
the institution. The piece was a direct comment on the sorry state of affairs in the
aftermath of the 1985 earthquake. Despite two years passing, buildings throughout the city lay in rubble or were barely standing, and many remained covered
by this ubiquitous scaffolding; the work implicitly criticized the Mexican govern-
ment's inability to remedy the disastrous situation. *Scaffolding for Our Modern Ruins*

won first place in the salon. Due to a controversy surrounding other work in the exhibition, the salon was temporarily shuttered soon after the exhibition opened. This second Alternative Spaces was also the last.

After the closing of Alternative Spaces, there was no place in the city, officially sanctioned or otherwise, in which to show work of the sort that Orozco and a few colleagues were making. So in 1989, together with independent curator Guillermo Santamarina, Orozco organized an exhibition that showcased installation-based art. *A propósito* opened in April at the Museo del Ex-Convento del Desierto de los Leones, a former Carmelite monastery located on the outskirts of Mexico City. It featured the work of fourteen artists. The subtext of the show was an homage to Joseph Beuys, whose "everyone is an artist" credo was well suited to this experiment. Beuys's work was represented by a small selection of photographs and a single poem. Beyond that, the connection to Beuys was loose. As Orozco has recalled, "Nobody did a real homage to Beuys in their own work; instead they made work that was related to the space." Orozco's own installation physically related to the space as much as it evoked the history of the site. High on the white wall of a spare room, Orozco hung a taxidermied elephant head; he placed in the center of the room gnarled and knotted tree trunks, themselves evocative of body parts. Aware that the room had once served as a chapel, Orozco positioned the elephant head in place of a crucifix, with the pile of wood visually doubling as its body.

Despite the success of *A propósito*, established art critics and commercial galleries in Mexico City remained uninterested in Orozco's variety of art, and the next years presented few opportunities for him to exhibit his work in his native country. Nonetheless, several important works date from this time, among them *Recaptured Nature* (1990), a giant balloon made from salvaged inner-tube tires conceived to travel, deflated, to New York for an exhibition at the Museum of

OPPOSITE:
*My Hands Are My Heart.* 1991.
Two silver dye bleach prints,
each 9 1/8 × 12 1/2" (23.2 × 31.8 cm).
Edition of 5

ABOVE:
*My Hand Is the Memory of Space.*
1991. Wooden ice cream
spoons, dimensions variable

Contemporary Hispanic Art; *My Hands Are My Heart* (1991), an economical yet elo-quent sculpture of clay squeezed to resemble a heart, and *My Hand Is the Memory of Space* (1991), a floor-bound sculpture consisting entirely of wooden ice cream spoons radiating outward while tracing the outline of Orozco's hand. The wooden ice cream spoons used to construct the latter work were ever-present in Mexico City, and their lozenge shape reminded Orozco of fingers. Configured as they were, they became an outward extension of a hand, now represented only as a negative space, a trace or a memory of where Orozco's hand once was.

Orozco's interest in photography continued. Although he was frequently sus-picious of photography as an enterprise, he had been exposed to it early through the work of artist Graciela Iturbide, the mother of Manuel and Mauricio Rocha, two of Orozco's closest friends since childhood. Iturbide's partner, Pedro Meyer, was also a well-known photographer. Nonetheless, Orozco was reluctant to pur-chase a camera: "I always thought that Mexican artistic photojournalism was a little too classist, racist, and sexist. If a photographer took a photo of a naked woman or an Indian, they would title the work *A Shadow* or *An Angel . . .* or else they would name it after the town where the image was taken (I guess as a man-ner to say the photographer was there in a far and exotic place). But, of course, if the photo was a portrait of a white man or woman, it was titled *Don Fulano de Tal y Cual*, including all three last names! I always found repulsive how the camera was, consciously or unconsciously, used as a tool for exploitation."

In 1991, together with his girlfriend, Maria Gutierrez, Orozco decided to go to Brazil, where they would spend two months. Prior to his departure Orozco pur-chased his first camera, a small, cheap Nikon Auto Focus. Later that same year, he took one of his best-known photographs, *Crazy Tourist*. Taken in a small village in Bahia, Brazil, the photo is of a deserted marketplace—empty save for the solitary

*"Photography provides yet another means by which Orozco has freed sculpture of its weight. Throughout his work the two mediums enjoy a slip-sliding relationship, collapsing into each other to the degree that one cannot discuss them separately. This holds true from the time of Orozco's first work in Mexico, where he performed 'actions' resulting in sculptural tableaux that he then photographed. The sculptural situation existed for the sake of the photograph it would always be, while the situation itself was in most cases short lived."*

Ann Temkin, "Afterword," in *Gabriel Orozco: Photogravity* (1999), p. 175

ABOVE:
*Green Paper.* 1991. Silver dye bleach print, 16 × 20" (40.6 × 50.8 cm). Edition of 5

OPPOSITE:
*Sleeping Dog.* 1990. Silver dye bleach print, 20 × 16" (50.8 × 40.6 cm). Edition of 5

oranges Orozco placed one per table. As the oranges recede into space they generate a constellation of points, each related to the other. In this work Orozco transforms a typically bustling marketplace into an abstract tableau. *Crazy Tourist* is both a sculpture, the product of the generative action of positioning the oranges on the tables, and a photograph, the final image with which we are left. In this sense, photography is absorbed by Orozco's larger artistic enterprise. From this point forth, a camera would often accompany the artist on his meandering walks. If he encountered an interesting sculptural situation, or if he created one, the camera captured the image. And, while the photographic print certainly related to the sculptural situation pictured, Orozco considered the image self-sufficient and not second to the sculpture: "The point was to construct an image that recorded something that happened in reality. It was not about photographic composition or drama. It was more about sketches and immersions, and not about explaining an action through photography. I wanted to construct a self-sustaining image that generates meaning by itself and is not a mere anecdote of the action. I use color prints just because I see in color, and I always dislike the black-and-white aesthetic dramatization of reality in classic photojournalism."

*"This Cagean aesthetic of a universal equivalence of all textures, procedures and materials has had a tremendous impact on Orozco's conception of sculpture and photography in general, and on their interdependence in particular. From the beginning of his work, the multiplicity and simultaneity of seemingly incompatible materials and sculptural production processes attest to that impact."*

Benjamin H. D. Buchloh, "Cosmic Reification: Gabriel Orozco's Photographs," in *Gabriel Orozco* (2004), p. 76

ABOVE:
*Crazy Tourist*. 1991.
Chromogenic color print,
16 × 20" (40.6 × 50.8 cm).
Edition of 5

OPPOSITE:
Notebook 2, p. 66. Graphite
and cut-and-taped paper on
notebook page, 10 3/4 × 8 1/16"
(27.3 × 20.5 cm)

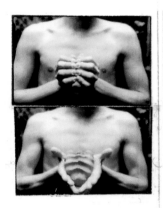

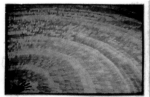

60

* EL ARTE SE VA
EXPANDIENDO COMO
EL UNIVERSO.

1 XII 92

4:47 P.M.

6:22 P.M. TIENDA SEÑORA. PAPEL ALBANENE. FICHAS GO.

6:44 P.M. REGRESÉ CON LA SEÑORA Y COMPRÉ LAS FICHAS DEL GO (SÓLO BLANCAS). TAMBIÉN DIEZ HOJAS DE PAPEL ALBANENE QUE TIENEN ALGUNA RELACIÓN AUNQUE AÚN NO LA DESCUBRO. LA CAJA DE LAS FICHAS ES CASI UNA ESFERA. DE MADERA. LA TAPA CIRCULAR ANUNCIA LOS ANILLOS DE LO QUE FUE UN ÁRBOL. CÍRCULO TRAS CÍRCULO EL PUNTO DE LA PRESENCIA.*
EL GO ES UN JUEGO DE TERRITORIALIDAD. LO INTENTÉ JUGAR UNA VEZ. HACE UNOS DIEZ AÑOS. CADA FICHA (PIENSO HOY) IMPLICA UNA PRESENCIA, OCUPAR UN ESPACIO. AL ~~DESPARRAMARLAS~~ ESPARCIRLAS EN CUALQUIER ESPACIO OCUPAREMOS UN TERRITORIO, SIN INTENCIÓN APARENTE. COMO LAS HOJAS CAÍDAS. COMO LOS CHICLES ESCUPIDOS EN LA ACERA. (AHORA PIENSO EN LA FOTO QUE TOMÉ DE LAS HOJAS DE ÁRBOL JAPONÉS CAÍDAS EN LA ACERA ENTRE LOS PUNTOS NEGROS DE LOS CHICLES. EL AZAR (O ~~EL DESTINO~~ LOS MOTIVOS DEL UNIVERSO) LOS PUSO AHÍ. AHORA ES DEMASIADO TARDE — LAS HOJAS SE HAN IDO CON EL OTOÑO — PERO ME HUBIERA GUSTADO PONER UNA FICHA DE GO EN CADA CHICLE ESCUPIDO MARCANDO UN TERRITORIO ININTENCIONADO Y LA PRESENCIA DE UNA PRESENCIA. LO HARÉ MAÑANA SIN LAS HOJAS. SÓLO FICHAS DE GO BLANCAS SOBRE CADA CHICLE ESCUPIDO ~~EN UN E~~ EN CUALQUIER BANQUETA. ESCUPIR TERRITORIOS. BUSCO EN EL DICCIONARIO LA PALABRA GO EN INGLÉS: (YA LA HABÍA BUSCADO Y POR ESA PALABRA COMPRÉ LAS FICHAS):

ESCUPIR TERRITORIOS

GO: 1. (TO MOVE ALONG, TRAVEL, PROCEED. 2. (TO WORK PROPERLY, OPERATE) (THE CLOCK IS GOING)
3. (TO ACT, SOUND, ETC. AS SPECIFIED. 4. (TO TURN OUT; RESULT. 5. (TO PASS (AS OF TIME).
6. (TO BECOME. 7. TO BE EXPRESSED; SUNG, ETC. 8. TO HARMONIZE; AGREE. (BLUE GOES WITH
GOLD). 9. TO BE ACCEPTED, VALID, ETC. 10. TO LEAVE; DEPART. 11. TO COME TO AN END; FAIL.
ETC. ~~Y OTROS MÁS QUE ... ALGUNA RELACIÓN~~ ES IRRELEVANTE.
• GO BACK; GO FOR; TO GO. • GO

GO. (GABRIEL OROZCO) (ODIO ESCRIBIR MI NOMBRE). GO

⊚ ⊙ ⊙ ⊙ ⊝ ⊝ ⊝ GO. GO GO GO GO

CORCHOLATAS EN EL SUELO. ESTRELLAS. CHICLES. GOTAS. GOTAS. GO. GO. GO.

## 1992: Migrations

OPPOSITE:
Notebook 2, p. 139.
Ballpoint pen, cut-and-pasted
printed paper, and coffee
stains on notebook page,
10 3/4 × 8 1/16" (27.3 × 20.5 cm)

ABOVE:
*Recaptured Nature*. 1990.
Vulcanized rubber, approx.
29 1/2 × 41 5/16 × 33 7/16"
(75 × 105 × 85 cm). One of
three versions

*"In* [Recaptured Nature] *(1990) two inner tubes take the form of a single, air-filled sphere, but this morphological transformation leaves all the elements that make up a tire intact. Created by the same gluing and vulcanizing methods used to make conventional inner tubes, the ball only emphasizes the flexible and resilient qualities of rubber and the expansive and cushioning properties of air that make these objects particularly suited to rolling smoothly across a surface. What's more, by emphasizing the tubes as containers of air, rather than things contained in something else, Orozco reverses their familiar position, the better for us to study or even admire them. What is normally ignominiously hidden is puffed impressively to capacity, and in its proud, effulgent presence attains a kind of loopy magnificence."*

Laura J. Hoptman, "Options 47: Gabriel Orozco" (1994), n.p.

SHORTLY AFTER RETURNING FROM BRAZIL IN THE WINTER OF 1991 Orozco received an unexpected visit at his home in Mexico City from Catherine de Zegher, then director of the Kanaal Art Foundation, in Kortrijk, Belgium. De Zegher had traveled to Mexico to survey contemporary art in the capital and to select work by living artists to include in a forthcoming exhibition, *America, Bride of the Sun*, organized by the Royal Museum of Fine Arts, Antwerp, for which she was the co-curator, together with Paul Vandenbrock. The exhibition examined five hundred years of Latin American art and coincided with the five-hundred-year anniversary of the discovery of the Americas. A historical survey, it was unusual for its thematic rather than chronological structure. As de Zegher later explained, "This exhibition could also be considered as an attempt to focus our attention on the European side of imperialism, to question Western hegemony and the mechanics by which Europe consolidated its empire and continues to consolidate it. Capitalism may have changed, I mean the very way land is conquered is different . . . but the motivations remain the same."[1] To make this point, the contemporary art was displayed throughout the exhibition rather than isolated in its own area. When the show opened in February two of Orozco's sculptures, *Recaptured Nature* (1990) and *My Hands Are My Heart* (1991), were included alongside work by Cildo Meireles, Lygia Clark, and Lucio Fontana as well as sixteenth- and seventeenth-century masterworks.

*Recaptured Nature*, an air-filled sphere of vulcanized rubber, was constructed entirely from the inner tubes of truck tires, which Orozco found in an industrial junkyard just outside of Mexico City. With the help of a mechanic who regularly repaired tires, Orozco split the inner circumference of one inner tube and then, using rubber from another tire, patched it together to form an inflatable sphere. The goal was straightforward: according to Orozco it was "an exercise in topology in which everything can become everything else, where each shape can develop into something different." But the work was also an object seized from and rooted in reality. As the artist has said, "It's not a Platonic sphere, pure, and perfectly

geometric; it's very much an object of nature, dirty, recovered." Indeed, the memory of the material's previous function is imprinted on the scratched and soiled surface of the work.

*My Hands Are My Heart* carries a different imprint: a terracotta sculpture, it bears the impression of Orozco's body. To create the sculpture Orozco squeezed a ball of clay in the palms of his hands, forming a heart-shaped object that reveals the processes of its making. As with the floor sculpture *My Hand Is the Memory of Space* (1991), the body is defined by the displacement of mass and presented as an absence. For the exhibition in Antwerp, Orozco's terracotta heart was placed in a vitrine in close proximity to Frida Kahlo's *Annotations and Memories* (1943), a self-portrait in oil depicting Kahlo's face contained within a cracking anatomical heart. In contrast to this fantastical treatment, Orozco strikes a keen balance between the base materiality of the object and its possible poetic implications. In a lecture Orozco gave in Mexico City in early 2001, he referenced a notebook entry in which he wrote, "The artist is first and foremost a consumer. The materials he consumes and the way in which he consumes them influence the development of his work and the subsequent implications. This consumption system is the first technique the artist has to define. Having abandoned my studio or workshop, I became a consumer of anything at hand and a producer of what already exists."[2] The clay that Orozco used here is not a traditional art material but clay taken from a brick factory in Cholula, Mexico. Like nearly all of Orozco's sculpture, it was made from scavenged components. And despite its new incarnation as an art-object, the material nonetheless carries the memory of its previous function, adding a layer of meaning that looks beyond the sculpture's physical parameters. As Jean Fisher aptly noted, "Orozco and others in the exhibition tend to use urban refuse as a medium, less perhaps for its esthetic than for its political potential."[3] *My Hands Are My Heart* is a complex but humble object whose poetic

TOP:
*Futon Homeless*. 1992
Silver dye bleach print,
16 × 20" (40.6 × 50.8 cm)
Edition of 2

ABOVE:
*My Hands Are My Heart*. 1991
Fired clay, 6 × 4 × 6"
(15.2 × 10.2 × 15.2 cm)

OPPOSITE:
Notebook 2, p. 126. Graphite,
cut-and-taped printed paper,
and toothpaste spit on
notebook page, 10 3/4 × 8 1/16"
(27.3 × 20.5 cm)

VOY EN EL FERRY: 3:15.P.M. TRABAJÉ TRES HORAS. TENGO
HAMBRE. (ESTOY VIENDO LA ESTATUA DE LA LIBERTAD, LA CHAPA-
RRITA). ODIO CARGAR CON MI CÁMARA. ODIO DEPENDER DE
ELLA. NECESITO OTRO LENTE. UN SEMIGRAN ANGULAR. LO QUE
VEN MIS OJOS. ES INTENSO ESTE TRABAJO, ESTAS TRES
HORAS. IR RECORRIENDO Y VIÉNDOLO TODO. (AHÍ VIENE
LA ISLA). TODO EN TODAS PARTE. ENCONTRAR. VISUALIZAR
EN GRANDE Y EN PEQUEÑA ESCALA. TENSIÓN CONSTANTE.
RECUERDO: ENTRE 2:00 Y 2:30 ME ENCONTRÉ CON UN TERRE-
NO-ALMACÉN DE MATERIALES DE CONSTRUCCIÓN. MONTÍCULOS
ALFOMBRADOS. FOTO. RECUERDO "LADRILLOS EN TERRENO BALDÍO=
ALFOMBRAS Y PIEDRAS EN MONTÍCULOS. PAISAJE. MONTAÑAS.

> "A bicycle, circling round and round, crosses a manhole cover en route and passes through two puddles, one almost dried up, the other still flush. The wet bicycle tires draw circling lines of movement on the dry pavement, paralleling the gesture of the painter's brush on canvas. The trail drawn by the tires gives way to the branches and fragments of grafting reflected in the water, extending reflection both literally and figuratively as immediate, concrete mirroring and a deepening of thought processes. Before the rays of the sun can put a speedy end to his actionist scenario, Gabriel Orozco shoots a picture of this profoundly elementary rendition of the overlapping cycles of body, spirit and nature: Extension of Reflection (1992)."

Bernhard Bürgi, "The Extension of Reflection," in *Gabriel Orozco* (1996), p. 7

LEFT:
Detail from Notebook 1, p. 72. Felt-tip pen and printed paper on notebook page, 5 7/8 × 4 1/8" (15 × 10.5 cm)

OPPOSITE:
*Extension of Reflection*. 1992. Chromogenic color print, 16 × 20" (40.6 × 50.8 cm). Edition of 5

*Foam*. 1992. Silver dye bleach print, 16 × 20" (40.6 × 50.8 cm). Edition of 5

potency proceeds from the modesty of its materials and the simplicity of Orozco's gesture.

*America, Bride of the Sun* was a pivotal exhibition for the artist, and "the beginning of many things," as Orozco has said. "It was the first time I had a show with such good artists, in a world-class museum. For me, it was the first international exhibition on that high of a level." The show provided a small but significant amount of international recognition, and it was meaningful to Orozco that it was sited in Europe rather than North America: "I was passing through Europe and *then* coming to New York; the European filter was important and interesting." Shortly before the exhibition closed in late May Orozco left Mexico City for New York. Prompting the move were personal as well as professional reasons—his soon-to-be wife, Maria Gutierrez, had recently begun to study at New York University. Just as significant, however, was Orozco's admission that there was little notice of his work in his native Mexico City, and certainly no market. As he remembers, "There was not a single gallery in Mexico interested in my work, zero. And besides [Guillermo] Santamarina, there was not a single curator understanding my work. I wanted to do many things, but in Mexico, where I had so little support, it was not clear how I could do them." By contrast, even

P. 66:
*Five Problems*. 1992. Silver dye bleach print, 16 × 20" (40.6 × 50.8 cm). Edition of 5

*Cats and Watermelons*. 1992. Chromogenic color print, 16 × 20" (40.6 × 50.8 cm). Edition of 5

P. 67:
Notebook 2, p. 124. Ballpoint pen, graphite, cut-and-taped printed paper, and photographs on notebook page, 10 3/4 × 8 1/16" (27.3 × 20.5 cm)

ESPUMA + ESPUMA. ÁRBOLES Y VIDRIOS AZU
SOMBRA DEL CIELO. PASTA DE DIENTES
SUBIR EL ÁRBOL O COLGARSE DE LA
EN LA TIERRA.

prior to his arrival in New York, Orozco's work had already garnered the attention and the support of critics and curators, among them Benjamin Buchloh, whom Orozco had met in Antwerp. In many ways the cultural landscape of New York in the early 1990s was primed to support Orozco's work. The art community was still recovering from the art market crash of 1990, and ready for an alternative to the Neo-Geo and Neo-Expressionist paintings that had dominated the previous decade. Orozco's quiet, barely there sculptures and sculptural interventions provided a point of contrast.

As New York became Orozco's adopted city, Orozco became its adoptee. However, this mutual embrace was complicated by Orozco's reluctance to define himself as a "New York artist." This rejection was not only an attempt to circumvent the expectations such labels carry, whether that of the exotic outsider or the perennial art world insider; for Orozco it was also a turning away from the sensibilities of the previous decade. The artist has said, "This labeling was a way of selling a package, the tendency to present a new generation of artists from New York. I was very much against that kind of packaging. The eighties were quite cruel, quite unfair, and quite frivolous in that respect. As a '90s artist, I was very much against the '80s." Speaking of himself and of like-minded colleagues, Orozco continued, "We behaved differently, we made art differently and I think for a little while we managed very well to get rid of a mentality that was very '80s. The '90s were a time of globalization and multiculturalism. I don't like these names, but there were some good intentions—in trying to open up cultural institutions and the art industry to look at the world in a more open way." These principles, established early in Orozco's career, at once reflected and responded to the cultural zeitgeist. In November of 1992 Bill Clinton successfully challenged incumbent George H. W. Bush to the office of the President of the United States, and soon Cold War politics were replaced by a new era of globalization. In a 1997 article titled "Nomads," art historian James Meyer similarly characterized the 1990s as an era of "unprecedented mobility and migration, the expansion of multinational companies and entertainment/news oligarchies, the spread of communication technologies," and argued a link between the culture at large and the art it produced, citing Orozco's oeuvre as "thematizing a peripatetic existence in staged, poetical figurations of transience."[4] Considered in this context, Orozco's reluctance to fully identify as a "New York" or a "Mexican" artist was not so much a rejection of either culture but rather a rejection of an exhausted and rigid worldview that made less and less sense as national boundaries became increasingly penetrable and national identities more fluid.

In October 1992 Orozco participated in an exhibition titled *Si colón supiera!* . . . (*If Columbus Only Knew!* . . .), organized by the Museo de Monterrey, Mexico. The exhibition's curators, Olivier Debroise and Rina Epelstein, focused on the ephemeral nature of contemporary art. Orozco showed two new works: *Yielding Stone* and *Dial Tone*. Although *Yielding Stone*—a solid ball of gray plasticine equivalent in weight to the artist's body—was conceived in New York, he constructed the work in Monterrey. The work was not considered finished until Orozco rolled it through the streets and a patina of dirt, pebbles, and debris formed on its surface. Displayed in the museum gallery, it continued to collect dirt and dust, incorporating foreign particles until they became aggregate components of the body of the work. The idea was inspired in part by a trip to The Museum of Modern Art; Orozco has recalled, "In that impeccable museum, I was amused to find trash and dust hidden in intermediate spaces, missed by the eyes of the public. This relationship of force between resplendence, which is what is visible, and dust, which is the dullness that covers and turns into a thing in itself, is one of my favorite motifs." *Yielding Stone* embraces this motif by allowing the hidden and the undesirable to become the subject of the work.

*Dial Tone* engages two central strategies of Orozco's: those of topology and appropriation. For this work Orozco removed the pages of a Monterrey phone book and cut them down to remove all of the names until only columns of

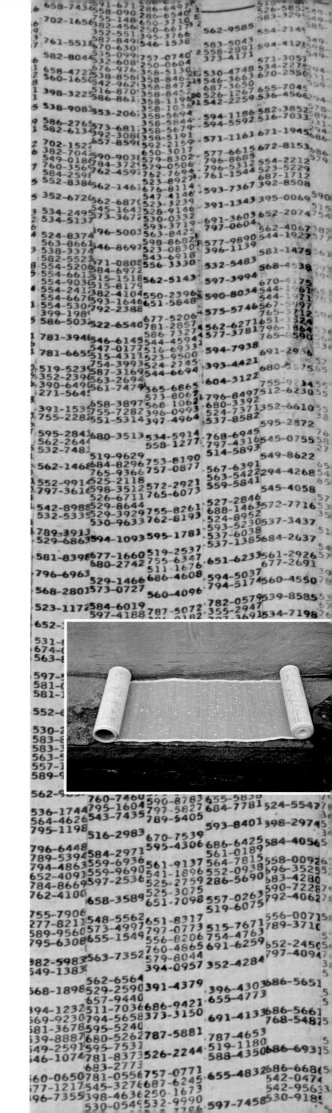

numbers remained. He then pasted these columns, one abutting the other, on a sheet of Japanese paper 82 feet (25 meters) long. The work retains the attributes of a telephone book, but one reimagined as a Japanese scroll. As Orozco has explained, "When you get close you can see a kind of grid or a kind of landscape. At some point, I called it *Phone River* because you unroll this thing and you see a torrent of numbers. It represents everybody in the city, they just don't have a name." Whether using inner tubes, phone book pages, or any of the many found objects that appear regularly in his work, Orozco's physical manipulations never conceal an object's original function or transform its principal identity. Rather, the found object returns as a reconfiguration of the original. As Orozco has said, "These objects, they keep being what they were after I've cut them and reassembled them, they keep functioning. There is a continuity to the characteristics of the materials."

Following the show in Monterrey, Orozco returned to New York and began preparing for a group exhibition at the New Museum of Contemporary Art that would open shortly after the start of the new year. And while several of Orozco's works would travel to Mexico throughout the course of the 1990s, the majority of the artist's activities took place outside of Mexico for the rest of the decade.

ABOVE:
*Maria, Maria, Maria*. 1992.
Phone book page with
erasures, 11×9⅛"
(27.9×23.2 cm)

RIGHT:
*Dial Tone* (detail). 1992.
Cut-and-pasted phone book
pages on Japanese paper,
11"×10' 10" (27.9×330.2 cm).
Artist's proof

INSET:
*Dial Tone*. 1992. Cut-and-pasted
phone book pages on Japanese
paper, 11"×34' (27.9×1,036 cm).
One of three versions

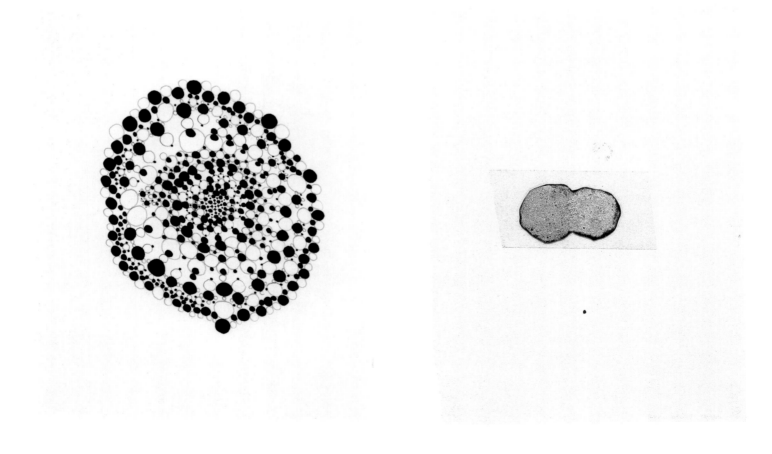

RIGHT:
*Horse*. 1992. Chromogenic
color print, 20 × 16"
(50.8 × 40.6 cm). Edition of 5

OPPOSITE, CLOCKWISE FROM TOP:
*Horseshit*. 1992. Silver dye
bleach print, 16 × 20"
(40.6 × 50.8 cm). Edition of 5

Untitled. 1992. Ink, graphite,
toothpaste spit, and tape on
paper, 11 × 8" (27.9 × 20.3 cm)

Untitled. 1992. Graphite
and ink on paper, 10 ½ × 8 ¼"
(26.7 × 20.9 cm)

## 1993: First Was the Spitting

"A plasticine ball was rolled on the streets, allowed to receive the imprint of any markings on the pavement, even to accept whatever pebble or dust stuck to it, so that at the end of its tour the ball had turned into a lump of material marked with the accidents it encountered as it rolled over the urban surface."

Miguel González Virgen, *Of Games, the Infinite and Worlds: The Work of Gabriel Orozco* (2003), pp. 96–97

"The stone relayed the outside impress of a changing world, the kick of the spectator, the paw of the dog. It shrugged off pictures. Orozco speaks of it variously. He told me that it is like the stone in nature on which animals sit."

Molly Nesbit, "The Tempest," in *Gabriel Orozco* (2000), p. 124

IN JANUARY THE EXHIBITION *IN TRANSIT*, organized by France Morin with Kostas Gounis and John Jeffries, opened at the New Museum of Contemporary Art in New York. A group show that included more than twenty-five artists, the exhibition focused on the complex and often transitory nature of the urban experience. As the accompanying brochure explained, "The subject of *In Transit* is both the involuntary movement of human beings through urban spaces, and the practices through which spaces are produced, shaped and represented."[1] Orozco showed a second version of *Yielding Stone* (1992), the plasticine sphere embedded with dirt, rocks, and other detritus from the city street. Although the first version was included in the exhibition the previous year in Monterrey, Mexico, the work was conceived with *In Transit* in mind. For the exhibition in New York Orozco rolled the greasy sphere down Broadway, and once sufficiently dirty it was placed in the museum. While installed it was still susceptible to the curious, probing fingers of museumgoers as well as the dust present in even the most pristine gallery space. As Orozco has explained, "It is a body that is vulnerable to time, to the city. . . . The work demonstrates the process of its making. . . . It, itself, is doing the work." This surrogate body, standing in for Orozco's own, is continually subject to the processes of change. Every speck of dust or dirt that lands on its surface, however minimal, becomes part of the work.

After *Yielding Stone*, Orozco would use plasticine again in several subsequent sculptures. An oil-based modeling clay that does not dry or harden when exposed to air and which cannot be fired, plasticine is often employed by sculptors in preparatory studies or as a molding material for plaster casts. Its malleability generally makes it unsuitable for the creation of permanent sculpture. By molding the plasticine into a sphere, rolling it in the street, and allowing dirt to gather on its surface, Orozco accentuates the innate properties of the medium: "The beginning of the work is also the end of the work. That's just what it is—a mound of plasticine. Every time you see it, it's going to be damaged, it's going to be fingerprinted, it's going to be different. It is a non-definitive proposition, the opposite of a static monument but sculpture as a body in motion." With *Lost Line*, another sculpture made from plasticine, movement is mapped onto the work's surface. Orozco began with a small ball of the material and gradually added new layers, rolling the growing mass into a lumpy sphere. As he rolled the ball, he wound white cotton packing twine around its circumference. These thin white lines remain visible in the completed work. *Lost Line* was made on the occasion of Orozco's first solo exhibition, in Kortrijk, Belgium, which opened in April. The exhibition, curated by Catherine de Zegher and sponsored by the Kanaal Art Foundation, took place in an abandoned brewery. Orozco also showed two other plasticine sculptures, *Orange Without Space,* an orange skin stuffed and covered with black plasticine, and *Soft Blue,* a blue plasticine sphere with the letters CCCP inscribed in its surface, as well as *Recaptured Nature* (1990).

The sustained intensity with which Orozco engages circles and spheres, evident in a number of the works on view in Kortrijk, is nowhere as apparent as in his drawings and notebooks, where there are pages filled with little circles growing organically from the center of the paper. As the artist has explained, "I think the circles started as a way of cleaning myself. It was a mental exercise of

*"Similarly of the body are his early drawings that utilize spit as a medium. By mixing his saliva with toothpaste, Orozco makes visible something that would otherwise disappear once it dried on paper. In* First Was the Spitting *(1993), a four-part work on graph paper, he spat near the centre of each page, encircling the stains with marks in graphite and pen, as if the organic elements were dictating the shape of the drawings in outward spirals. In some parts of these compositions, Orozco re-drew the lines of the grid over the spit, superimposing an order onto what is otherwise organic."*

Rochelle Steiner, "Path of Thought," in *Gabriel Orozco* (2004), p. 122

CLOCKWISE FROM TOP LEFT:
*Lost Line*. 1993. Plasticine and cotton string, approx. 19" (48.3 cm) diam. One of three versions

*Soft Blue*. 1993. Plasticine and Letraset, approx. 4 1/2" (11.4 cm) diam. One of three versions

*Orange without Space*. 1993. Plasticine and orange, approx. 12 3/4 × 15 1/2 × 15 1/2" (32.4 × 39.4 × 39.4 cm). One of three versions

OPPOSITE, CLOCKWISE FROM TOP LEFT:
*First Was the Spitting I–IV*. 1993. Ink, graphite, and toothpaste spit on four sheets of graph paper, each 16 1/2 × 12 3/4" (41.9 × 32.4 cm)

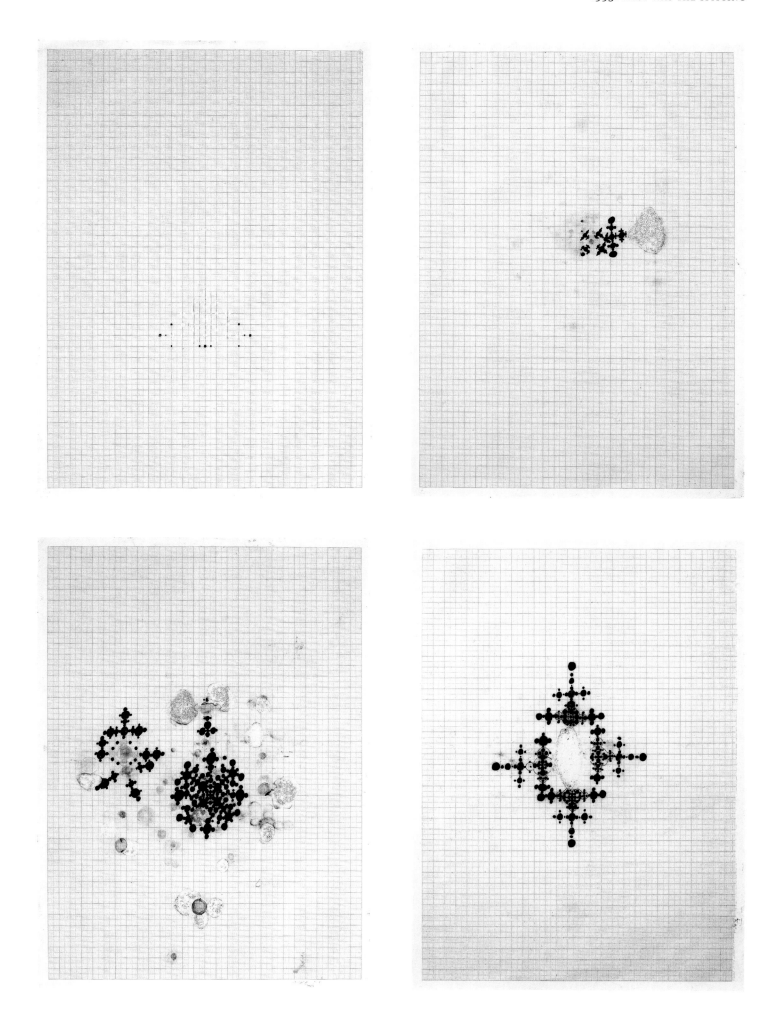

PÁGINAS 120 Y 121: TRANSPORTACIÓN TERRESTRE

LA OS UN AUTORRETRATO.

TUE 18 I 94

RELOJ CORTADO

(PÉNDULO)

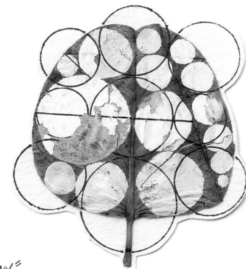

~~HACER~~ HACER UN ÁRBOL ~~(MONDRIAN)~~ (MONDRIAN)

PRODUCE: TO BRING ABOUT. CAUSE TO
HAPPEN OR BE:
"HIS WORDS PRODUCED A VIOLENT REACTION"
TO BRING TO VIEW: TO PRODUCE EVIDENCE
TO MANUFACTURE: TO MAKE
TO EXTEND OR LENGTHEN, AS A LINE (MANZONI)
ECONOMY: TO CREATE (ANYTHING WITH EXCHANGEABLE VALUE
TO YIELD OR GENERATE AN APROPRIATE PRODUCT OR RESULT.

emptiness, a kind of meditation through drawing where your brain is concentrated but not thinking too much." While preparing for the exhibition in Kortrijk, Orozco produced dozens of drawings populated with circles. Among them are drawings like *First Was the Spitting*, a four-part work that begins with Orozco spitting toothpaste foam onto a sheet of graph paper and then surrounding the stain with small circles drawn in pencil and ink.[*2] As Orozco has described it, "The bubbling, it starts with that, the universe being a big bang from a bubble and the bubble grows—it's a kind of universe in expansion. I started to spit on graph paper, on a grid, the spit dried and you could see all of these bubbling things. I continued with black ink and graphite, creating a diagram that started with the spitting." In these drawings the dried spit, the irregularly drawn circles, and the precise machine-made grid are not defined through a relationship of contrasts and oppositions; instead they exist on a long continuum: the stain, the circles, and the grid each contains and is contained within the others. This complex and complementary relationship of abstract geometry and natural or organic forms, already apparent in these early drawings, has followed Orozco throughout his career. It is a theme to which he would return in many subsequent works, most notably in *Black Kites* of 1997.

In June the Venice Biennale opened. This exhibition presented an opportunity for Orozco to introduce his work to a broad range of international visitors. He made his debut in the Aperto—a portion of the Biennale dedicated to exhibiting work by younger, emerging artists—with two works, *840 lbs Net Black Plasticine*,

OPPOSITE:
*Pinched Ball*. 1993. Silver dye bleach print, 16×20" (40.6×50.8 cm). Edition of 5

*Breath on Piano*. 1993. Chromogenic color print, 16×20" (40.6×50.8 cm). Edition of 5

Notebook 4, p. 133. Ballpoint pen, graphite, gouache, and leaf on notebook page, 10 3/4 × 8 1/16" (27.3×20.5 cm)

a mammoth cousin of *Yielding Stone*, and *Empty Shoe Box*. For the latter Orozco took a simple, white cardboard shoe box, placed the lid underneath it, and positioned the box on the floor in the center of his allotted exhibition area. The miniature quality of the sculpture was an impish comment on the tiny display space. Francesco Bonami, a member of the Biennale's curatorial team, has remembered: "I suggested to Orozco to glue the box to the floor. It was clear to me that the poor ephemeral piece would not survive the milling throngs during the opening. People would crush the thing, distractedly seeking more evident signs of contemporary art. . . . Orozco looked at me calmly, if a little worried. I understood right away that my suggestion was not only silly, but showed quite awkwardly that I didn't get anything about his work."[3] Elsewhere Bonami has written, "It was only when I kicked it that I understood clearly the *Empty Shoe Box*. Its meaning rolling away, not sinking, just momentarily vanishing."[4] At first Orozco's shoe box could be understood simply as a Duchampian readymade, *reductio ad absurdum*. Closer consideration reveals that the proportions of the shoe box neatly rhymed with those of the exhibition area. The box's clear articulation of space is central to an understanding of this work in particular and to Orozco's conception of sculpture in general. His preference for everyday objects comes from their unique ability to intensify the reading of space and volume. In *Empty Shoe Box* the viewer finds an object encountered countless times before, whose size, shape, and weight is a known and familiar quantity. Orozco depends on the viewers' almost innate knowledge of the object to throw the surrounding space, the space *not* occupied by sculpture, into focus: "When the shoe box was left opened—volume became real, it was not a *representation*." With *Empty Shoe Box*, Orozco tosses aside all notions of sculpture's monumentality and permanence and instead embraces the real, transient, and ordinary space of the everyday.

MEMORIA DEL ESPACIO

"*The empty shoe box on the floor is essentially a koan: it forces the observing spectator to ask him or herself: 'What is an empty shoe box doing here? What does it mean? What could I be missing?' And this is exactly what it contains: what is missing.*"

Miguel González Virgen, *Of Games, The Infinite and Worlds: The Work of Gabriel Orozco* (2003), p. 105

Notebook 2, p. 183.
Ballpoint pen and graphite on notebook page, 10 3/4 × 8 1/16" (27.3 × 20.5 cm)

OPPOSITE:
*Empty Shoe Box*. 1993. Shoe box, 4 7/8 × 13 × 8 1/2" (12.4 × 33 × 21.6 cm). Installation view of 45th International Art Exhibition: The Cardinal Points of Art, Venice Biennale, 1993

OCUPAR UN ESPACIO VACÍO CON UN ESPACIO VACÍO.
CAJA ZAPATOS BLANCA EN PABELLON MUROS BLANCOS
ESPACIO VACÍO EN ESPACIO VACÍO.
ABANDONAR. OCUPAR.
SE RESUELVE CAMINANDO.
ESTO ES LO QUE ESTÁ SUCEDIENDO.
NO HAY VACÍO.
PRESENCIA + PRESENCIA DEL ESPECTADOR
RELACIÓN INTERIOR-EXTERIOR
　　　CAJA — PABELLON
　　　MUSEO — CIUDAD
　　　CUERPO — ESPACIO

ABANDONAR UN ESPACIO VACÍO EN UN
ESPACIO VACÍO. NO HAY VACÍO.

EL INTERIOR DE LA PIEL

"*The empty box, a container of objects that have disappeared, had been of course one of Orozco's paradigmatic objects since the very beginning. Most programmatically and stunningly, he had presented it in* Empty Shoe Box *(1993), an object that has gained—with hindsight all the more so—an epistemological authority approaching the status of Duchamp's first, pure unadulterated readymade. The reasons for the quietly compelling attraction of an utterly banal object are of course manifold, yet one primary explanation could be found in the fact that the presentation of an empty container, rather than the object itself, traces the very shift from use value to exhibition value that has occurred in the culture at large.*"

Benjamin H. D. Buchloh, "Gabriel Orozco: Sculpture as Recollection," in *Gabriel Orozco* (2006), p. 177

Orozco next participated in *Real Time*, a group exhibition organized by Gavin Brown at the Institute of Contemporary Arts, London, together with Rirkrit Tiravanija, Andrea Zittel, and Lincoln Tobier. Orozco exhibited *Yielding Stone* and *Recaptured Nature*, positioning the latter in the lobby near the building's entrance. Situated in this unspectacular thoroughfare, the object did not immediately register as sculpture. Similarly, a work titled *Melon* consisted of a melon placed high on a shelf in the museum's bookshop. These objects were accompanied by a fifty-nine-minute video, *Before the Waiting Dog*. Although Orozco seldom uses video in his work, the action captured by the camera was similar in spirit to his photographs of impromptu sculptures made from materials found on the street.

In *Before the Waiting Dog* the still camera is replaced by a video camera, which Orozco slings over his shoulder so that it is facing behind him. The viewer follows Orozco, always outside of the frame, as he rearranges items on the shelves

"Not the monument, not the picture: Gabriel Orozco often mixes these categories with mundane life. . . . In this practice of incongruent objects in an imploded field, Orozco may transfer the attributes of one medium to another medium, as in Yielding Stone, where the indexicality associated with photography becomes the property of sculpture. So too a sculptural process may prepare a photographic tableau, as in Island within an Island (1993) where the (de)compositional strategy of installation art sets up the photograph—in this case a miming of the Lower Manhattan skyline in the background with found debris in the foreground. Folding medium onto medium, space onto space, island onto island, Orozco often wins critical pleasures from the otherwise painful ironies of dislocation and dispersal. After the events of 11 September 2001 this work of subversive mimicry has also taken on new meaning as an image of remembrance, of coming-after and living-on."

Hal Foster, Design and Crime (and Other Diatribes) (London: Verso, 2002), pp. 142–43

OPPOSITE:
*Empty Shoe Box.* 1993. Silver dye bleach print, 16×20" (40.6×50.8 cm). Edition of 5

*From Roof to Roof.* 1993. Silver dye bleach print, 16×20" (40.6×50.8 cm). Edition of 5

ABOVE:
*Island Within an Island.* 1993. Silver dye bleach print, 16×20" (40.6×50.8 cm). Edition of 5

of a British supermarket. Eventually, out of the corner and in the blink of an eye, strange configurations come into view—kitty litter becomes the unlikely inhabitant of a tower of toilet paper, a dog printed on a box of dog food surveys a bounty of bananas from the elevated perch of a vegetable scale—introducing a bit of chaos into the highly structured landscape of the supermarket.

That summer several of Orozco's photographs were included in a group exhibition at Marian Goodman Gallery in New York. From the time Goodman and Orozco had been introduced to each other by Benjamin Buchloh the previous year, Goodman took an interest in the artist's work, and had been generous with both her time and advice. The exhibition made clear that Orozco's photographs fall into two categories. The first are images resulting from an intervention by which Orozco manipulates objects in his environment into sometimes poetic, sometimes humorous assemblages. As a complement to this strategy, Orozco also takes straightforward snapshots of things in the world just as he finds them. Among the photographs on view at Marian Goodman were *Extension of Reflection* (1992) and *Empty Shoe Box* (1993), which shows a box similar to the one included in the Biennale on the roof of his apartment in New York sitting atop a layer of snow.

In September *Projects 41: Gabriel Orozco* opened at The Museum of Modern Art in New York. The show was an ambitious undertaking. The exhibition series had been established in 1971 as a forum to introduce audiences to young and largely unknown artists. Lynn Zelevansky, then a curatorial assistant at the Museum, approached Orozco in 1992 and invited him to participate. As early as March the artist was making regular visits to the Museum, looking not only at the gallery spaces but also at how visitors interacted with the work on view and how they moved from room to room, both inside and outside of the galleries. Although Projects exhibitions generally take place in a single gallery, Orozco asked that he not be restricted to this space. He has explained, "Because I was doing work

that was about site specificity, time specificity, interventions into the space of everyday life, with everyday objects, an empty white cube in a museum was not that interesting." Instead, he envisioned placing his works as he did in the ICA in London: in the interstitial spaces—corridors, hallways, the public areas where art was generally not found. As Orozco has said, "The moment you enter into a gallery you are entering a realm of illusion, you enter into a white screen, and there you are ready to see art. But before going into the galleries you are in between things, so I thought it was interesting to act in those exact moments where expectations were very low and when people were not expecting to see art."

After long discussions with the administration, Zelevansky secured permission for Orozco to show his work outside the confines of the Museum's galleries. Orozco installed an unfurled *Dial Tone* (1992) in the empty space between the Museum's escalators. As visitors ascended or descended the escalators they passed by a river of numbers. Similarly, Orozco placed *Recaptured Nature* and *Lost Line* on the Museum's second- and third-floor platforms previously occupied by large-scale sculptures like Rodin's *Monument to Balzac*. Inhabited by Orozco's comparatively unassuming objects, these areas retained their marginal character, places to pass through rather than final destinations. In the Sculpture Garden Orozco suspended a hammock between two trees, treating this rarefied space for viewing art as just an ordinary garden. The work's title, *Hammock Hanging Between Two Skyscrapers*, reflects his initial hope to hang the hammock between two Midtown buildings; in the end, however, securing the necessary permits proved impossible. A "recipient for a body," the hammock alluded, at least obliquely, to the other sculpture in the garden, most of which "somehow related to a body or represented a body." Orozco added that he "never had much admiration for that type of sculpture—sculpture that looks like a stiff figurine." For the visitor reclining in Orozco's hammock, the stiff figurines inhabiting the garden quickly fell outside the field of vision and were replaced by a vista of rooftops and open sky.

"He made the project space at the Museum of Modern Art, New York, expand into episodes that erupted quietly around and outside the museum. He tried hanging a hammock from two skyscrapers but settled for two trees in the sculpture garden. He asked the occupants of the apartments across the street to put fresh oranges on tumblers in their windows. And when they did, the oranges sat behind the glass windows, living up to their title, Home Run. Here was a game beyond baseball, a game that could score without breaking windows or surfaces, a game that left museum aesthetics behind. There was no stylistic thread linking all of this, no consistency that could be packaged into the kind of commodity we call a 'line of work.' "

Molly Nesbit, "The Tempest," in *Gabriel Orozco* (2000), pp. 124, 127

*Home Run* further expanded the space of the exhibition. To realize the work, Orozco asked the occupants of a few private buildings across from the Museum to place oranges in their windows for the duration of the exhibition. The Museum would provide the oranges, which were delivered fresh each week so that they could be eaten. (Orozco did not want to waste a single orange in the name of contemporary art.) Dozens of people became the artist's collaborators and the mundane act of placing an orange in a window became extraordinary when realized on this large scale. Although there was a wall label acknowledging the work, *Home Run*, even more than the other works in the exhibition, was something one encountered almost accidentally. To see it required a heightened awareness, and *if* the sculpture came into view, Orozco hoped, "You would see it and think, 'What is that?' " The placement of the oranges rendered their identity as sculpture precarious: they resided both within an institutional context (as a work by Gabriel

OPPOSITE:
*Melon.* 1993. Silver dye bleach print, 16 × 20" (40.6 × 50.8 cm). Edition of 5

ABOVE:
*Home Run.* 1993. Oranges, dimensions variable. Installation views of *Projects 41: Gabriel Orozco,* The Museum of Modern Art, New York, 1993

*"Surrounded by sculptures literally cut vertically or horizontally into the air, Hammock seemed to be sagging under the atmosphere's weight, neither exactly touching the ground nor convincingly suspended above it. Though Hammock made one conscious of the existence of the empty air around it, the work itself was unobtrusive. This flimsy sack did not stand out among the bronzes, and many visitors to the museum failed to notice it until they were almost upon it. To give it substance, Hammock needed a body to lie down in it, but like the missing sixty-two centimeters in La DS, the obvious absence of such a body was what in fact allowed Hammock, sandwiched as it was in space, to be read as a pouchlike pucker between earth and sky."*

Laura J. Hoptman, "Options 47: Gabriel Orozco" (1994), n.p.

RIGHT, TOP TO BOTTOM:
*Hammock Hanging Between Two Skyscrapers.* 1993. Cotton hammock, dimensions variable

*Recaptured Nature.* 1990. Vulcanized rubber, approx. 29 1/2 × 41 5/16 × 33 7/16" (75 × 105 × 85 cm). One of three versions

*Dial Tone.* 1992. Cut-and-pasted phone book pages on Japanese paper, 11" × 34' (27.9 × 1,036 cm). One of three versions

Installation views of *Projects 41: Gabriel Orozco,* The Museum of Modern Art, New York, 1993

OPPOSITE:
Notebook 2, p. 112. Ballpoint pen, graphite, photograph, and cut phone book page on notebook page, 10 3/4 × 8 1/16" (27.3 × 20.5 cm)

THE
VISITOR.

HAMACA
DIRECTORIO
BICICLETA
PELOTA
CORAZÓN RÍO

ACCIÓN

OBJETO
FOTO
TEXTO
ESCULTURA
PIEDRA

CUERPO
PICO
TIEMPO
ESPACIO
MOVIMIENTO
GEOMETRÍA.

EL TEXTO
EL CAMINO
EL PUENTE
LA PELOTA
LA PIEDRA

POSADEROS

OBSERVACIÓN.

EL CHARCO
LA BURBUJA
LA PIEDRA
LA GOTA
EL RÍO

FLOTA
TRANSCURRE
RECORRE
EROSIONA

TODO EL CIELO
TODO EL SUELO
EL AIRE
EL AGUA

LA PUERTA ABIERTA

DETENIMIENTO.

*"A car for just two people, a driver and a backseat passenger. A claustrophobic feeling as a reflection of failed dreams, speed, coolness, progress. A regression inside a modernist nightmare. A traumatic reminder an instant before the sound-breaking disappointment of time. Vanished wishes of a ravenous technical era. La DS, Tati's Mon Oncle, footnotes of a visionary mind at the end of a blurring millennium. A contemporary shock with an endless soundtrack of excruciating, screeching wheels."*

Francesco Bonami, "Gabriel Orozco: *La DS*," *Flash Art* (1994), p. 95

ABOVE:
Detail from Notebook 4, p. 90. Cut-and-taped electrostatic print, 11 1/16 × 4 13/16" (28.1 × 12.3 cm)

RIGHT:
*La DS.* 1993. Modified Citroën DS, 55 3/16" × 15' 9 15/16" × 45 5/16" (140.1 × 482.5 × 115.1 cm). View from interior

OPPOSITE:
Notebook 4, p. 119. Gouache, printed paper, and photograph on notebook page, 10 3/4 × 8 1/16" (27.3 × 20.5 cm)

Orozco, cited in the wall label and the exhibition brochure) and outside of it (as objects in the windows across the street from the Museum). The success of the sculpture rested in the balance Orozco struck in reconciling these conflicting positions, which he achieved by placing enough oranges to negate the possibility of coincidence. *Home Run* so forcefully challenged the distinction between art and life as to throw the relevance of this distinction into question.

Orozco's first solo museum presentation was immediately followed by his first solo show in a commercial gallery, Galerie Chantal Crousel in Paris. The artist traveled to Paris in October and soon began to work on *La DS*, a modified 1960s Citroën DS. Together with an assistant, Philippe Picoli, Orozco spent virtually the entire month of November in a garage cutting the car lengthwise into thirds, removing the center third, and carefully reassembling the two remaining sections back into a whole. Although the newly narrow shell hyperbolized the promise of speed, by removing the engine Orozco had rendered the vehicle inert. When the exhibition opened in early December, this epitome of aerodynamic design could not move an inch. Visitors to the gallery were invited to touch the car and even climb inside, though it now only had room for two passengers, one in the front and one in the back.

Orozco's decision to use a Citroën DS, commonly called "*la DS*" (the letters phonetically doubling as "*déesse*" — the French word for "goddess"), was deliberate. Since it first rolled off of the assembly line in the 1950s, at a moment when the country was still recovering from the economic and psychic aftershocks of World War II, the futuristic DS became a symbol of French ingenuity. And although production of the DS model ceased in 1975, the car still held its iconic status in French popular culture, and thus had a special resonance for a French audience. Orozco relied on this collective cultural memory when he split the vehicle apart and then sutured it back together, subjecting it to a process he bluntly terms "extraction and reconfiguration." Although the phrase succinctly explains the methods by which the Citroën became *La DS*, it also underscores how *minimal* this process was, even when deployed on a maximal scale. In the end, the core identity of the car was preserved. "It is still the same object but it's revealed in a more accelerated, or more physical way," as he has said. As a sculptor, Orozco prefers to alter rather than create anew, a tactic evident not only here, but in virtually all of his work. After the exhibition closed in late January 1994, *La DS* toured to several European institutions, becoming Orozco's best-known work to date.

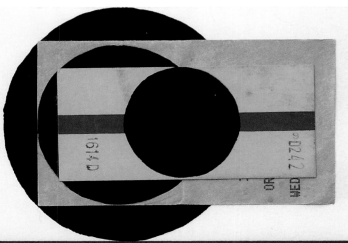

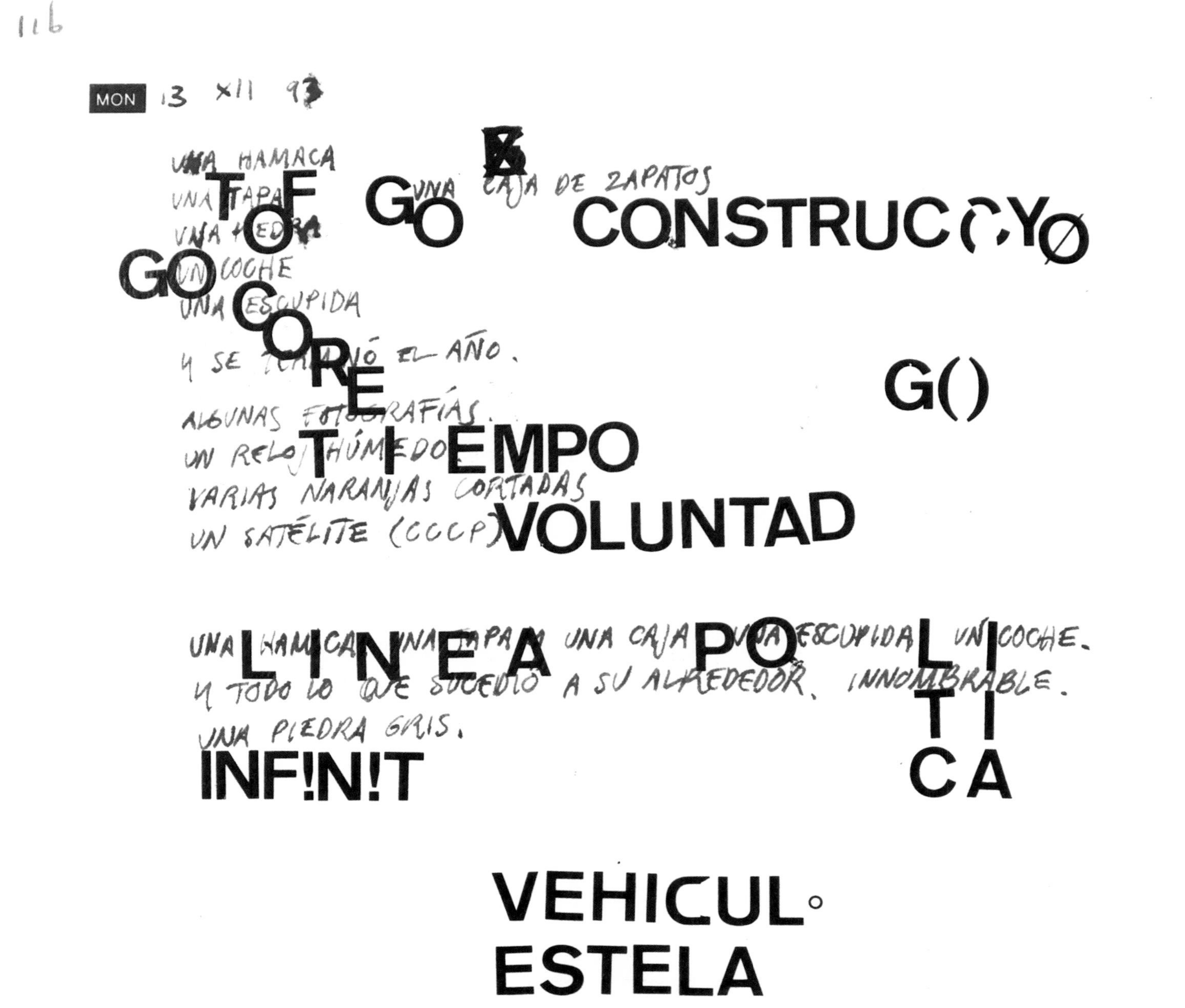

MON 13 XII 93

UNA HAMACA
UNA TAPA
UNA PIEDRA
UN COCHE
UNA ESCUPIDA

Y SE TERMINÓ EL AÑO.

ALGUNAS FOTOGRAFÍAS.
UN RELOJ HÚMEDO
VARIAS NARANJAS CORTADAS
UN SATÉLITE (CCCP)

T F GO B UNA CAJA DE ZAPATOS
TO GO CONSTRUC C Y Ø
GO CO RE G( )
TI EMPO
VOLUNTAD

UNA HAMACA UNA TAPA UNA CAJA UNA ESCUPIDA UN COCHE.
LINEA PO LI TICA
Y TODO LO QUE SUCEDIÓ A SU ALREDEDOR. INNOMBRABLE.
UNA PIEDRA GRIS.
INF!N!T CA

VEHICUL○
ESTELA

Notebook 4, p. 116. Felt-tip pen
and transfer letters on notebook
page, 10 3/4 × 8 1/16" (27.3 × 20.5 cm)

OPPOSITE:
La DS. 1993. Modified Citroën
DS, 55 3/16" × 15' 9 15/16" × 45 5/16"
(140.1 × 482.5 × 115.1 cm)

"Orozco's treatment of it goes even further toward
advancing the notion of this car as a 'sculptural aerolite.'
But making the piece available to the public—visitors
were free to touch, to open the doors and trunk, even to
sit in the seats—constituted a divergence from the usual
relation between the work of art and the spectator; it was
more like a vehicle in a salesroom. The spectator's status
became strangely uncertain, divided between the role of
driver—but a driver with limited powers (only because
this DS no longer has a motor)—and the role of viewer,
but a viewer on whom, for once, there was no weight of
noli me tangere. Seated like an old child behind the
steering wheel of this obstinately immobile, giant toy, one
found oneself in one of the most disorientating situations
that an art gallery can offer."

Jean-Pierre Criqui, "Gabriel Orozco: Galerie
Crousel-Robelin/BAMA," Artforum (1994), pp. 95–96

# 1994: Portable Puddle

**T**HE YEAR BEGAN WITH AN INVITATION FOR OROZCO to participate in *WATT*, a group exhibition at the Witte de With Center for Contemporary Art in Rotterdam curated by Gosse Oosterhof and Chris Dercon. The exhibition included work by twenty-nine artists, almost all of whom were in the early stages of their careers. It was an opportunity for figures as dissimilar as Jake and Dinos Chapman, Douglas Gordon, and Tacita Dean to exhibit alongside one another in the hope that these unexpected juxtapositions would generate new insights into the work on view. Orozco arrived in Rotterdam in late January, one week prior to the show's opening, armed with nothing. Interested in working with whatever was on hand, in one week's time he created three sculptures with materials found or purchased locally: *Ironing Board*, *Frozen Portable Puddle*, and *Four Bicycles (There Is Always One Direction)*.

The first two were ephemeral sculptures, in existence only for the duration of the exhibition and preserved as photographs thereafter. For *Ironing Board*, a site-specific sculptural intervention, Orozco placed a store-bought ironing board on the roof of the building across the street from the gallery. As with *Home Run* the previous year, in situating his work beyond the confines of the gallery space Orozco drew attention to sites typically unseen. In its new context, rising above the building's precipice, this quotidian object subtly evoked the building's past, when servants occupied the top floors. It suggested a springboard, Orozco has recalled, "like somebody was going to jump." *Ironing Board*'s seemingly haphazard placement belies the forethought and deliberation with which Orozco approaches his work. *Frozen Portable Puddle* illustrates his simultaneous flexibility and openness to chance encounters. This work, a loosely circular arrangement of thin white plastic record sleeves Orozco purchased at a nearby thrift shop, was installed on the roof of the gallery. After carefully positioning the discs on

Notebook 4, p. 179. Graphite and photograph on notebook page, 10 3/4 × 8 1/16" (27.3 × 20.5 cm)

OPPOSITE:
*Frozen Portable Puddle*. 1994. Silver dye bleach print, 16 × 20" (40.6 × 50.8 cm). Edition of 5

*Portable Puddle*. 1994. Three silver dye bleach prints (one shown), each 16 × 20" (40.6 × 50.8 cm). Edition of 5

the damp surface, Orozco left the work on the roof overnight. By morning, the discs were covered with a thin sheet of ice. At once organic and inorganic, *Frozen Portable Puddle* blurred the distinction between these two poles.

The third sculpture, *Four Bicycles (There Is Always One Direction)*, relies on a similar strategy of "extraction and reconfiguration" as *La DS*, from the previous year. And like *La DS* it is emblematic of the place it was made. As Orozco observed, Rotterdam was a land of bicycles. During his time there he, like many of the city's residents, spent hours on a bike, and as a result the bicycle became the focus of his next work. He purchased four classic Dutch bicycles and removed their seats and handlebars. He then fit the bicycle frames together by inserting the seat support of one into the handlebar support of another, forming a freestanding structure stabilized by gravity and a single kickstand. For Orozco it was important that the bicycles not be welded together because "that would be cheating . . . if you weld, the [initial] structure doesn't matter, whatever you do it's going to hold." Unlike Picasso's *Bull's Head* (1943), an early precedent that also consists of bicycle parts (notably, the handlebars and bicycle seat missing from Orozco's construction), Orozco's bicycles are not divorced from their original use and transformed into something else. As Orozco has said, "I'm not inventing, just reinterpreting." Indeed, as in Marcel Duchamp's *Bicycle Wheel* (1913), the bicycles used to construct the work are not only plainly visible and identifiable, they are named in the title of the work. The formation "works as a kind of object for motion, an object that is meant to be moving," yet the bicycle's actual function is rendered moot: this fantastical perpetual-motion machine is locked into a permanent state of stasis, not unlike *La DS*. Together with *La DS*, *Four Bicycles*

31 - 11 - 94

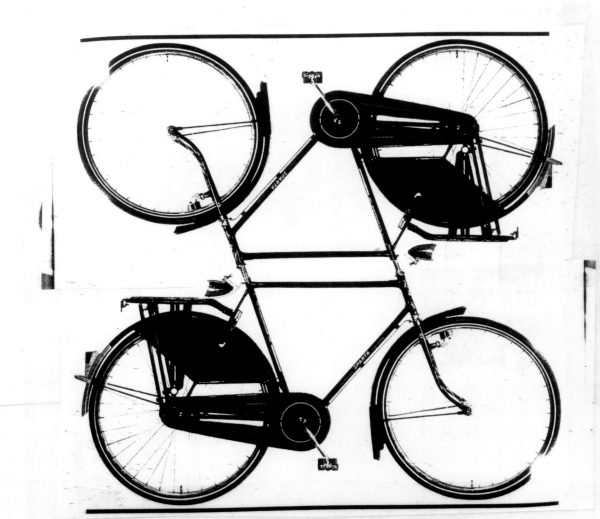

Notebook 4, p. 147.
Felt-tip pen, cut-and-taped
electrostatic print, and
napkin on notebook page,
10¾ × 8¹⁄₁₆" (27.3 × 20.5 cm)

OPPOSITE:
*Ironing Board*. 1994.
Silver dye bleach print,
16 × 20" (40.6 × 50.8 cm).
Edition of 5

View of *Four Bicycles (There
Is Always One Direction)* in a
workshop, Rotterdam, 1994

signaled Orozco's growing interest in exploring the themes of transportation in his work — themes that would continue to resurface intermittently throughout the coming years.

After *WATT* closed, *Four Bicycles* was exhibited in New York as part of a summer group exhibition on view at Marian Goodman Gallery. This was the second time Orozco's work was displayed at the gallery, and a few months in advance of his first solo exhibition there. Concurrently, at the Hayward Gallery in London, a suite of Orozco's photographs hung alongside photographs by Bernd and Hilla Becher, Andreas Gursky, Thomas Struth, Jeff Wall, and others in an exhibition titled *The Epic and the Everyday: Contemporary Photographic Art*. Of all the artists included Orozco was one of only two for whom photography was not a primary medium (Robert Smithson was the other). Orozco was also one of the few who did not work on a monumental scale. His photographs, deceptively simple images taken with an automatic Nikon camera, were printed no larger than 16 by 20 inches (40.6 by 50.8 centimeters), a size that allowed them to be comfortably visible when hanging on a gallery wall but still maintain the casual, everyday character of snapshots. Years later Benjamin Buchloh, writing about Orozco's photography, observed, "Gabriel Orozco resuscitates the Conceptualists' original dismissal of photographic artistry and craft, and he continues their deskilling of the photograph: his images are distinguished neither by the high resolution generated by advanced digital camera and printing techniques, nor by extreme care and preparation in the preliminary phases of image selection and production."[1] James Lingwood, the exhibition's curator, described Orozco's photographs in the show's accompanying publication as ordinary, ephemeral observations.[2] The seeming everydayness of photographs featuring sleeping dogs, broken bricks, puddles, and the like belies the evocative power of these pictures. A particularly salient example is *Breath on Piano* (1993), an image of condensation on a closed piano keyboard lid, which makes acutely clear not only the fleeting nature of time but the photographer's ability to stop it and capture an image of a moment already lost.

Orozco and Maria Gutierrez married on August 2 at City Hall in New York.

During the summer months Orozco prepared for a solo exhibition at Marian Goodman Gallery, his first in a New York commercial space. As was typical, he paid great attention to the site where his work would be displayed. The gallery, located on the fourth floor of an office building on Fifty-seventh Street, contains two gallery spaces separated from one another by a long hallway: the north gallery, the first space into which visitors enter, and the south gallery, located toward the rear of the floor. Orozco decided that in order to properly introduce New York audiences to his work he would need to include earlier objects but not the best known. He chose to exhibit *My Hands Are My Heart* (1991), *My Hand Is the Memory of Space* (1991), and *Lost Line* (1993) in the south gallery, and to create something new for the north. "I wanted to disappoint. I wanted to clean up all that people would think about me, so then I could start from zero and move on a free platform," Orozco has recalled. "I was not going to be big big big grow grow grow. I was not going to cut cars now, then big cars, then trucks, and then cut an airplane. I wanted to do many different things and different *types* of things." Orozco showed *Yogurt Caps*, a new work consisting of four transparent, blue-rimmed Dannon yogurt lids stamped with a still legible expiration date and price tag. Orozco centered one on each of the four walls of the room, then hammered them in place. The lids, one of which had been pinned to the wall of Orozco's apartment for about a year and which he had been reluctant to throw away, demarcated the space of the gallery, but just barely. Orozco has remembered of the opening, "At the beginning, people arrived. They came to this big-deal gallery, they stepped in and peeked through and saw nothing, really. A little thing. They couldn't get it, and then they left to the other room." While Orozco certainly dashed expectations, he didn't altogether disappoint. Dan Cameron, reviewing the show for *Artforum*, wrote, "Orozco's art may come

OPPOSITE:
*Four Bicycles (There Is Always One Direction)*. 1994. Bicycles, 6' 6" × 7' 4" × 7' 4" (198.1 × 223.5 × 223.5 cm)

ABOVE:
Detail from Notebook 5, p. 43. Cut-and-taped photograph, 4 3/16 × 2 3/8" (10.7 × 6 cm)

104

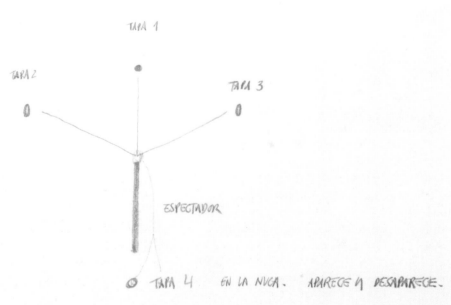

*"If one looked carefully, one saw them, transparent,
blue-rimmed, four vacant circles of garbage, plastic
blanks. The container they had capped was gone.
The yogurt eaten. Stamps and stickers gave a
price, ninety-nine cents, and an expiration date,
three from September and one from May, for in the
spring Orozco had tried out the idea of the cap in
his kitchen. The gallery required four, like compass
points, except that from any one point the viewer
would only ever be able to see three. The fourth
would have to nag behind, in the mind. But was
this an address to the mind? Each cap was installed
mouth high. As if there might be a memory of taste."*

Molly Nesbit, "The Tempest," in *Gabriel Orozco*
(2000), p. 155

Notebook 6, p. 104. Graphite
on notebook page, 10¾×
8¹⁄₁₆" (27.3×20.5 cm)

INSET:
*Yogurt Caps* (detail). 1994.
Four yogurt lids, each lid
3¹⁄₈" (7.9 cm) diam.

OPPOSITE:
*Ball on Water*. 1994.
Silver dye bleach print,
16×20" (40.6×50.8 cm).
Edition of 5

*Coins in Window*. 1994.
Silver dye bleach print,
16×20" (40.6×50.8 cm).
Edition of 5

"*The modest punctuation of the white cubical space performed by these Yogurt Caps (1994)—discreet almost to the point of invisibility—produced perplexity and discomfort for most viewers, who were forced to contemplate the startling blankness of the room in the absence of any recognisable art objects on the floor or the walls. The gesture has been received by some as deeply disappointing and by others as extremely courageous— a glib and cynical manoeuver or a brilliant critique of the commercial gallery system?*"

Miwon Kwon, "The Fullness of Empty Containers," *Frieze* (1995), p. 54

*Yogurt Caps.* 1994. Four yogurt lids, each lid 3⅛" (7.9 cm) diam. Installation view at Marian Goodman Gallery, New York, 1994

*"How do you take the weight out of sculpture? The question provides one way to consider the complex project that Gabriel Orozco has set for himself during the final years of this millennium. … A consideration of lightness begins with Orozco's many pieces that involve the literal subtraction of mass. Most sensational, perhaps, was the exhibition at the Marian Goodman Gallery in New York, in 1994, where four clear Dannon yogurt container lids rimmed in blue hung on the white walls of an otherwise vacant room. It was a poem about nothing that, beautifully, could thus be one about everything too. A presence, however slight, was the key to seeing the emptiness of the room, as just a single sound is needed to manifest silence. "*

Ann Temkin, "Afterword," in *Gabriel Orozco: Photogravity* (1999), p. 173

Plexiglas Rods
Laminate (Woodgrain)
Stainless Steel
Stainless Steel/Woodgrain

TRES
CORTES

Circular Discs
Stainless Steel
Stainless Steel
Flush Panels (Woodgrain) w/Aluminum Molding

directly out of his experience of the world, but once it takes on physical form, it seems to offer a kind of poetic refuge — not from the world itself so much as from the inability to conceive of a transcendental moment without a corresponding need to erect a monument in its place."[3] Despite the simplicity of the gesture, for Orozco the work was immensely significant: "*Yogurt Caps* was my research of space, spectatorship, the viewer, the poetic, the emptiness, the body in movement, the white box as container, the container in general, the circle. . . . Everything was in that work."

Concurrent to the show at Marian Goodman Gallery, a solo exhibition of Orozco's work, organized by Laura Hoptman and Richard Francis, was on view at the Museum of Contemporary Art in Chicago. The MCA had invited Orozco to participate in its Options series, which introduces audiences to emerging artists. Along with showing earlier works, Orozco created a new sculpture: *Elevator*. With the help of Elaine Budin at Marian Goodman Gallery, he found a contractor in Chicago willing to salvage an elevator from a building that was being demolished. Orozco has noted, "I thought it would be easy to find an elevator, a second-hand elevator. I was a bit naive because obviously there is not a second market; second-hand elevators don't exist. They are all custom made: you build a building and you order an elevator and when the building is destroyed, the elevator is gone." To create this ambitious sculpture Orozco worked with a team of assistants to cut the elevator horizontally in half, remove a section, and suture it back together. The interior height of the resulting form matched that of Orozco's body. Entering the cabin induced a feeling of vertigo and the sensation that the elevator was simultaneously rising and falling. As he has explained, "I like to play with the physicality of the object but also our relation to the memory of that object. We all have memory of an elevator. When it goes up and down you feel it in your stomach, so when you go into this elevator you remember that feeling. . . . It's not just the cutting of the object per se, it's also cutting the memory of that object, you are transforming the memory."

Nylite
Laminate (Designer Color)
Laminate (Woodgrain)
Flush Panel (Woodgrain)

**ELEVATORS**

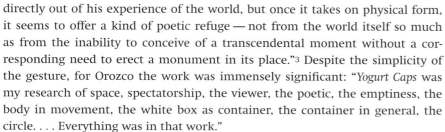

OPPOSITE:
*Elevator*. 1994. Modified elevator cabin, 8' × 8' × 60" (243.8 × 243.8 × 152.4 cm)

ABOVE:
Detail from Notebook 6, p. 115. Photograph, 4 × 6" (10.2 × 15.2 cm) (cropped)

RIGHT:
Notebook 4, p. 161. Graphite and cut-and-taped printed paper on notebook page, 10 3/4 × 8 1/16" (27.3 × 20.5 cm)

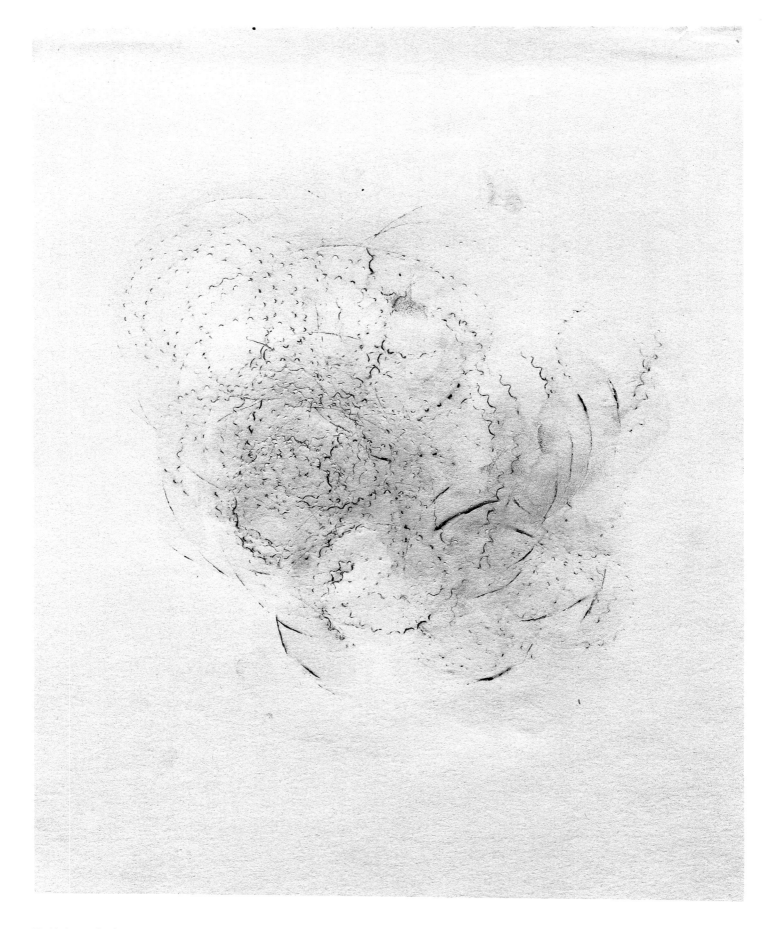

Untitled. 1994. Bottle cap
rubbing on paper, 10 1/2 × 8 3/4"
(26.7 × 22.2 cm)

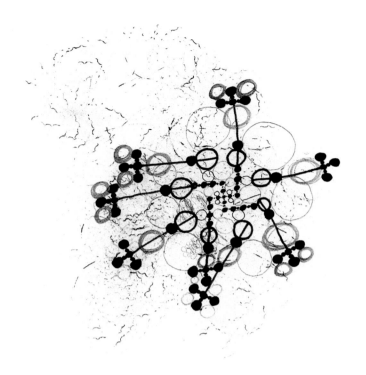

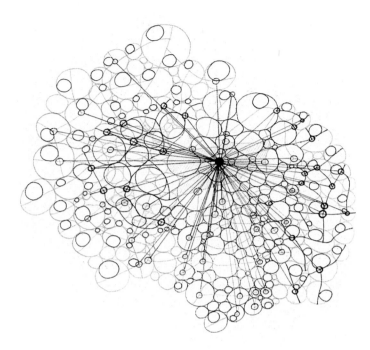

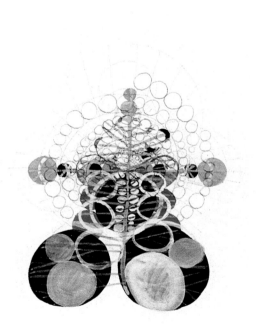

Untitled. 1993. Synthetic polymer
paint, graphite, and marker on three
sheets of paper, each sheet 10½×8"
(26.7×20.3 cm)

Untitled. 1994. Graphite and
paint on printed paper on paper,
10½×8¼" (26.7×20.9 cm)

# 1995: Bubble Maker

**E**ARLY IN 1995, curator Hans Ulrich Obrist and the Musée d'Art Moderne de la Ville de Paris invited Orozco to create a new work for Migrateurs, an exhibition series the museum described as "interventions by young artists." For the show Orozco filled two mateless socks with papier-mâché, removing the fabric sheath once the material had hardened. The result was an exceedingly humble sculpture that, at first glance, appears entirely organic. Orozco would employ a similar strategy of creating casts years later when working on his series *Galaxy Pots* (2002) and *Spumes* (2003).

Shortly before the closing of Migrateurs, a solo exhibition of Orozco's work opened in Italy at the Galleria Monica De Cardenas in Milan. In addition to the photographs and drawings on display, Orozco created a new work, *Habemus Vespam*, a sculpture of a Vespa motorbike carved from Sarnico stone at a local workshop. The title of the work is a pun on the Latin "*Habemus Papam*," or "We have a Pope," the pronouncement accompanying the naming of a newly elected Pontiff. Orozco's phrase could be read as a satirical comment on consumerism in Italy reaching a height of religious proportions: We have a Vespa! Orozco was inspired by the stone lions in Venice's Piazza San Marco, and wanted to make a work with which people could interact. He has said, "Public sculptures are somehow accessible to the body, they can be touched. People sit on the stone and erode the work." Like so much of Orozco's sculpture, *Habemus Vespam* is a receptacle for the body. This was the third time that Orozco used a vehicle as the subject of his work. Such sculptures, Benjamin Buchloh has observed, "constitute a typology whose 'public' status appears to be already guaranteed by its mere affiliation with transportation, urban circulation, and consumer-culture design."[1]

In April Orozco moved to Berlin, where he would reside for one year thanks to a grant from the DAAD (Deutscher Akademischer Austausch Dienst, or German Academic Exchange Service) Berlin Artists-in-Residence program. Shortly after arriving in Germany, Orozco purchased a used yellow Simson Schwalbe KR51 scooter. This popular model was produced during the 1960s in East Germany, and by the 1990s had gained cult status. Virtually everywhere Orozco went he encountered another yellow Schwalbe. As a means of documenting his wanderings

TOP:
*Two Socks*. 1995. Papier-mâché, 6 ¹¹/₁₆ × 11 × 4 ³/₄" (17 × 28 × 12 cm)

ABOVE:
*Shoes*. 1993. Shoes, shoelaces, and metal, 6 ¹¹/₁₆ × 11 × 4 ³/₄" (17 × 28 × 12 cm)

OPPOSITE:
Notebook 6, p. 55. Graphite on notebook paper, 10 ³/₄ × 8 ¹/₁₆" (27.3 × 20.5 cm)

12 VIII 74

around the city, Orozco would park his scooter next to a nearly identical one and snap a photo, leading to *Until You Find Another Yellow Schwalbe*. Of creating works specific to his surroundings, Orozco has remarked, "It is very important for me to base my work on what is happening in my life, not in a narrative way or an anecdotal way, but to be aware of where I'm living and what is happening around me. Not having a technique that is always the same and not having a proper studio makes me focus on the moment I'm living in and the place I'm living in, which I then try to use to make the work." After about two months Orozco had accumulated a group of photographs. Although they all feature the same subject — two yellow Schwalbe scooters — the images otherwise vary from one to the next. The most noticeable distinction between them, aside from an obvious change in background, is the change in angle of the scooters' positions, and because the photographs are typically displayed in one long, linear sequence, the scooters appear to rotate in space. Orozco likens this to a series of film stills: "When you walk through the line of photographs it's almost like walking through a film. There is something static and something moving. It was about movement."

*Until You Find Another Yellow Schwalbe* is also a complex rumination on place. Relics from the time when the Berlin Wall divided the city into East and West, these vehicles punctuated the urban landscape of the newly reunified Berlin. Orozco's search for another yellow Schwalbe was, itself, an exercise in reunification. By bringing together the Schwalbe scooters, objects still culturally identified as products manufactured by the former East German state, Orozco invoked Germany's divided past. He stressed this point when, after taking the photos, he left pamphlets on the scooters inviting the unknown owners to a meeting of yellow Schwalbes set to take place in the parking lot of the Neue Nationalgalerie in Berlin on October 3, the five-year anniversary of German reunification. Despite having distributed numerous flyers as well as placing an announcement in a magazine for motorcycle enthusiasts, only two Schwalbe owners and their scooters joined Orozco in the parking lot, a gathering documented in the fortieth and final photo of the series.

*Horses Running Endlessly* was also made in Berlin under the auspices of the DAAD grant. An exaggerated chessboard, its field of 256 squares in four colors is four times as large as the standard board. And, unlike a standard board, knights are the only pieces in Orozco's game of chess. Of all the game's pieces, the knight is unusual; it can move vertically and horizontally in a single turn, potentially creating a circular or spherical pattern on the board. Writing about the work, Francesco Bonami observed, "*Horses Running Endlessly* create a series of circles among themselves and on the chess board. It's impossible to detect these circles materially, but the horses' movement indicates it clearly."[2] By altering the game, the rigid system of rules morphs into an organic and pointless trajectory reminiscent of Orozco's own meandering travels on the Schwalbe scooter.

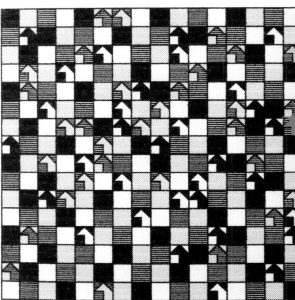

Orozco's yearlong stay in Berlin was interrupted periodically by invitations to participate in exhibitions abroad, including the 1st Kwangju Biennale, in Kwangju, South Korea, which opened in September. Although Orozco arrived in Kwangju about a week prior to the exhibition's opening unsure of what to make, he had with him notebooks filled with drawings, many of which featured colored circles and circular forms. The artist has said, "I've had circles in the work I was doing since 1991 but this was something I did in my notebook, in my spare time. They started as a kind of mental exercise. It was like meditating through drawing." And while this interest in circularity was already detectable in his earlier works, such as his untitled toothpaste drawings (1992–93), *Yogurt Caps* (1994), and even *Horses Running Endlessly*, it generally resides beneath the surface. In the Kwangju work, circles became the dominant motif. Working with a local sign maker, in less than one week Orozco completed ten light boxes, all of which featured a variation of the circular pattern. Despite foregrounding this abstract iconography, the work also related to the place where it was made. Orozco's light boxes called to mind the light box advertisements found everywhere on the streets of the city.

*"By introducing a carefully chosen, specific object (in continuation and in opposition to the principle of the readymade) and matching it with the principles of doubling and serial repetition in the random chance encounters of these vehicles in a vast urban territory, this work not only introduced a complex variation (and critical revision of three formal paradigms of Dada, Surrealist, and Minimalist procedures), but it also shifted from the dramatic performance of an act of public fissuring (in La DS) to an act of public fusion."*

Benjamin H. D. Buchloh, "Gabriel Orozco: The Sculpture of Everyday Life," in *Gabriel Orozco* (2000), p. 98

OPPOSITE, TOP:
*Habemus Vespam.* 1995. Sarnico
stone, 45 1/4 × 70 7/8 × 24 13/16"
(115 × 180 × 63 cm)

OPPOSITE, BOTTOM:
Detail from Notebook 7,
p. 91. Printed paper, 3 15/16 × 4"
(10.1 × 10.2 cm)

ABOVE:
*Until You Find Another Yellow
Schwalbe.* 1995. Forty chromogenic
color prints, each 12 7/16 × 18 5/8"
(31.6 × 47.3 cm)

52

6 11 95

SOPORTES (JUEGOS DE MESA):

JUEGO EN EL PALO DE ESCOBA.
JUEGO EN EL ESQUÍ
JUEGO EN LA CAFETERA EXPRESS.
JUEGO EN EL CENICERO CIRCULAR (BARAJA CIRCULAR (MEMORIA)).

FICHAS:
JUEGO DE LOS RELOJES DE ARENA

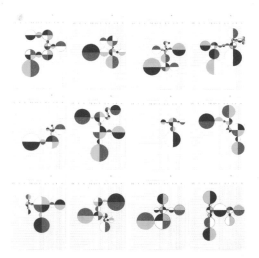

CABALLOS AZULES, ROJOS, & BLANCOS Y AMARILLOS

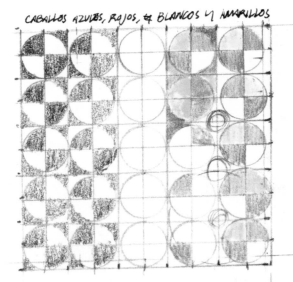

Notebook 7, p. 52. Ballpoint pen,
graphite, and colored pencil
on notebook page, 10¾ × 8¹⁄₁₆"
(27.3 × 20.5 cm)

INSET:
*Twelve Korean Notebook Pages*. 1995.
Gouache and graphite on twelve
sheets of notebook paper, each
sheet 7 × 5" (17.8 × 12.7 cm)

EL JUEGO DE LOS CABALLOS ROJOS, AZULES,
BLANCOS Y AMARILLOS. (INFINITO).

ABOVE:
*Horses Running Endlessly*. 1995.
Wood, 3 3/8 × 34 3/8 × 34 3/8"
(8.7 × 87.5 × 87.5 cm). One of
three versions

BELOW:
*Light Signs (Korea)*. 1995.
Synthetic polymer paint on
plastic sheet, and light box,
39 3/8 × 39 3/8 × 7 3/4" (100 × 100 ×
19.7 cm). Two of ten versions

*"Rather than a reasonably conceivable variant of the
traditional chess game, Gabriel Orozco's* Horses Running
Endlessly *(1995) calls to mind something resembling
Mondrian's* Broadway Boogie Woogie *remade by
a hallucinating Bobby Fischer. . . . The configuration
of the pieces is rich in potential transformations. On a
conventional chessboard, the knight can successively occupy
all the squares without ever passing through the same
one twice. I do not know whether this possibility exists on
Orozco's oversized version, but I imagine nevertheless the
simultaneous setting in motion of the pieces and the quasi-
infinite potential configurations. Moreover, each viewer is
free to modify the given configurations as he or she wishes
(at least according to the allowable moves of the knight).
Like a Calder mobile one could activate with a fingertip or
merely a breath,* Horses Running Endlessly *is a machine
to produce diversity."*

Jean-Pierre Criqui, "Like a Rolling Stone,"
*Artforum* (1996), pp. 88, 91

When the biennial opened to the public, the critical reaction was one of bewil-
derment. One visitor recalled, "Looking for his work among a confusing array
of different works . . . I stopped in front of some lightboxes with neo-geo circles.
From a distance it was impossible to comprehend who would have created such
oddities—discovering that these works were attributed to Gabriel Orozco was a
very disconcerting experience."[3] Perplexing at the time, *Light Signs (Korea)* directly
presaged Orozco's renewed interest in painting, which he would use to further
develop this circular motif.

After returning briefly to Berlin, Orozco left again to prepare for his first solo
exhibition at the Galerie Micheline Szwajcer in Antwerp. The original concept for
the show was straightforward: Orozco would present a series of drawings. During
installation, however, Orozco noticed how heavily trafficked the street in front
of the gallery was. While the gallery was located in a quiet, residential section
of Antwerp, the local residents often found it difficult to park their cars, which
would sometimes stand double-parked, blocking traffic further still. *Parking Lot*
was Orozco's practical response to this annoying situation. He proposed transforming the gallery into a fully functioning garage. The building, itself a renovated space retrofitted with a large door, was ideally suited to the role. When
emptied, the main space could accommodate at least seven cars, possibly more. A
standard "P" sign in front indicated that parking was available to the public. Once
inside and parked, the vehicle's owner would step up to the gallery office, which
was transformed by the addition of a plexiglass ticket window, and exchange his
or her car keys for a ticket (though parking was free of charge). An intervention
into both public and private space, *Parking Lot* simultaneously altered the function

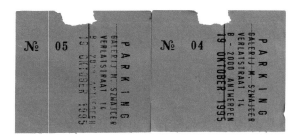

*"The relationship between public and private in Orozco's work is always ambiguous and confusing, but never misleading. In* Parking Lot, *he transformed the Szwajcer Gallery in Antwerp, Belgium, into a parking lot, allowing the public to be contained by the private, working bluntly upon the inside/outside dimension of reality with no compromises or negotiations. The gallery became a parking lot, the exterior was absorbed by the interior and the mirror exploded, representation finally subsided to its functionality."*

Francesco Bonami, "Sudden Death: Roughs, Fairways and the Game of Awareness— Gabriel Orozco," *Parachute* (1998), p. 31

of the gallery and the traffic circulation of the neighborhood. Orozco had long been actively involved in blurring boundaries, from his very early impromptu sculptures created in the streets of Mexico City to *Home Run* (1993) and *Ironing Board* (1994), works positioned outside the sanctioned institutional space. With *Parking Lot*, he brought the outside in. The only thing distinguishing the gallery from an ordinary, if small, parking lot was a series of Orozco's *Finger Ruler* drawings that hung on the walls. The gallery maintained *Parking Lot* for the scheduled duration of the exhibition, after which it resumed its standard operations.

Toward the end of the year Orozco left Europe for India, where he would travel for two months.

TOP LEFT:
Detail from back cover of Notebook 8. Parking stubs, each 2³/₁₆ × 2⁵/₁₆" (5.5 × 5.9 cm)

ABOVE:
*Parking Lot.* 1995. Installation at Galerie Micheline Szwajcer, Antwerp, 1995

*"In order to trace in a clear, objective, and impersonal way the parallel, vertical lines on a piece of paper, Orozco uses a ruler but encounters resistance from his own finger/eye in attempting to draw those straight lines. Between instrumentalization and impulse, he follows his fingertip and thus incorporates erroneous discontinuity as a chink in the perfectly straight line. Again and again, with the poetry, precision, and sparseness of Orozco's work, the irrational seems to pierce through the 'objective' order."*

M. Catherine de Zegher, "The Os of Orozco," *Parkett* (1996), p. 66

RIGHT:
*Finger Ruler 1.* 1995. Graphite on paper, 11×8" (27.9×20.3 cm)

BELOW:
*Dog Circle.* 1995. Silver dye bleach print, 16×20" (40.6×50.8 cm). Edition of 5

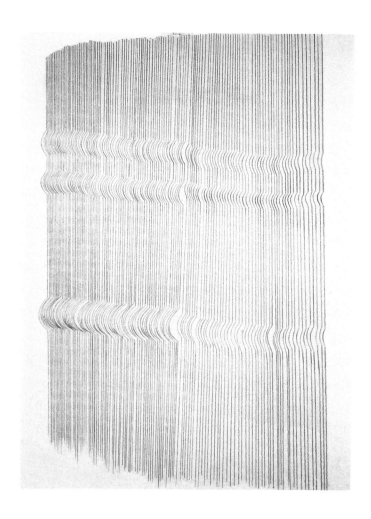

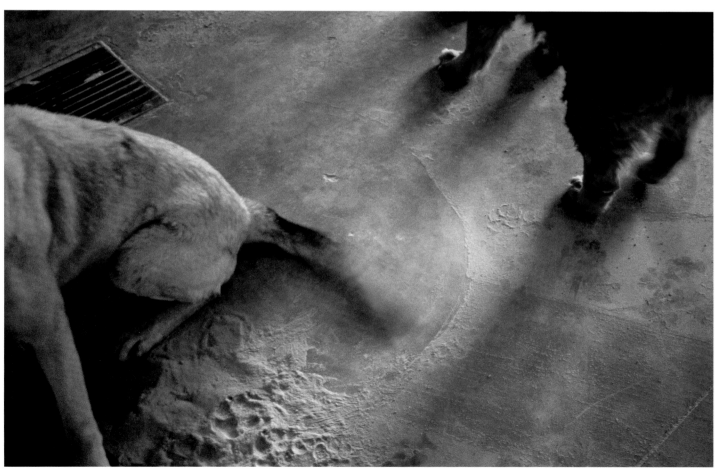

# 1996: Player for an Empty Club

IN AN EXHIBITION AT THE KUNSTHALLE ZÜRICH IN MAY, Orozco showed *Working Tables*, an installation that reflects broadly on his process of making sculpture — a process that involves countless ongoing tests and experiments. Since the early 1990s he had been placing the products from these tests in standard shoe boxes. On this occasion he removed the leftovers of earlier projects from the shoe boxes that were lining his apartment and laid them out on a pair of tables, presenting not so much the objects themselves as their shared condition: all are things that *might* be on their way to becoming sculpture. There were primitive lumps of plasticine, models for sculptures that Orozco would later execute in another scale or medium, found objects—yogurt lids, chess pieces, a toy Citroën.

The artist describes a sculpture as "a platform for an action; it's not just an object but . . . an object that you are using." The *Working Tables* required of the viewer considerable effort, in part because they cannot be comprehended in a glance. One must think through the making and unmaking of these disparate, rough, often unfinished pieces, forging new relationships among them—whether causal, instrumental, associative, or simply rhythmic. "The objects themselves are small," Briony Fer has written, "but the span of the connections among them suggests an immensity of scale; their juxtapositions of handmade and commodity forms, natural and synthetic materials set up what Orozco once emphatically called an 'organic world.' As viewers, we are asked to shuttle from one order of magnitude to another."[1]

The Zurich exhibition traveled to the Institute of Contemporary Arts in London in June. Concurrently, Orozco presented in London a project titled *Empty Club*. Working with Artangel, a British organization that commissions temporary artists' projects, he took over the interior of 50 St. James's Street in London. Orozco had chosen the building with a geopolitical frame in mind: working with Artangel's codirector, James Lingwood, he deliberately sought out a centrally located but empty building from the eighteenth or nineteenth century, the era epitomizing British imperial self-confidence. The building they chose had begun its life in 1828 as Crockford's Temple of Chance, one of London's first official gambling dens. There wealthy men socialized and made business deals, and through their games acted out in a formalized manner the higher-stakes gambles they made offstage: industrial investments in the north of England and

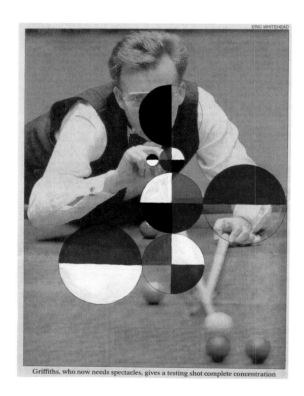

Griffiths, who now needs spectacles, gives a testing shot complete concentration

TOP:
Gabriel Orozco with
*Carambole with Pendulum*
(1996), at the exhibition
*Gabriel Orozco: Empty Club*, 50
St. James's Street, London,
1996

ABOVE:
*Atomist: Complete Concentration*.
1996. Gouache and graphite
on newspaper clipping,
7 × 5 1/8" (17.8 × 13 cm)

OPPOSITE:
*Carambole with Pendulum*.
1996. Modified billiard
table and billiard balls,
35" × 10' 1 3/4" × 7' 6"
(88.9 × 309.2 × 228.6 cm).
One of three versions

Detail from inside cover
of Notebook 7. Postcard,
4 1/8 × 5 7/8" (10.5 × 15 cm)

commercial enterprises in the East and West Indies. The club gained in respectability throughout the nineteenth century—eventually closing the casino—but during the twentieth century declined along with the fortunes of the privileged classes. It closed in 1976, and reopened in the 1980s as an office building. It was for rent when Orozco and Lingwood found it: the "Building for Let" sign remained in the window throughout the exhibition.

For *Empty Club* Orozco filled the space with modified games. On the first floor of the building he installed *Carambole with Pendulum*. Carambole is a type of billiards—a French game similar to American pool or British snooker, except that the table has no pockets and the game requires just three balls. The work's conceptual origins were French as well: though Orozco first showed it in London, he had conceived it for the Centre de la Vieille Charité in Marseille. He altered the

billiard table in response to the former chapel's architecture, rounding the edges of the table so that it was oval rather than rectangular in form, mimicking the church's egg-shaped interior. He suspended one of the balls from the ceiling so that it would swing like a pendulum. (The ceilings in the chapel were extremely high, so when installed there the following year *Carambole with Pendulum* evoked the exceptionally long Foucault pendulum, which had been developed in the mid-nineteenth century as a means of demonstrating the Earth's rotation.)

The references to the Marseille chapel's architecture were lost in the building at 50 St. James's Street, but nonetheless Orozco's alterations to the billiard table changed the mode of play in thought-provoking ways. To score points in billiards players must hit one ball so that it strikes the two others—nearly always banking against the table's edge along the way. A curved edge complicates the physics of this maneuver. When the pendulum ball is hit, moreover, it begins to swing unpredictably, introducing an element of chaos into this supremely rational game. What had been a model of Newtonian mechanics—the regularized, predictable movement of the heavens or of atoms—becomes instead an exercise in improvisation in the face of chance, one that resonated deeply within the walls of the former "temple of chance."

On the second-floor walls hung a selection of *Atomists*—the title refers to the ancient Greek atomistic theory of matter and motion—a series of newspaper reproductions of sporting events modified with networks of circular forms. The photographs centered on sports that had begun in Britain but had become more

TOP:
*Working Tables, 1993–1996.*
1996. Mixed mediums,
dimensions variable.
Installation view at
Kunsthalle Zürich, 1996

ABOVE:
Tabletop, artist's house,
Tlalpan, Mexico City, 1995

OPPOSITE:
Views of *Carambole with Pendulum* from top

Installation view of *Carambole with Pendulum*, Chapelle du Centre de la Vieille Charité, Musée de Marseille, 1997

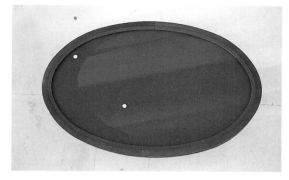

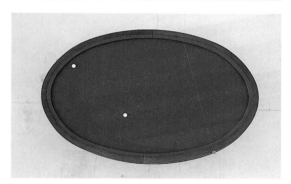

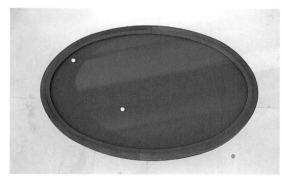

*"Orozco's predilection for curves, spheres and ellipses—
all present in* Oval Billiard Table*—could be restated
alternatively as a reticence towards rectilinearity; the
point is that these two geometries suggest rather different
relations of bodies to space-time. At base, it is the Cartesian
grid which seems to be incompatible with the sensibility
projected by Orozco's work, not simply because the grid
tends towards fixity as opposed to the sphere's infinite
movement of inflections; but also because it maps the
world-as-object from the perspective of a coherent, centred
subject, one that the artist's work consistently resists."*

Jean Fisher, "The Play of the World," in *Gabriel
Orozco: Empty Club* (1998), p. 20

popular in the former colonies—especially cricket and soccer (a personal favorite of Orozco's). A few of the works in this larger series were small-scale and
done by hand: Orozco ran through his printer either original newsprint photographs or photocopies of such images in order to print designs on them, and
then painted them with gouache. As time went on, he began to scan the newspaper images into his computer and then develop his geometric designs on-screen
before enlarging and printing them. In all cases he thought of the circular forms
as blow-ups of the dots used in the original printing process.

One floor above, Orozco set up a long, narrow alley of artificial potted
trees modified with circular "leaves" that related to the forms criss-crossing
the *Atomists*. The works—called *Moon Trees*—were inspired by a solar eclipse
he had seen in New York's Central Park. "It's a kind of natural phenomenon
translated into an artificial object which probably helps us to see that object
in a different way," he told Benjamin Buchloh. "It's just an artificial thing but
it also looks so natural. It has to do with growing, the infinite and the artificiality of perception, or how through artificiality we perceive nature and
then nature becomes artificiality."[2] On the top floor he installed a model of
a cricket field. Positioned approximately three and a half feet off the ground
with a surface area of roughly six and a half by five and three-quarters feet
(two by one and three-quarters meters), *Cricket Model*, complete with a miniature stadium, was populated by dozens of similarly scaled immobile metal
figurines. Along the perimeter Orozco affixed miniature trees to the backs of

the figures, creating human-tree hybrids that somewhat forebodingly encroached on the field of play. The concept was inspired by a dream Orozco had that recalled the scene in *Macbeth* in which soldiers disguised as trees arrive to defeat Macbeth, who has been told that he would not be vanquished "until Birnam Wood comes to Dunsinane."

Many of the works that appeared in *Empty Club* traveled to New York in September for Orozco's second exhibition at Marian Goodman Gallery. The objects functioned differently outside the English context in which they had first been displayed (and *Carambole with Pendulum* functioned differently in both places than it would when displayed in Marseille), and critics responded less to their implied histories of sport and empire than to the art historical precedents in the work of early-twentieth-century artists, especially Piet Mondrian and the Russian Constructivists. Orozco has argued that his work — even when designed with a specific site in mind — is never simply site-specific because it is always meant to circulate in the world and accrete new meanings. "It starts from a specific situation," he has told Fer, "and then it starts to travel. It is important that the work gets out into the world and gets exposed to the erosion of different

Crews battle to establish an early advantage at the start of the boys junior eights, which was won by Westminster, at Holme Pierrepont

TOP:
*Atomist: Heavy Whipping.* 1996. Gouache and ink on newspaper clipping, 6⅜ × 6¾" (16.2 × 17.2 cm)

ABOVE:
*Atomist: Making Strides.* 1996. Gouache and ink on newspaper clipping, 8¼ × 8¼" (20.9 × 20.9 cm)

RIGHT:
*Atomist: Crews Battle.* 1996. Gouache and ink on color electrostatic print, 6¼ × 8¾" (15.9 × 22.2 cm)

*Atomists: Asprilla.* 1996. Ink-jet print, 6'6¾" × 9'7" (200 × 292.1 cm). Edition of 3

OPPOSITE:
Detail from Notebook 8, p. 100. Felt-tip pen on photograph, 4 × 6" (10.2 × 15.2 cm) (cropped)

*Moon Trees.* 1996. Wood, paper, and plastic, approx. 8'4" × 66" × 66" (254 × 167.6 × 167.6 cm). Three of nine versions

Asprilla, the Newcastle United substitute, attempts an overhead kick despite the close attention of Calderwood at St James' Park yesterday. Photograph: Marc Aspland

places. Specificity becomes a temporal development. . . . It comes from a center, a cultural center. That doesn't mean a very powerful cultural center. Every culture is a center and every culture is very local in many ways. And then it goes out into the world, and starts to travel."[3]

In October Orozco flew to Iceland to make a site-specific work at The Living Art Museum in Reykjavík as part of a two-person exhibition with Rirkrit Tiravanija. Orozco purchased a parachute at an Army-Navy store on Canal Street in New York and brought it with him to make *Parachute in Iceland*. Tethering the silky white parachute at one end, he allowed the wind to lift it into the Icelandic air so that it hovered sideways just above the rich, black volcanic earth. He took photographs of the parachute from each of the four cardinal points, creating works like the bright, almost Pop-like *Parachute in Iceland (South)* and the romantic, delicately moody *Parachute in Iceland (East)*, which he shot in the long, indeterminate, northern light with a glacier rising behind it.

Another memorable photograph from this year originated as an installation commissioned by the Museum of Contemporary Art San Diego for the sculpture garden of its newly renovated building in La Jolla. As with *Hammock Hanging*

*Between Two Skyscrapers* (1993), Orozco used humor to question the special status of the museum garden. With *Long Yellow Hose*, he called attention to the garden's pristinely manicured expanse—no easy feat in such an arid climate—by running a 1,200-foot-long (365-meter-long) bright yellow hose all around the grounds. The work recalls the sort of casual, ad hoc irrigation system one might see in developing countries. Because the museum has an irrigation system that is both fully functional and more or less invisible, Orozco's hose was an unnnecessary extra, one that disrupts the seeming effortlessness of the garden's Edenic setting.

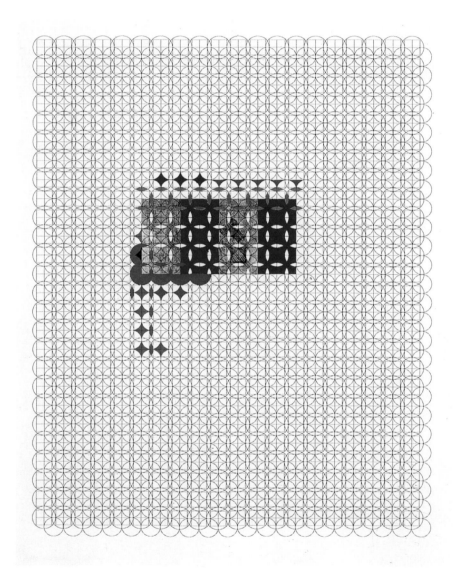

ABOVE, TOP TO BOTTOM:
*Parachute in Iceland (North).* 1996
*Parachute in Iceland (East).* 1996
*Parachute in Iceland (South).* 1996
*Parachute in Iceland (West).* 1996

Silver dye bleach prints, 16 × 20"
(40.6 × 50.8 cm). Editions of 5

RIGHT:
*Puddle 68.* 1996. Synthetic polymer paint and graphite on ink-jet print, 11 × 8 1/2" (27.9 × 21.6 cm)

OPPOSITE:
Notebook 7, p. 63. Stickers and postcards on notebook page, 10 3/4 × 8 1/16" (27.3 × 20.5 cm)

OPPOSITE, INSET:
*Light through Leaves* (for *Parkett*, no. 48). 1996. Ink-jet print, 20 × 32 3/16" (50.8 × 81.8 cm). Edition unknown

*"Since the mid-1990s, he has been producing computer-generated drawings, which he calls* Puddles *(1996–1997). These start off as templates of circles and grids generated by the click of a mouse. Then, at the centre of each one, he adds more circles and half-circles, ellipses and eclipses, and it begins to unravel. Orozco creates a template and then colors bits of it in, from the centre outwards, by hand. . . . Adding these elements destroys the coherence of the whole. Beginning at the centre, he destroys the centre."*

Briony Fer, "Spirograph: The Circular Ruins of Drawing," in *Gabriel Orozco* (2004), pp. 18, 20

GENTILE E GIOVANNI BELLINI

OPPOSITE:

*Common Dream.* 1996. Silver
dye bleach print, 16×20"
(40.6×50.8 cm). Edition of 5

*Long Yellow Hose.* 1996. Silver
dye bleach print, 16×20"
(40.6×50.8 cm). Edition of 5

Notebook 7, p. 137. Photographs
on notebook page, 10¾×8¹⁄₁₆"
(27.3×20.5 cm)

*"But much of the work falls in-between: the possibilities exist for the subjects to be found
'just as is' or the intervention to be so gentle that one is either not at first aware of it,
or not always sure of it. The circle of sheep shot in India in* Common Dream, *1996,
captures an uncanny natural formation in which the older animals form a protective
circle to shade the younger ones from the heat. Even when they are humorous, there is a
profound sense of lifecycles in Orozco's images. This is apparent in that powerful image
of a profoundly sleeping dog, in the sculptural forms of dead leaves in lushly abundant
forests of Costa Rica, and in his many images of food, excrement, life, and death."*

Phyllis Rosenzweig, "Gabriel Orozco: Photographs," in *Gabriel Orozco: Photographs*
(2004), pp. 12–13

EMPTYING THE MIND ON ITS WAY TO THE VOID FULLNES, WHICH IS EMPTY OF ANY EXISTENTIAL

THOUGHT.

# 1997: Emptying the Mind

I N THE WINTER OF 1996 one of Orozco's lungs collapsed. Though he recovered fully after a painful procedure and a week in the hospital, the experience affected him profoundly. He was "a young man, skinny and healthy" who had never spent time in the hospital before, and he was struck by how irrational and accidental it all seemed. Upon his release, he wanted a break from his usual ambitious levels of activity. "I wanted to spend time indoors. It was wintertime; I wanted to make it a very slow process, enjoy this process, go into this thing." "This thing" was *Black Kites*, a sculpture made from a human skull that Orozco purchased at Evolution Nature Store in SoHo. Except for a few brief diversions—in January he went to the Centre de la Vieille Charité in Marseille to install a billiard table similar to the one he had shown the year before with Artangel, while in March he produced a new installation of *Working Tables* for the Whitney Biennial—he spent most of the several months following his hospitalization studying the skull and then covering it, inside and out, in a dense, shiny graphite grid.

*Black Kites* calls to mind the iconographic tradition of the *memento mori* as well as the skulls that permeate Mexican art and culture. As Orozco explained to Benjamin Buchloh, however, his interest was the reality rather than the symbolism of death: "I was intrigued by something real, that is not a fake, something natural, real death (if that is possible)."[1] The elemental reality of the sculpture's materials is significant too: it was essential to Orozco to begin with a real skull, which consists largely of calcium, and to overlay it with another dense, mineral

"A mysterious entity, silent and profound. Orozco reinvents a Mexican tradition, neither quoting it nor following any inspiration. He looks at the origins not of his culture but of the abstraction of any origins. The past is now ahead and the future is behind us. We cannot look at this 'thing' simply for what it is, we are forced to look at it as a black hole, a crack in the linear vision of civilization."

Francesco Bonami, "Sudden Death: Roughs, Fairways and the Game of Awareness," in *Gabriel Orozco: Clinton Is Innocent* (1998), pp. 21, 23

"What is strange about the skull is not its iconography alone, but also that fact that you treat a bodily fragment as a ready-made. The skull is a found human body part. The drawing is the added element. So that's a very strange conception of what a sculpture is. . . . Then to add onto this peculiar structural reversal the feature of drawing and design in the way you do by claiming that peculiar parallel to Op Art and what that represents for you at this moment: that makes this a doubly-strange object."

Benjamin H. D. Buchloh, "Benjamin Buchloh interviews Gabriel Orozco in New York," in *Gabriel Orozco: Clinton Is Innocent* (1998), pp. 99, 103

*Black Kites*. 1997. Graphite on skull, 8 1/2 × 5 × 6 1/4" (21.6 × 12.7 × 15.9 cm)

substance, in this case, graphite. Working out the materials' black-and-white checkerboard play became a kind of meditation and, ultimately, a guide to the perception of the object. "You can really follow the drawing and go around the work and you can look at it for a very long time. You can travel through the head. . . . The drawing's strange behavior in the eyes and in the back. So you can imagine the eyes being black holes, or something like that."

If the grid offers a topography of the skull, the converse is also true: the skull's contours transform the regularity of the grid. What begins as a fairly regular lattice in the front goes on to loop and split into lozenges on the back and sides. Order, however rigorously applied, cannot entirely shake its opposite. *Path of Thought*, a photograph that Orozco took of the work in its early stages, further emphasizes the organic irregularities underpinning the sculpture's graphic logic. The skull sits spotlit on a table under a strong raking light that brings out the jagged edges of the fused cranial plates and mineral weathering of the bone itself—features that are in no way contained by the elegant graphite contours that Orozco seems almost to have etched into its surface. In both the sculpture and the photograph, Orozco continues his investigation of the relationship between natural irregularity and the ordering systems of abstract thought evident in his graph paper drawings of 1993 and works such as *Horses Running Endlessly* (1995) and the *Atomists* (1996).

Orozco made *Black Kites* for Documenta 10, the contemporary art exhibition that takes place every five years in Kassel, Germany. At the same time he was also included in Sculpture Projects Münster, a decennial exhibition that has emphasized large-scale, temporary installations of public sculpture since 1977, when artists such as Joseph Beuys, Richard Serra, and Michael Asher were working out close-knit, critical relationships between artworks and their surroundings. Orozco's ambitious proposal for the exhibition was *Half-Submerged Ferris Wheel*: it was to be a Ferris wheel, at least 40 feet (about 12 meters) in diameter, one half of which would be below ground. For one half of the cycle, viewers would have seen the landscape continuously, provokingly, transformed, and then at the very moment that they were literally plunged into the site everything would have disappeared from view. This broken cycle physically echoes the bisected circles that have appeared throughout Orozco's career, while conceptually the work reconsiders many of the questions of fate and fatality that arise in *Black Kites*.

RETÍCULA BLANCO Y NEGRO. A CUADROS (AJEDREZ).
EN RODILLOS. COMO PLATAFORMA. DE FONDO. PAISAJE. NADA COMO NADA.
NEUTRALIZAR EL MURO. LA SUPERFICIE. LA CONCIENCIA. Y LUEGO...
ACTUAR. HACIA LA NUEVA NADA. VACÍO — LLENO — VACÍO.
TOTAL     NEUTRO     LUZ — OSCURO —          BLANCO — NEGRO — BLANCO
                     OSCURO — LUZ — OSCURO    NEGRO — BLANCO — NEGRO

5.11.96 → 13.11.96.

# H O S P I T A L          PNEUMOTORAX ESPÓNTANEO.

15.10.96
 CRÁNEO.
 PELÍCULA.
 RUEDA DE LA FORTUNA.

16.11.96
 LIBRO: AGENDA + CUADERNO + CATÁLOGO.          CRONOLOGÍA PERSONAL
                                                COMPENDIO.

22.11.96

RUEDA DE LA FORTUNA ENTERRADA

SUMERGIDA EN CANAL
SEMICIRCULAR

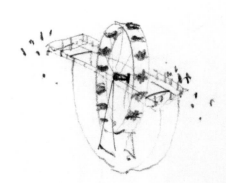

23.11.96

DESARROLLO TENIS EN VITRINAS.
PIANO ELÉCTRICO.

Notebook 9, p. 16. Graphite on
notebook page, 10¾ × 8¹/₁₆"
(27.3 × 20.5 cm)

Describing the work to the exhibition's curator Kasper König, Orozco wrote of "the ferris wheel idea (half and half) (day and night) (light and dark) (under and over) (life and death) (earth and sky) (horizon) (movement) (circle)."[2] *Half-Submerged Ferris Wheel* was too expensive to realize at Sculpture Projects Münster; instead, the artist's proposal was published in the accompanying catalogue. König installed a smaller version of the work at the EXPO 2000 in Hannover, and Orozco hopes to realize it fully in the future.

In September Orozco returned to Galerie Micheline Szwajcer in Antwerp, the space he had turned into a parking lot in 1995. In a group show with Mona Hatoum and Ann Veronica Janssens, he installed *Ventilators*, a series of ceiling fans with partially unfurled rolls of toilet paper streaming from each blade. Visually exciting yet somewhat gangly, the fans had their genesis in the some-times absurd cultural disjunctions that arise during travel. When Orozco and his wife had visited India the year before, they found that hotel proprietors, whether in budget or deluxe hotels, greeted them similarly. "They would wel-come us to our room, and instead of taking our luggage they would give us keys and toilet paper. . . . At that point I started to play around. In the room, of course you have all these ventilators, or fans, and you turn on the light and you launch

ABOVE:
Ceiling fan with a roll of toilet paper in a hotel, Bangalore, India, c. 1996

BELOW:
*Half-Submerged Ferris Wheel*. 1997. Ferris wheel, dimensions variable. Installation view of EXPO 2000, Hannover, 2000

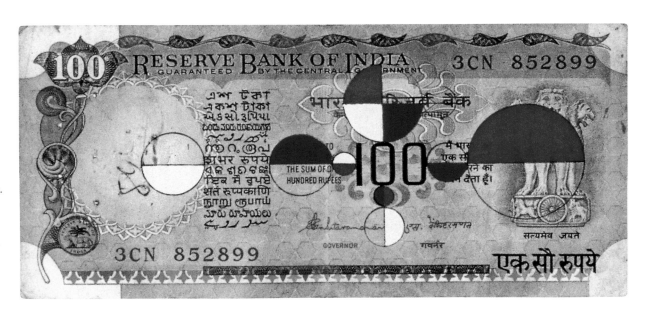

the toilet paper from the ventilator." *Ventilators* focus that absurdist sense of play into a spiral of energy: mischievous, a little perverse, yet still connected to the more serious issues of cyclical time that arise in other works.

In November the exhibition *Gabriel Orozco: Recordings and Drawings* opened at the Stedelijk Museum in Amsterdam. The recordings consisted of about five hours of video shot in New York and Amsterdam. To make the project's forty- to sixty-minute segments, Orozco walked the cities' streets with his video camera, capturing brief, arresting sequences of events. And like many of the other works he had exhibited that year, they reveal a tension between artistic control and composition and the vagaries of the real world. Orozco would notice something interesting and would begin to "trace certain intentions with the camera, and then suddenly the tension between my intentions and reality becomes too great and the whole thing breaks down," at which point he would turn off the camera.[3]

In early December Orozco had an exhibition at Anthony d'Offay Gallery in London. Games featured prominently, as they had in the Artangel show the year before, but here they served more as structuring principles than as points of reference. Orozco constructed two works on-site: *Kitchen Maze Door*, a colorful space through which viewers could choose either direct or meandering routes, and *Circle Mats,* Astroturf circles, small and large, that evoke childhood games like leaping from one stone to another. Both works suggest rules but neither lays them out explicitly, leaving them to be invented or imagined.

Hanging on the walls of the maze were a number of gouache drawings: works, like *Ventilators*, that had their roots in Orozco's trip to India. On that trip he had been very taken with Tantric drawings and miniature paintings, and soon he began working on new versions of his drawings. For pictorial supports he used airline tickets and Indian rupee bills—pieces of paper that served as evidence of circulation, movement, or exchange and yet in some cases seemed utterly insubstantial: "When I started to do it with Indian paper I was very much aware of how non-valuable it was. In that time one rupee was like a fraction of a fraction of a fraction. . . . In a way it didn't even exist." To draw on the bill was to rescue it, "at least as an image so it's not so un-valuable and devaluated. . . . In a way a little bit romantic."

The floor of one room at d'Offay was strewn with eight *Pinched Stars*—aluminum sculptures whose elaborate shapes suggest a gestural or biomorphic expressionism. Far from treating gesture as a metaphorical sign of the artist's feelings, however, the stars' forms literally capture the smallest, seemingly least consequential of gestures: the meeting of two fingers. Orozco began with a small

JAYA PRAKĀŚA

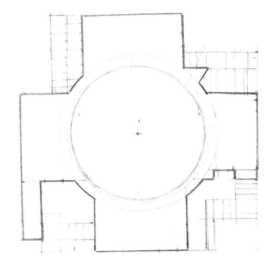

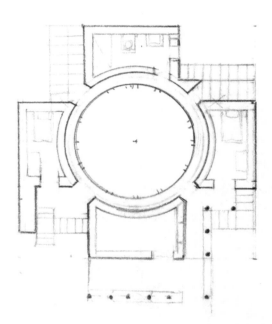

AGUAPRACASA

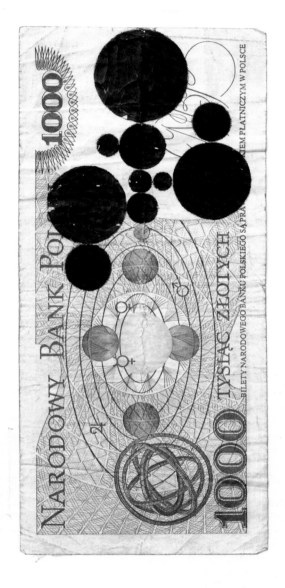

Notebook 8, p. 33. Graphite,
gouache, printed paper, and
banknote on notebook page,
10¾ × 8 1/16" (27.3 × 20.5 cm)

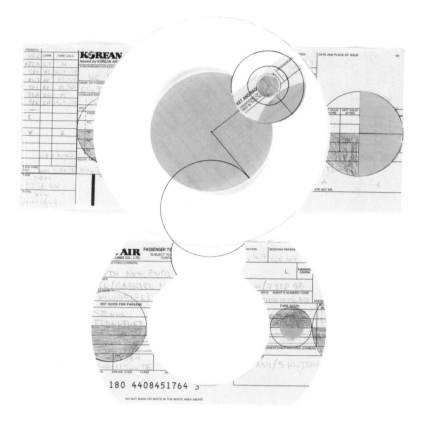

*Pinched Stars I–VIII.* 1997.
Aluminum, dimensions
variable. Each variation,
edition of 3

LEFT:
*Korean Air.* 1997. Ink and
colored pencil on cut-and-
pasted printed paper on
paper, 11×8½" (28×21.6 cm)

piece of wax, which he pinched between his thumb and forefinger, creating a form that he then turned over to professional ceramists who made large-scale replicas. These were, in turn, cast in shiny aluminum, giving them an industrial sheen. In an interview with the artist, Buchloh observed that "there is an authentic gesture at the beginning" of this process, but that Orozco then feeds this "into a very elaborate process, perverse in a sense because these are now industrialized artisanal production processes. That's what makes them even stranger since they now look like modernist abstract sculpture and you don't quite know how they got their authenticity. . . you end up with a hybrid that is neither here nor there."[4] On top of this conceptual perversity and hybridity there is, Orozco insisted to Buchloh, another layer: "The *Pinched Stars* look clumsy or intricate, like a piece of shit. It's very scatological in the end."[5] The *Pinched Stars* were the first works Orozco made that took a freeform shape — the first that one might readily describe as *looking* scatological. But Orozco later explained that a wide-ranging, far from classically defined perversity runs implicitly throughout his work, from the geometric paintings to the Conceptual photography to, of course, *Ventilators.* He said, "I feel much more connected to the infantile, geometric approach to life you find in European art before World War II. I am interested in the way the art of the early avant-garde was based on childhood experience and had more connection with reality. . . . Dada is for perverted kids, who shit and pee on the table. I feel much closer to that."[6]

SEPTIEMBRE 95

MICHAEL, RIRKRIT Y YO JUGANDO PELOTA-TAPA EN KWJANGJU.

Notebook 8, p. 20. Graphite and
photographs on notebook page,
10¾ × 8¹⁄₁₆" (27.3 × 20.5 cm)

OPPOSITE, TOP:
*Focos Philips*. 1997. Silver dye
bleach print, 16 × 20"
(40.6 × 50.8 cm). Edition of 5

OPPOSITE, BOTTOM:
*Columpio*. 1997. Silver dye
bleach print, 16 × 20"
(40.6 × 50.8 cm). Edition of 5

# Clinton is

# Innocent

*Clinton Is Innocent.* 1998.
Synthetic polymer paint on
wall, dimensions variable
Installation view of *Clinton Is
Innocent,* Musée d'Art Moderne
de la Ville de Paris, 1998

OPPOSITE:
*Clinton Is Innocent.* 1998.
Ink-jet on newspaper clipping,
11¾ × 8½" (29.8 × 21.6 cm)

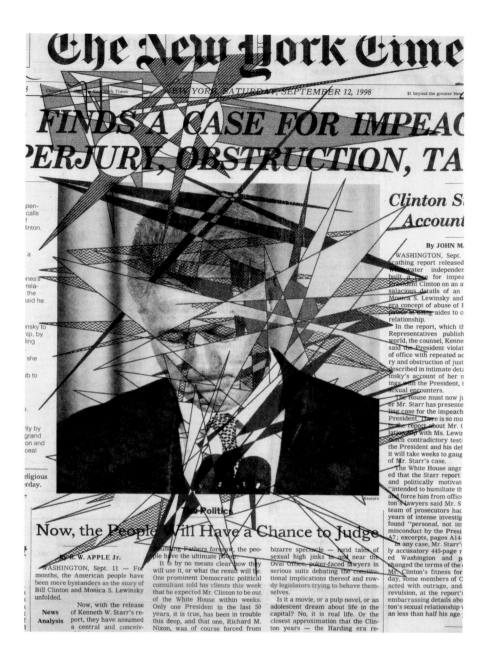

## 1998: Free Market Is Anti-Democratic

*"Returning now to 'Clinton is Innocent,' the debate that raged in the United States and reached a peak in the summer of 1998—that is to say at the very moment that G.O. wrote his pet phrase in giant letters on the wall of a museum that was hosting an exhibition of his work, in an exotic land where screwing in the office was strictly a personal affair—did not concern the innocence or guilt of the man who was then president of the U.S. . . . but only concerned the indictable nature or not of what had been revealed. . . . Consequently, Clinton's innocence did not need to be proven nor refuted: as it turns out, it was a pointless notion."*

Jean-Pierre Criqui, "The G.O. File (Excerpts)," in *Gabriel Orozco: Trabajo* (2003), p. xxiii

IN EARLY 1998 OROZCO WAS LIVING IN PARIS, preparing for a large exhibition at the Musée d'Art Moderne de la Ville de Paris, organized by Angeline Scherf. The exhibition, which opened in May, took place during the escalation of the Whitewater investigation and the Monica Lewinsky scandal. It was called *Clinton Is Innocent*. Orozco printed this declaration in big letters across a specially built curving title wall, using a font that recalled a *New York Times* headline. Many works in the exhibition had an air of carefully aimed fragility and naiveté: *Maman*, for example, a miniature French-style house with pianos inserted in its two sides, and *Kiss of the Egg* (1997), a steel infinity sign suspended from the ceiling with a little stand for an egg at the juncture of the two loops. Visitors were invited to interact with both works: they could stand inside the house of *Maman* or play its pianos; with the *Kiss of the Egg* two visitors could each step into one of the figure-eight's loops and kiss the egg at the center. Since the egg was precariously balanced the two people would have to kiss it simultaneously and with great care not to knock it down, transforming the familiar, intimate gesture into one that

Installation view of *Gabriel Orozco:*
*Clinton Is Innocent*, Musée d'Art
Moderne de la Ville de Paris,
1998, showing *Ventilators* (1997),
*Blackboard Drawings* (1997–98),
*Dandelions* (1998), and *Pinched Stars*
(1997)

FOREGROUND:
*Kiss of the Egg.* 1997. Steel, cable, and egg, 28½×47¼×22" (72.4×120×55.9 cm). Edition of 3

BACKGROUND:
*Maman.* 1998. Two pianos, slat roof, masonry tile, wood, metal, chair and mixed media, 120× 104×55" (304.8×264.2×139.7 cm)

Installation view of *Gabriel Orozco: Clinton Is Innocent*, Musée d'Art Moderne de la Ville de Paris, 1998

BELOW:
*Ping-Pond Table* (detail). 1998. Modified Ping-Pong table, water lilies, soil, stones, and water, 30"×13' 11¾"×13' 11¾" (76.2×426.1×426.1 cm). One of three versions

was more public, but also more precarious. As it happened, very few eggs broke over the course of the exhibition.

Orozco wanted the exhibition to give the impression of a large promenade or an open landscape. Viewers were invited to wander amid a scattering of *Pinched Stars* (1997), which were spread out on the floor like space-age rocks, and a new series of flowering white branches called *Dandelions*. Orozco had worked with the renowned Parisian artificial-flower factory Maison Guillet to make these fractal-formed structures. Each one consisted of seven branches radiating from a central core, each producing seven more stems, and each of those repeating the pattern once again before culminating in small circular petals to create an elegant bloom. Overhead, six *Ventilators* (1997) twirled. Hanging on the walls of the same gallery were *Blackboard Drawings* (1997–98), computer-generated patterns screenprinted in white on blackboard surfaces. Each geometric design was, like the structure of the *Dandelions*, governed by some very simple, arbitrarily chosen rule. Chalk and erasers resting on the ledge below each blackboard encouraged viewers to draw on the printed grids: sometimes elaborating on their logic, sometimes creating interruptions to that logic. In some cases people commented on other works in the gallery or wrote slogans whose tone reflected the proclamation about President Bill Clinton's innocence with which the show began.

In a glass-walled room known within the museum as "the aquarium," Orozco suspended *Color Travels through Flowers.* The work consisted of leaves of paper left

*"Orozco's game, at some point in the past, would seem to have diverged from its nominal likeness and taken a path to a world 'incompossible' with it. Indeed, the work produces the unsettling sense of being confronted with some other, cryptic or hermetic order for which the game rules have not been provided. The consequence of this mutation of relations is that the people who are watching or playing, unable to map themselves within an entirely familiar field, lose a sense of certainty—and become 'decentred.'"*

Jean Fisher, "The Play of the World," in *Gabriel Orozco: Empty Club* (1998), p. 19

over from the process of creating artificial blooms at Maison Guillet. Each page had been used to dry silk petals after dyeing, and had been stained with many different richly saturated colors. Orozco collected the sheets—which are ordinarily discarded once they become full of ink—while working on *Dandelions* in the factory. When installed in the museum the sheets floated freely from wires lined up across the room. Orozco has compared the experience of walking through the space to that of moving through markets in which sellers have hung their wares casually over the frames of tightly packed stalls. Viewed together, they have a loose, repetitive order.

Visitors to the exhibition could also play *Ping-Pond Table*, an altered Ping-Pong table with four rounded ends and a pond of water lilies in the place of a net. In Orozco's version of the game, four to eight people can participate rather than the usual two or four, and the rounded edges of the table increase the players' mobility. The ball does not simply have to overcome the net's vertical barrier, but must travel the pond's distance (and do so at the peril of becoming wet, slippery, and slightly messy). The game is therefore not only more challenging than traditional Ping-Pong, but involves a new sense of dimensionality—forcing the body of the viewer/player to engage with space (and time) in a more emphatic manner. Orozco has explained, "It's designed for a good game. It is of course a slower game because you have a big pond in the center, and even if you know how to play Ping-Pong, you quickly realize that the movements are different, the timing is different, the whole thing changes. And that's why time, the notion of time, is altered completely. And I think that happens in many of my works, like *Carambole with Pendulum* and *Yogurt Caps* or even *Black Kites*."

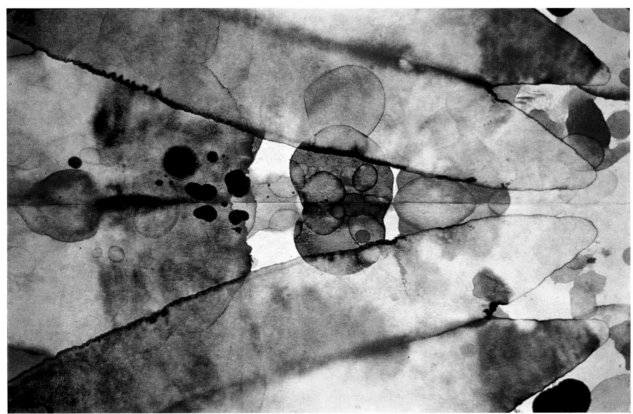

*Color Travels through Flowers*. 1998. Dye on paper, dimensions variable. Installation views of *Clinton Is Innocent*, Musée d'Art Moderne de la Ville de Paris, 1998

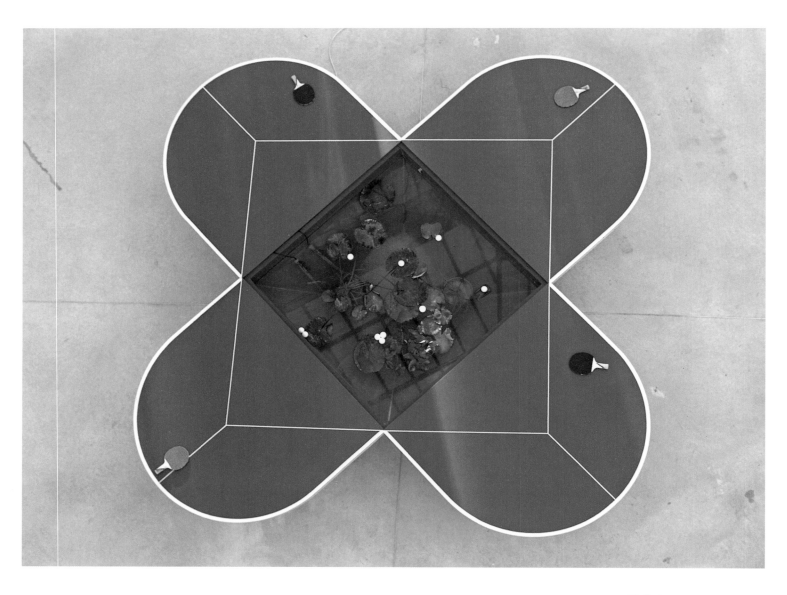

Orozco has pointed out his interest in the fact that games such as Ping-Pong, cricket, billiards, and chess refer to a culturally specific idea of the civilization that produced them. His alterations tinker with those models, repurposing them while maintaining their wider reference and at times extending some connections. Some of the materials used are also culturally specific. Especially when installed in Paris, the water lilies at the crux of *Ping-Pond Table* easily brought to mind Claude Monet's *Water Lilies*. In these paintings Monet recorded the landscape not as he found it but as he had designed it, capturing nature as constructed by man. The paintings thus hold the natural and the artificial in a complicated and typically modern relationship—one that Orozco plays off of and amplifies by placing a bit of "nature" at the center of *Ping-Pond Table*. The table's overall form also looks beyond its literal borders: it is shaped like a lotus, a Buddhist symbol for the origin of the universe. While *Ping-Pond Table* is decidedly not a religious statement, it does gesture toward a cosmic scale, and consequently insists that we think through our experience with the game in relation to the wider world.

Throughout the exhibition in Paris, visitors could hear a recording of Orozco playing the piano—careful improvisations performed by an artist who had no experience with the instrument. To make these recordings Orozco had gone to a professional studio one day a week for two months; brief selections from the recordings played in the galleries. The music itself was calm and contemplative, but that repose was as fragile as the egg in *Kiss of the Egg*. The open invitation to play the pianos in *Maman* meant that the exhibition might erupt into aural chaos at any moment.

TOP:
*Ping-Pond Table*. 1998. Modified Ping-Pong table, water lilies, soil, stones, and water, 30" × 13' 11¾" × 13' 11¾" (76.2 × 426.1 × 426.1 cm). One of three versions

ABOVE:
Marcellus Hall, illustration originally published in the *New Yorker*, January 11, 1999, p. 10, with the caption "Free-form Ping-Pong courtesy of Gabriel Orozco, at Marian Goodman"

In the summer Orozco returned to New York and began *Penske Work Project*. He rented a truck from Penske and for about a month drove it around New York, accompanied by a small team, including Juan Carlos Martín, a young Mexican film director who started to follow Orozco everywhere to make a film about his daily practice. Orozco would stop at every Dumpster to collect material for a work that he would make on the spot and store in the truck until final delivery to the gallery space. Much of the garbage had originally come from demolition, construction, or industry: there were plastic buckets, heavy-duty fans, scraps of metal, chunks of drywall. Orozco has described the process: "It's a kind of game to drive this truck around the city, and I have to make the work with the found object and I have to come to a solution right there on the spot. So I work for a little while, sometimes thirty minutes, sometimes two hours, until I come up with a solution that I like, that I find finished. Then I take a Polaroid of it to be sure that I will remember it, and I store it in the truck. Then I go to the next place."

Orozco exhibited *Penske Work Project* at Marian Goodman Gallery in November. Three days before the opening he received word that his father had died of a heart attack. Orozco flew home to Mexico City and returned to New York in time to finish the installation. Titled *Gabriel Orozco: Free Market Is Anti-Democratic*, the exhibition consisted of almost one hundred objects, displaying *Penske Work Project* alongside *Dandelions* and *Pinched Stars*. The latter works lent some of their elegance to the *Penske* assemblages. In turn the *Penske* works gave the Parisian sculpture a fresh materiality. Orozco also reinstalled *Yogurt Caps* (1994), which had first gone on view at the gallery four years before.

*Penske Work Project* in progress. New York, 1998

ABOVE:
Juan Carlos Martín. Stills from *Gabriel Orozco*. 2002. Film, 80 mins.

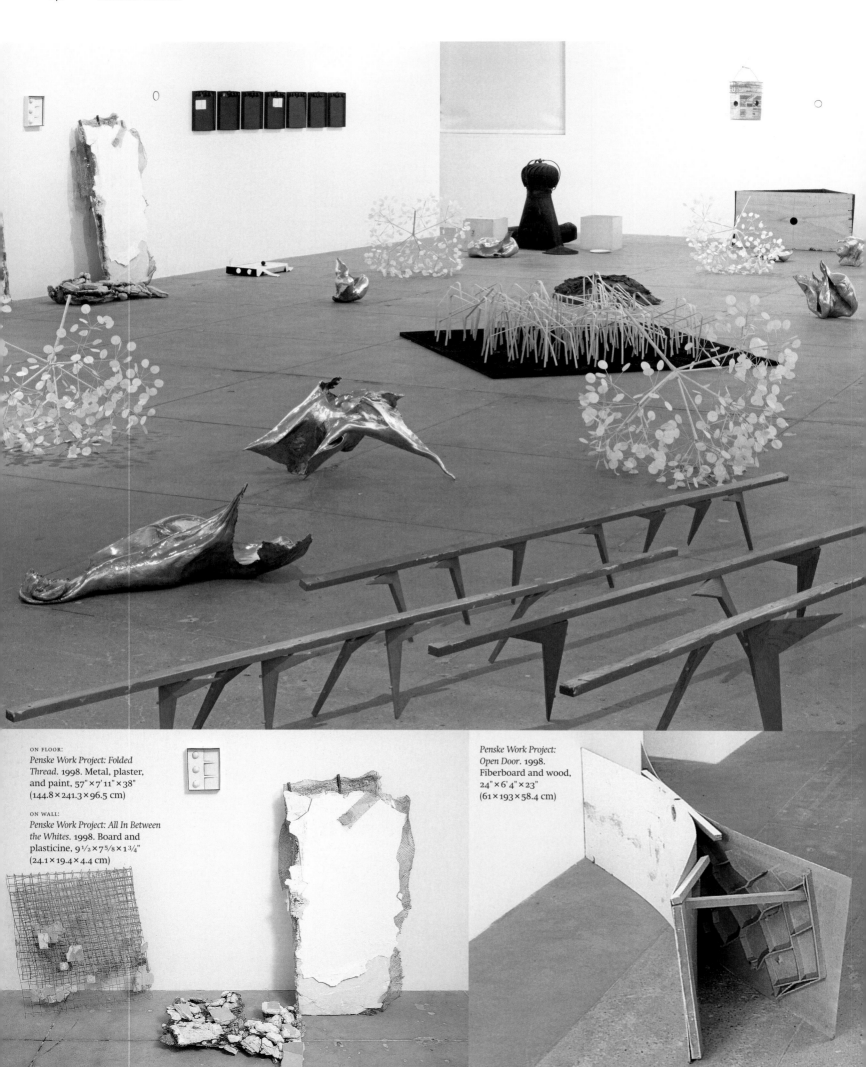

ON FLOOR:
*Penske Work Project: Folded Thread*. 1998. Metal, plaster, and paint, 57" × 7' 11" × 38" (144.8 × 241.3 × 96.5 cm)

ON WALL:
*Penske Work Project: All In Between the Whites*. 1998. Board and plasticine, 9 1/2 × 7 5/8 × 1 3/4" (24.1 × 19.4 × 4.4 cm)

*Penske Work Project: Open Door*. 1998. Fiberboard and wood, 24" × 6' 4" × 23" (61 × 193 × 58.4 cm)

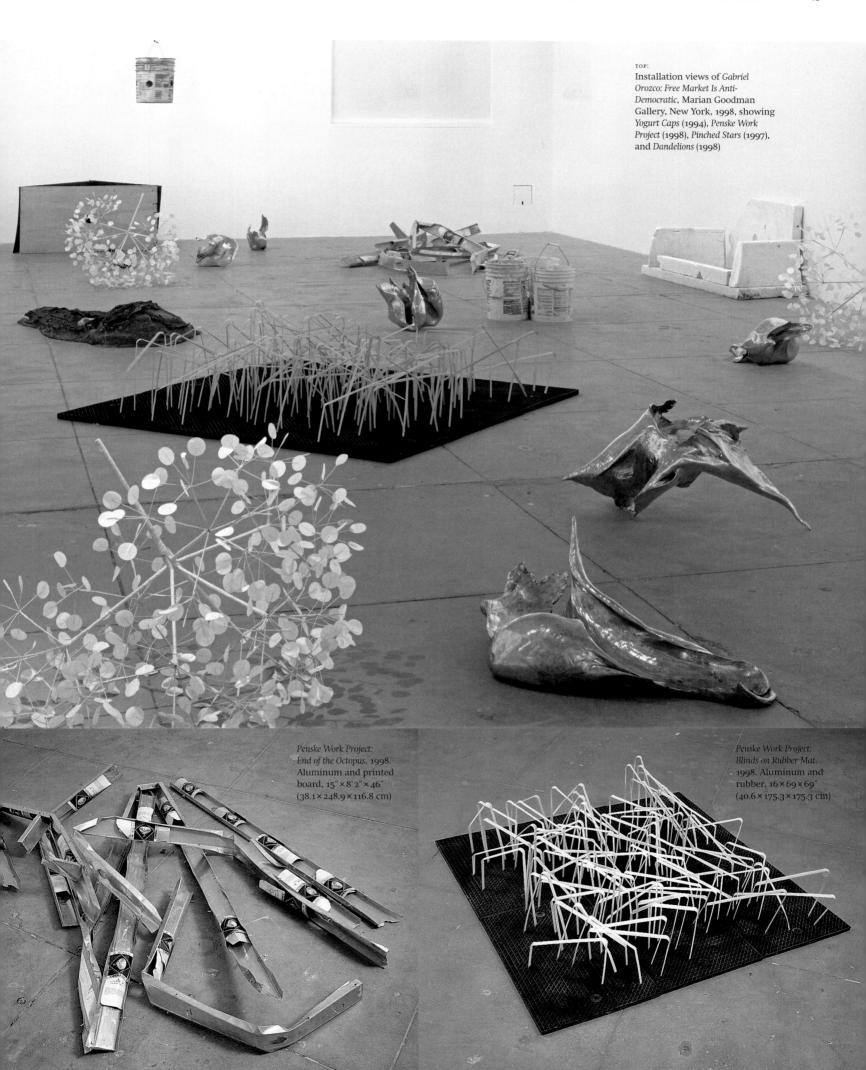

Installation views of *Gabriel Orozco: Free Market Is Anti-Democratic*, Marian Goodman Gallery, New York, 1998, showing *Yogurt Caps* (1994), *Penske Work Project* (1998), *Pinched Stars* (1997), and *Dandelions* (1998)

*Penske Work Project: End of the Octopus.* 1998. Aluminum and printed board, 15" × 8' 2" × 46" (38.1 × 248.9 × 116.8 cm)

*Penske Work Project: Blinds on Rubber Mat.* 1998. Aluminum and rubber, 16 × 69 × 69" (40.6 × 175.3 × 175.3 cm)

The Marian Goodman exhibition also contained several drawings, including one that looked forward to future projects: a sketch of the eighteenth-century Jantar Mantar observatory in New Delhi, a sprawling complex that includes a giant stone platform with two large hemispheres carved into its surface. Orozco imagined filling one of these indentations with water, and pictured this thought in his drawing *Aguapracasa* (Water for the house). This architectural rendering shows the newly aquatic observatory both in plan and elevation. Later *Aguapracasa* would become the model for his Observatory House, which would be built on a Mexican beach in 2006.

LEFT:
*Eroded Suizekis 3*. 1998. Cut-and-pasted printed paper, 11¼ × 8⅛" (28.6 × 20.6 cm)

TOP:
*Penske Work Project: Fish Aquarium*. 1998. Plastic and printed board, 13¾ × 11½ × 11½" (34.9 × 29.2 × 29.2 cm)

ABOVE:
*Penske Work Project: Bucket Fractal*. 1998. Three plastic buckets and garbage, 20½ × 23 × 23" (52.1 × 58.4 × 58.4 cm)

OPPOSITE:
Notebook 9, p. 15. Ballpoint pen, graphite, gouache, and ink-jet print on notebook page, 10¾ × 8 1/16" (27.3 × 20.5 cm)

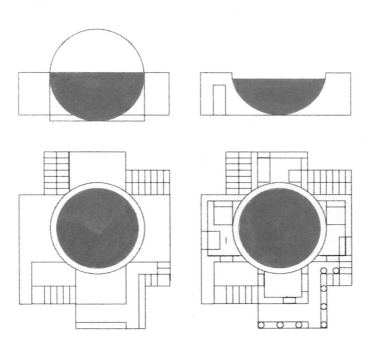

AGUAPRACASA:

# 1999: Photogravity

**O**ROZCO SPENT THE FIRST WEEKS OF 1999 on a secluded beach in the Mexican state of Oaxaca, far from the urban environment in which he had made *Penske Work Project* the previous fall. Much of that project's character had come from the dense, urban profusion of New York's industrial-strength detritus. Everything Orozco used in making the work had been discarded, ejected from the mainstream economy. It was at this point that the artist intervened, recycling the materials by returning them to circulation as art objects.

Orozco engaged a similar process of recovery while in Oaxaca to create *Carta Blanca*, a work that also began with the collection of trash. In this case Orozco collected cans that had washed ashore and oxidized to an almost uniform gritty orange-brown. He had picked them up partially out of annoyance with the litter, but instead of simply throwing them out, he brought them—all hundred or so—back to his cabana. He wanted to make a large-scale work with them but was not yet sure what form it would take. He was on the beach with a number of friends, and Juan Carlos Martín was there with a production crew shooting a documentary on Orozco. They were a large group, working, relaxing, and drinking a fair amount of Carta Blanca—the only kind of beer they could get in the region, a cheap brew with a red-and-gold label. As they drank, the humid air began to peel the labels off the bottles and Orozco began playing with them, gluing them to the rusty cans he had found on the beach. "And then I decided to put my friends to work," Orozco has said. "During two days I would buy them all the beer they could drink if they would give me the labels, and we all got very drunk. And, they worked very hard."

This "hard work" brought about a retrieval similar to that of *Penske Work Project*. The tin cans had long since lost the function of their given role; some were so decayed that holes had rusted right through them. Pasting the bright, shiny labels on these abandoned objects, as if to renew them as commodities, was utterly absurd. But it is through this somewhat comic gesture that the cans left the beach ecology and entered the art economy. When Orozco exhibited *Carta Blanca* at Portikus Gallery in Frankfurt am Main, Germany, he also brought sand from Mexico to form a kind of miniature beach beneath the cans on the floor.

ABOVE, TOP TO BOTTOM:
*Sandball and Chair III.* 1995. Silver dye bleach print, 16 × 20" (40.6 × 50.8 cm). Artist's proof

*Sandball and Chair I.* 1995. Silver dye bleach print, 16 × 20" (40.6 × 50.8 cm). Edition of 5

*Sandball and Chair II.* 1995. Silver dye bleach print, 16 × 20" (40.6 × 50.8 cm). Edition of 5

RIGHT:
*Concha con Conchas.* 1999. Steel and shells, 33 × 28 ½ × 37" (83.8 × 72.4 × 94 cm)

The rest of the exhibition continued along the same thematic lines. Near *Carta Blanca* stood another sculpture made of Mexican beach findings, *Concha con Conchas*—a pile of shells and the frame of a classic modernist shell-shaped beach chair that had washed up on the shore, having lost its woven rope seat. (The same chair frame appears in the related photographs *Sandball and Chair I–III*, 1995.) Just above the floor on the back wall of the gallery hung *Paper Foam Waves*, twenty-five pieces of white paper that Orozco had cut with a compass cutter—a compass with a disk-shaped blade on one end that would mechanically cut perfect circles as he rotated it around a point. He had been using compasses throughout his career to create many of the circles often present in his drawings. In a sense he was drawing here too by creating hard-edged, clean-lined contours. Traditionally, though, drawing has been valued for its form-giving qualities; here it becomes part of a methodical, progressive disintegration. The sheet furthest to the left had a single bit removed from one side, the next one had the same piece missing plus one other, again and again until the last sheet had dissolved almost to a frothy lace.

Installation view of *Exhibition No. 91: Gabriel Orozco*, Portikus Gallery, Frankfurt am Main, 1999, showing *Carta Blanca* (1999) and *Paper Foam Waves* (1999)

RIGHT:
Juan Carlos Martín. Stills from *Gabriel Orozco*. 2002. Film, 80 min.

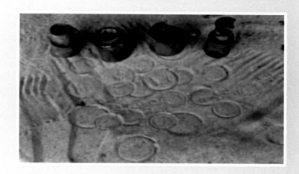

ABOVE:
*Double Relief.* 1999. Silver dye bleach print, 16 × 20" (40.6 × 50.8 cm). Edition of 5

OPPOSITE:
*Inner Circles of the Wall.* 1999. Graphite on plaster, dimensions variable

*Inner Circles of the Wall* (detail). 1999. Graphite on plaster, dimensions variable

Installation views at Galerie Chantal Crousel, Paris, 1999

An exhibition at Galerie Chantal Crousel that opened in May took the renovation of the gallery as an opportunity to explore the idea of the ruin. Some of the ruins were classical: the exhibition included *Double Relief* and other photographs taken on an earlier trip to Egypt. Others reflected the state of the gallery-as-construction site. Upstairs Orozco lined up remnants of a demolished plaster wall against the newly finished wall. He placed other shards—inscribed with compass-drawn circles—on the massive wood tables that he had designed to fit around the gallery's two central structural columns. Downstairs he installed *After the Table*, four flat painted-plywood constructions—leftovers from the making of the gallery's tables. Hanging on the walls were drawings from a series that Orozco called *Havre-Caumartin* after a Paris Métro station of the same name. Its walls, covered in round white mosaic tiles, had first caught his attention in the early 1980s. He and several assistants worked on the drawings together, placing large sheets of Japanese rice paper on the station wall and rubbing their surfaces with graphite so that rows of circles would show through. The results are less reproductions of the walls than eroded versions of them, made visually interesting by the levels of pressure applied by the different hands doing the rubbing, the time the fatiguing process required, and the texture of the paper onto which the pattern was transposed.

Over the summer Orozco worked with José Kuri and Mónica Manzutto to organize *Market Economics*, an exhibition in Mexico City's Mercado de Medellín that lasted a single day, August 21. This event marked the beginning of the gallery kurimanzutto. Orozco proposed that they rent a stall in a market for a day—one that would sell artworks rather than fruits and vegetables. A number of artists participated, most contributing works made of materials that one could buy at the market. The art was priced reasonably enough for ordinary shoppers to afford. The exhibition was successful on two counts: the artists did sell many of

View of *Havre-Caumartin* in
progress in the Paris Métro,
1999

Installation view of *Havre-Caumartin* (1999) at Galerie
Chantal Crousel, Paris, 1999

*Havre-Caumartin 1–3*. 1999.
Graphite on Japanese paper,
6' 6 3/4" × 39 3/8" (200 × 100 cm)

*"But Orozco's drawing nonetheless vividly demonstrates the twin action in his work, a ruination of centre and an infinite dispersal of its elements. His endless series of divergences and recombinations are continually in movement in ways that dislocate the normal coordinates by which things are linked together in the world."*

Briony Fer, "Spirograph: The Circular Ruins of Drawing," in *Gabriel Orozco* (2004), p. 24

OPPOSITE, CLOCKWISE FROM TOP LEFT:
*Butterfly Effect 9.* 1998. Cut-and-pasted printed paper, 11⅞ × 9¼" (30.2 × 23.5 cm)

*Eroded Suizekis 25.* 2002. Cut-and-pasted printed paper, 11¼ × 8⅛" (28.6 × 20.6 cm)

*Butterfly Effect 11.* 1998. Cut-and-pasted printed paper, 11⅞ × 9¼" (30.2 × 23.5 cm)

*Eroded Suizekis 5.* 1998. Cut-and-pasted printed paper, 11¼ × 8⅛" (28.6 × 20.6 cm)

RIGHT:
*Mixiotes.* 2001. Maguey membrane, rubber balls, plastic bags, and cotton string, dimensions variable

BELOW:
Views of *Market Economics,* Mexico City, August 21, 1999

their works to people out doing their weekly shopping, and the gallery began its trajectory to becoming one of Mexico City's most important art venues. Orozco's contribution was *Mixiotes*, a series of delicate hanging sculptures. For these works Orozco took the thin, membranous outer skins of maguey plants—a type of agave—and twisted them around translucent, plastic bags that each contain a rubber ball and that float in the air, suspended by a string. Hanging in the market and named after a food—*mixiotes* are a kind of rabbit-meat tamale cooked in an agave leaf—the works have a consumable aspect, which Orozco heightened by materials so ephemeral that he was not certain the sculptures would last more than a day.

That fall the exhibition *Photogravity* opened at the Philadelphia Museum of Art as part of its Museum Studies series. Orozco's installation explored the relationship between sculpture and photography, as well as that between ancient and contemporary art. The Philadelphia museum is home to a collection of pre-Columbian objects given in 1950 by Louise and Walter Arensberg, also the donors of the great collection of works by Duchamp, Brancusi, and other modern artists. By 1999 all but two of the pre-Columbian works had been in storage for many years. For *Photogravity*, Orozco wished to engage these objects with his own. He made black-and-white, life-size photographic reproductions of several of his works from the preceding years, each mounted on a backing board and a limb-like support that allowed it to stand freely on the gallery floor. *La DS* (1993) was there, as well as *Elevator* (1994), *Recaptured Nature* (1990), and *Yielding Stone* (1992).

*Photogravity*. 1999. Ink-jet
prints, foamcore, steel, rubber,
and wood, twenty-eight
parts, dimensions variable.
Installation views at *Gabriel
Orozco: Photogravity*, Philadelphia
Museum of Art, 1999

Orozco also used photographic reproductions of several pre-Columbian sculptures, which he had enlarged to approximately the same size as the reproductions of his own works. The resulting objects intermingled in the museum's gallery. Thin, light, and blank on their backsides, they were both photography and sculpture, and yet they did not provide the same viewing experience as either. Side by side, equalized, the two bodies of work seemed to inhabit a common art historical past. Their shared roots do not lie in a mythically unified native land, however, but in the mid-twentieth-century proliferation of photographically reproduced artworks—and in the history of the museum itself.

*"From the starting-point of your relations with that place, you produced your work in a context of specificity relating to a certain time, a phase, a moment. Hence the fact that a number of your works also express this idea: they do not just relate to a particular place, but also to the discourse of passage, of circulation. Various works have this meaning. Furthermore, in Mexico we were coming to terms with the fact that the cultural discourses at the time were not exclusively our own, and that they were much more dependent on historical and time-based circumstances. In this sense, the work that you were creating related in a way to a Mexican identity and did not break away from it. In the context of that time—in relation to official art and to what was happening in Mexican galleries—your work was totally and utterly different. Few artists had such a broad viewpoint with regard to use of materials, to working models and to their self-image."*

Guillermo Santamarina, "Gabriel Orozco in Conversation with Guillermo Santamarina, Mexico City, August 2004," in *Gabriel Orozco* (2005), p. 134

# 2000: The Prodigal Sun

OROZCO SPENT THE EARLY MONTHS OF 2000 preparing for his first major survey at an American museum. The exhibition, organized by Alma Ruíz at the Museum of Contemporary Art in Los Angeles, opened in June and later traveled to the Museo Internacional Rufino Tamayo in Mexico City and to the Museo de Arte Contemporáneo in Monterrey, Mexico. These latter presentations would be the first time that a substantial body of Orozco's work would be shown in Mexico. The retrospective brought together a decade of sculpture, drawings, and photographs, uniting in the flesh many works that had stood together in *Photogravity* the previous year.

For the MoCA installation Orozco took down all of the temporary partitions in the museum's main 7,000-square-foot (650-square-meter) gallery, putting *Working Tables, 1993–2000* at the center and creating constellations of objects around them. The effect was that of a giant *Working Table*, in which even the large-scale sculptures looked a little bit like models or maquettes, each work part of the larger whole that was the overall installation. The only work hanging on the gallery walls was *Yogurt Caps* (1994). Rather than request the original lids as a loan, Ruíz simply purchased new ones for the installation—the importance of the work being the conceptual gesture rather than the specific artifact. One cap was centered on each of the four walls, as they had been at Marian Goodman Gallery in 1994. In this context, the work became a kind of fragile container for the exhibition, one whose own hard-won coherence provided a fitting frame for a retrospective in which organizing principles did not come readymade for viewers.

ABOVE:
*Noodles in the Fence*. 2000. Silver dye bleach print, 16 × 20" (40.6 × 50.8 cm). Edition of 5

OPPOSITE:
Notebook 10, p. 53. Felt-tip pen, graphite, and napkin on notebook page, 10 3/4 × 8 1/16" (27.3 × 20.5 cm)

OPPOSITE, INSET:
Installation view of *Working Tables, 1993–2000* (2000) at The Museum of Contemporary Art, Los Angeles, 2000

MAYO 1999

EXPO MOLA LA

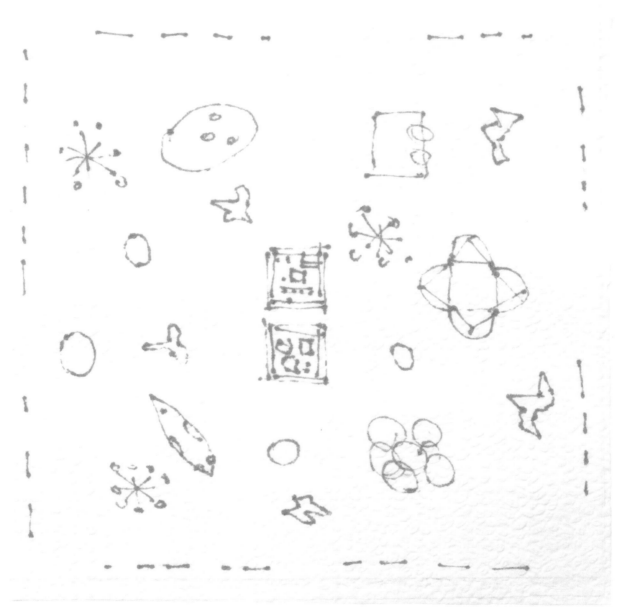

"If the first two galleries at MOCA invited museum-goers to play games—
the Ping Pond Table in the first gallery and Oval with Pendulum in the
second—the beautifully installed third gallery proposed another kind of game:
hide and seek. Where exactly do we find the art of Gabriel Orozco? In this
gallery 'reproduction' slid in next to original, study sidled up to art object, and
ephemera joined with monumental sculpture. In other words, Orozco took the
material conditions of the museum, including its strategies of canonization,
and submitted them to the same acts of unraveling and serendipity that inform
all of his work 'in reality.'"

David Joselit, "Gabriel Orozco: Museum of Contemporary Art,
Los Angeles," Artforum (2000), p. 174

NADA QUE ESCONDER
EL MUNDO NO TIENE NADA QUE ANI K
SIMOS NOSOTROS LOQUE NO LO VEMOS.

A bilingual catalogue accompanied the exhibition, containing essays by Ruíz, Benjamin Buchloh, Abraham Cruzvillegas, Gabriel Kuri, and Molly Nesbit. Orozco's friend and fellow artist Damián Ortega also drew a comic strip—titled "El pájaro: Para principiantes" (The bird: for beginners)—as an introduction to Orozco's work. Ortega's contribution was modeled on a series of comic books that had been popular in Mexico in the 1960s and '70s. Orozco and his colleagues were cognizant of the fact that while the international success the artist had achieved throughout the 1990s had drawn much attention in Mexico, there was very little real knowledge of his work in his native country. They were aware, too, that a few local critics had serious reservations about it. Ortega's comic addressed the difficulties in presenting Orozco's work in Mexico City: "A city where practically no one knows him except for an elite minority: his mom and his Aunt Lucha for instance. So the country's most acclaimed artist isn't renowned here. Fancy that!"[1]

The new work that Orozco planned for the exhibition in Mexico City played with the tradition of Mexican mural painting. He hired billboard painters to cover a gallery wall inside the Tamayo Museum with the red, black, and yellow sunburst logo of Sol, a popular Mexican beer. He titled this large-scale pseudo-advertisement *Mural Sol*. Using the same form with which Diego Rivera, José Clemente Orozco, David Alfaro Siquieros, and Orozco's own father had glorified those who had fought against imperialism and capitalism—from the Aztecs to the proletariat—Orozco instead depicted a product of capitalist consumer society. Some of the critics who saw the work in Mexico City viewed it as an attack by the "prodigal son" on his artistic forebears, but *Mural Sol* is perhaps better understood as an example of Orozco's attention to the way that the significance of forms changes over time. By the year 2000, mural scale had long since become billboard scale, and the graphic tradition of the muralists had been replaced by the visual language of advertising. Orozco did not treat the situation nostalgically but by equating muralism with advertising he advocated for forms of art not founded on monumentality or propaganda. The exhibition proved to be a triumphal homecoming and ushered Orozco into a newly prominent position within Mexico's cultural landscape.

The work of preparing these three exhibitions did not entirely curtail Orozco's peripateticism. After the opening at MoCA in Los Angeles, he and Gutierrez had traveled to Japan for a month. Orozco took many photographs there, including images of modest urban corners into which he had inserted plastic replicas of Japanese food. He also made photographs of *katagami*—print screens for kimonos—that the artist had found in antique shops.

Right after the opening of the show in Mexico City, Orozco accompanied his wife on what would be a yearlong stay in Costa Rica, where she was doing fieldwork for her doctoral dissertation on tropical forests and climate change. Most of Orozco's photographs and drawings from the end of 2000 until November 2001 had to do with his explorations of Costa Rica's rainforest.

TOP:
Damián Ortega, detail from "El pájaro: Para principiantes," originally published in Alma Ruiz, ed., *Gabriel Orozco* (Los Angeles: The Museum of Contemporary Art; and Mexico City: Museo Internacional Rufino Tamayo, 2000)

RIGHT:
Installation view showing *Four Bicycles (There Is Always One Direction)* (1994), in foreground, and *Mural Sol* (2000), in background, Museo Internacional Rufino Tamayo, Mexico City, 2000

INSET:
Cover of the exhibition catalogue *Gabriel Orozco* (Los Angeles: The Museum of Contemporary Art; and Mexico City: Museo Internacional Rufino Tamayo, 2000), showing the artist at four years old, Cuernavaca, Morelos, Mexico, 1966

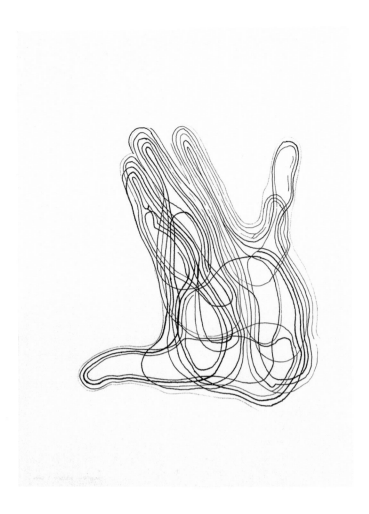

CLOCKWISE FROM TOP LEFT:
Untitled. 2000. Graphite and ink on paper, 11 3/8 × 8 1/4" (28.9 × 21 cm)

*Untitled (hand prints)*. 2000. Ink and gouache on paper, 12 × 9" (30.5 × 22.9 cm)

Untitled. 2000. Graphite and ink on paper, 11 1/2 × 8 1/4" (29.2 × 21 cm)

OPPOSITE:
*Sandwich Steps*. 2000. Silver dye bleach print, 16 × 20" (40.6 × 50.8 cm). Edition of 5

*Tree through Leaves*. 2001. Silver dye bleach print, 16 × 20" (40.6 × 50.8 cm). Edition of 5

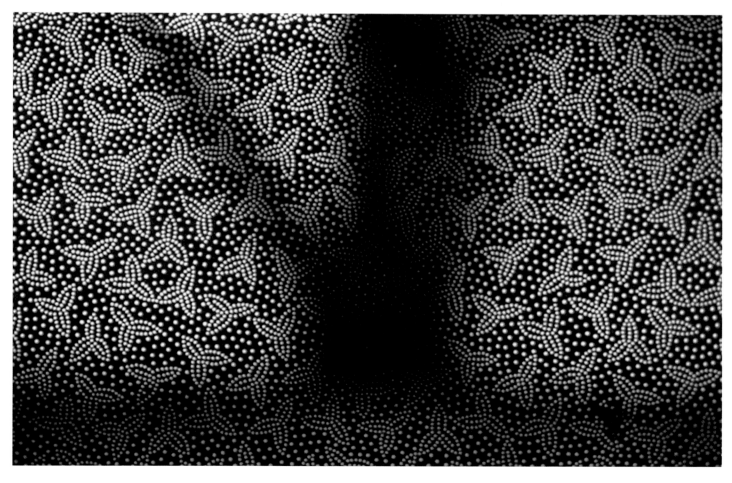

# 2001: Fear Not

SINCE LATE 2000, OROZCO HAD BEEN LIVING IN COSTA RICA, where he often accompanied his wife on her fieldwork. He was traveling through the Costa Rican rainforest on September 11, when airplanes attacked the World Trade Center towers in New York. While so many learned of the event in real time as it unfolded on television screens across the world, Orozco did not hear of it until a day or two later. He remained in Costa Rica for another month and a half, eventually returning to New York in November.

Despite wishing to stay in Costa Rica, Orozco did participate in two international exhibitions that opened in September. For the first, the Yokohama Triennial, he simply packed his luggage and went to Japan. Rather than creating a new work, the suitcase was displayed as his contribution to the show.

Orozco didn't travel to Istanbul for the opening of its biennial on September 21. After a prior visit to the city, he sent instructions for his contribution. The project was titled *Replaced Car Stoppers*, and it was intended to create a dialogue between the spaces of the city and the exhibition. The streets of Istanbul are lined with mushroom-shaped concrete forms that are meant to guide the city's notoriously chaotic traffic. They are distinctively local, but also modest and so ubiquitous as to be almost unremarkable. Orozco had collected a number of broken and uprooted ones and placed them outside of the exhibition's several venues, in interior corridors, on top of paved walkways, and in other unlikely spots. Their

*"He is an activist in the sense that his daily activity confronts the shortcomings of our perception of reality."*

Francesco Bonami, "Sudden Death: Roughs, Fairways and the Game of Awareness," in *Gabriel Orozco: Clinton Is Innocent* (1998), p. 21

stout forms, damaged by traffic and corroded around the edges by the exhaust of passing cars, had a vaguely archaic character. Orozco made replacements for the original barriers he had removed from the streets. These stand-ins — placed along the road with nothing to set them apart as art objects — had essentially the same form as the originals, but came to a rounded peak resembling a nipple. The new stoppers continued the regulatory function of the originals while also focusing the attention of passersby on something seen at a glance, bringing a level of whimsical uncertainty to the urban environment.

Orozco traveled to New York from Costa Rica to prepare for his December opening at Marian Goodman Gallery. The main work included in that exhibition, titled *Lintels*, was an installation of sheets of dryer lint hung as though on a set of clotheslines. Orozco had collected the lint over the course of about a year, augmenting the remnants of his own laundry with contributions from a New York Laundromat. Lint is the residue of the modern dryer, but here it was displayed as if it were the clothes themselves drying the old-fashioned way, in the open air.

*Lintels* is an almost uncomfortably personal work, full of hair (clumps of which were visible in a few places), skin cells, and the remnants of clothing. The sheets were delicate almost to the point of disintegration, and their fluttering fragility and responsiveness to even the subtlest of air currents also made them unexpectedly beautiful. "I always was quite appalled by this material," Orozco has said. "I didn't like it, but liked it. It's super clean but it's super dirty. It's residue but it's very complex and it's full of hair but also nails, it's full of residue from cotton and all that. . . . It doesn't smell, so it's kind of clinical but organic at the same time. So I think at the end it has associations with many things."

Some of those associations lead to other works by Orozco. *Yielding Stone* (1992), for example, incorporates dirt and other debris into its plasticine core. It had also been a dusty Mexico City that, after the 1985 earthquake, prompted Orozco to pick up a camera and begin thinking about it as a tool for making art. The

OPPOSITE, TOP:
*Lemon Game.* 2001. Silver dye bleach print, 16 × 20" (40.6 × 50.8 cm). Edition of 5

OPPOSITE, BOTTOM:
*Untitled (Yokohama).* 2001. Luggage, 29 × 22 × 12" (73.7 × 55.9 × 30.5 cm) Installation view at *Yokohama 2001: International Triennial of Contemporary Art*, 2001

BELOW AND RIGHT:
*Replaced Car Stoppers.* 2001. Concrete, dimensions variable. Installation views at *Egofugal: 7th International Istanbul Biennial*, 2001

meditation on dust, corporeality, and ephemerality in the *Lintels* also made them available to retrospective association: though Orozco had begun them well before September 11, the works were completed, installed, and experienced in a city still very much feeling the aftermath of the attacks. "Dust has been very important in my work in general: the idea of dust, the concept of dust, the reflection of dust, thinking about dust from the *Yielding Stone* on. And the dust in New York after this attack was very present and reminded me of the earthquake in Mexico from 1985 that was also very important in my life."

In the south gallery of Marian Goodman, Orozco suspended a newly made group of *Mixiotes* (1999)—translucent bags made from the outer skin of the maguey plant containing rubber balls—intermixed with *Bamboo Balls* (2001)— rubber balls from which bamboo leaves appeared to sprout. On the walls he installed drawings and photographs in careful grids, creating dialogues between them and the other works in the gallery. A photograph of the Costa Rican rainforest, for example, juxtaposed dead, dry leaves and lush new growth, and visually entered the orbit of the *Bamboo Balls*. Leaves appeared yet again in a series of drawings from this year called *Fear Not*, which also served as the title of the exhibition. Here Orozco conflated leaf prints and handprints, the veins of the former often supplanting the creases of the latter, as though suggesting an alternative form of palmistry.

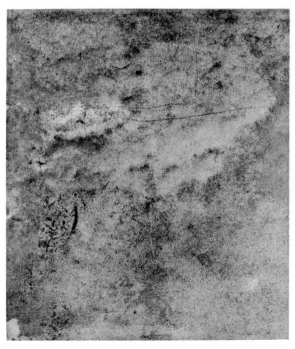

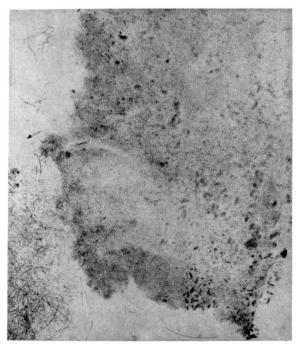

ABOVE:
*Lintels.* 2001. Dryer lint, dimensions variable. Installation view at Marian Goodman Gallery, New York, 2001

LEFT:
*Polvo Impreso.* 2002. Portfolio of twelve soft ground etchings with chine-collé, each 17 × 14 ½" (43.1 × 36.8 cm) (three shown). Loose portfolio edition of 25; bound portfolio edition of 25

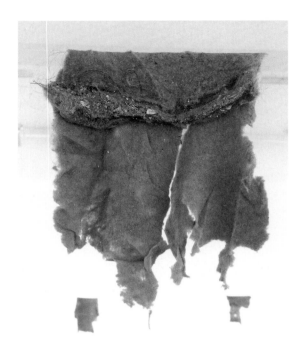

A collage titled *Eroded Suizekis* from 2001 was also included in the exhibition (Orozco had made the first in the series in 1998, and would make several more in the years to follow). A *suizeki* is a Japanese scholar's rock, an object found in nature but valued because its elaborate form makes it suitable for extended contemplation. Craggy-edged and often pierced with gaping holes, *suizeki* are almost always naturally eroded—a state of great interest to Orozco because it demonstrates the effects of time and matter on an object. Orozco has further "eroded" this image of *suizeki* using a compass cutter, a mechanical instrument that can cut perfect circles. The stone itself is disarticulated by Orozco's cuts, its contours pulled apart and then collaged back onto the pictorial surface. Orozco used this same procedure in *Kelly Kites*, also in the exhibition. He took standard letter-size reproductions of paintings by Ellsworth Kelly, excised sections of them with the compass cutter and then rotated and relocated the sections within the space of the composition. The results maintain the pristine quality of the original paintings' hard-edged geometries but insist on a sense of mutability and process.

A video titled *Jaipur Kites* was shown alongside *Kelly Kites*. In this case, the title was literal: Orozco shot the thirty-minute work during the 1998 kite festival in Jaipur, a noisy, populous city in Rajasthan, India. Like *Kelly Kites*, the video brings together four-square geometries and swirling activity as the small, colorful kites cut sharp, dizzying arcs across the thickly smoggy sky. Initially, the camera

*"Duchamp or no Duchamp, the intricate, exceedingly clean debris that accumulates in clothes dryers merits attention for its compound of human and textile filaments and dust. There is no end of painting-like subtlety in its textures and vestigial colors. When one starts looking at it with respect, its fragility stirs surprisingly tender feelings."*

Peter Schjeldahl, "Exquisite Debris: The Transforming Eye of Gabriel Orozco," *New Yorker* (2001), p. 102

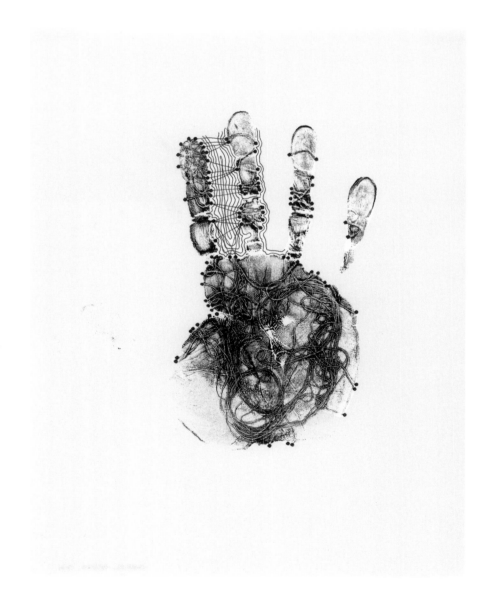

ABOVE:
*Lintels* (detail). 2001.

RIGHT:
*Fear Not.* 2001. Synthetic polymer paint and felt-tip pen on paper, 11×8½" (27.9×21.6 cm)

OPPOSITE:
*Suspended Leaf.* 2001. Silver dye bleach print, 16×20" (40.6×50.8 cm). Edition of 5

*Spider House.* 2001. Silver dye bleach print, 16×20" (40.6×50.8 cm). Edition of 5

narrows in on the kites' pathways through the sky, holding them in isolation even as the sound of aggressive car horns indicates the busy city below. Rows and rows of trees filled with kites testify to the difficulty of the task at hand. As Peter Schjeldahl has written, "The video's wordless soundtrack captures the noisiness of populous towns from which swarms of the brave toys struggle aloft. . . . Kites and buildings share astonishing yellows, pinks, greens, indigos, and electric blues, which glow with an effulgence of damp heat. Zooming and panning, the camera hungrily goes after the colors as if they were food. At one point, it lingers on a young girl as she tries repeatedly to launch a kite from a walled back yard. Her practiced motions become a dance of dedicated effort—she is an artist at work."[1] Near the end of the video, the soundtrack moves into a series of insistent birdcalls as the camera points at the sky, finding its path between birds and kites.

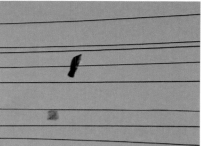

ABOVE:
*Vitral.* 1998. Silver dye bleach print, 16×20" (40.6×50.8 cm). Edition of 5

RIGHT:
Stills from *Jaipur Kites.* 1998. Video (color, sound) transferred to Beta Cam and DVD, 29 min., 1 sec. Edition of 3

OPPOSITE, TOP:
*Right Hand the Point.* 1996. Color slide

OPPOSITE, BOTTOM LEFT:
*Kelly Kites 6.* 2001. Cut-and-pasted printed paper, 11¾×9½" (29.8×24.1 cm)

OPPOSITE, BOTTOM RIGHT:
*Kelly Kites 8.* 2001. Cut-and-pasted printed paper, 11¾×9½" (29.8×24.1 cm)

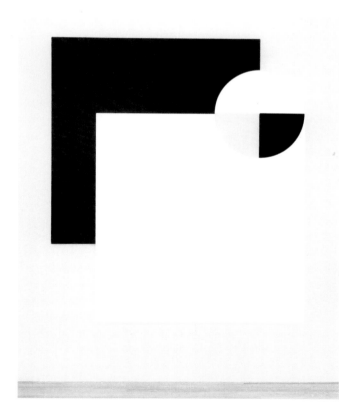

24 y 25 DE ABRIL.   2ª SESION CERÁMICA COSNE SUR LOIRE

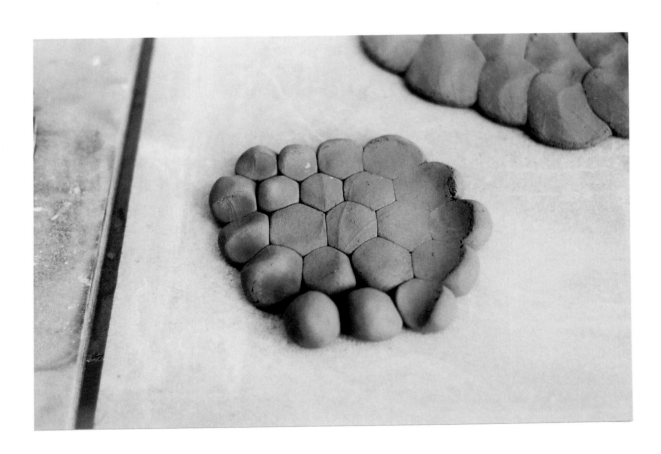

## 2002: Down to Earth

**A**T THE BEGINNING OF 2002 OROZCO TRAVELED TO MALI, inspired by pictures he had seen of people there making ceramic pots directly in the sand, without the use of a wheel. His interest was that of a sculptor, and while he made neither sculpture nor pots of his own while in Mali, he did take a number of photographs that articulated a model for sculpture.

The *Cemetery* photographs show a scene Orozco encountered in the desert around Timbuktu: a hillside strewn with bulbous clay pots, all of them broken. The site was a cemetery, and the pots were grave markers. Made of refined earth and slowly disintegrating into the terrain, such pots conflate their origins and final destinations, embodying the life cycle in order to commemorate it.

Orozco's sculpture, in general, shares the burial pots' acceptance of change over time, and also their distance from the grand Western tradition of memorial sculpture, historically built to transcend time or otherwise defeat it. The pots pose a positive, pragmatic alternative to failed eternity: as both containers and grave markers they signify universally, but do not pretend to have a single, universal, and unending significance. The cemetery, Orozco has said, "was an amazing discovery because the idea of the pot for me is very interesting, it's in all cultures, it's such a basic thing—made for conservation of food, but also of the dead. To see the pottery as graveyard markers was very nice, the way it was integrated into the landscape in a very casual way. In the end you see the little dunes of sand with pots on top and imagine the bodies resting underneath."

OPPOSITE:
Notebook 12, p. 106.
Ballpoint pen and
photographs on notebook
page, 10 3/4 × 8 1/16"
(27.3 × 20.5 cm)

ABOVE:
*Cemetery (View V)*. 2002.
Chromogenic color print,
16 × 20" (40.6 × 50.8 cm).
Edition of 5

While in Timbuktu Orozco also made *Total Perception*, a photograph of the interior of a mosque, said to be the oldest in the world. Its ceiling consists of loosely woven burlap and is supported by raw, rough-hewn sticks. Photographed from within the dark interior, the exterior detail is lost and the two visible doors open onto a white light so pure and bright it seems almost solid. Round holes permeating the walls at irregular intervals let more light through, focusing it almost like lenses on a projector. This constelled distribution of light captured in Orozco's photograph brings to mind a primitive planetarium, and with it an invitation to approach the macrocosmic through the microcosmic. Benjamin Buchloh has written, "Scattered projections of light fill this entire ritualistic space with the intensity of a desire for illumination and material transformation, a desire that is generally initiated in the circularity of shapes in Orozco's photographic and sculptural work."[1] Another photograph Orozco took in Mali, *Well*, seems almost to invert *Total Perception*: now we are on the outside in the blinding light, peering into a dark hole. The well's rim makes a striking form: at once reptilian and mouthlike, yet unmistakably made of wood. The rim is gouged with lines, each the mark of countless ropes bearing a heavy, water-filled bucket to the surface. To look at this form is to imagine the decades or centuries of use that brought it into being.

Orozco's experiences in Mali fed directly into his next sculptural project, *Cazuelas (Beginnings)*. In the spring he worked with Jean-Marie Foubert, a ceramicist in Burgundy. As always, he carefully selected the place where he made the work. As it had been for earlier works, the project Orozco had in mind was best-suited to an early-industrial workshop, and he chose a ceramics studio that used to be a brick factory. With expert efficiency, the head craftsman would use the workshop's mixer to produce exactly the consistency of clay that Orozco wanted to work with: a brick clay, more substantial and porous than the kinds

30

9 III 02

OLLAS OLLAS BARRO

15 GRUESAS BOLAS MANOS
3 " CIRCULOS CONCENTRICOS
20 DELGADAS VARIOS TAMAÑOS
12 MOLDES CIRCULARES
20 ACCIONES BOLA EN BASE DE BARRO
35 ACCIONES TUBO
9 LADRILLOS HUELLAS TENIS
4 LADRILLOS HUELLAS TUBO
1 HUEVO
1 ELEFANTE

140 PIEZAS

1.5 TONELADA BARRO
UNA SEMANA    4 - 8 MA
2

usually used for pots, called *mortar la cota*. Foubert would then turn clay on a potter's wheel while Orozco created a small arsenal of balls from the same material. When the pot on the wheel reached the right size, Orozco would throw the balls, "smashing them into it. It was like a game between baseball and basketball, trying to get the ball inside the bowl. The bowl was spinning, and the ball was a kind of meteorite. All at the same time, pitching and throwing, smashing the balls against the molds, and altogether they form a bowl. It was a reflection on pottery, erosion, movement, planetary space, etcetera."[2]

Because *mortar la cota* is so dense, it must dry for two months before being wood-fired. The firing process introduced other accidents, including cracks and uneven tonality. Many of the pots had been turned and distorted until they were no longer functional: holes had opened up in the middles of some, the sides of others split in two. In some cases, Orozco also fired the balls he had thrown at the pots while on the wheel. He rested these inside a few of the finished vessels, where they served as displaced relics of the sculptural process. Orozco exhibited these works that summer at Documenta 11 in Kassel, Germany.

As Orozco has pointed out, the wood-firing process used for hardening the clay is very similar to the traditional means of baking bread in an oven. When he returned to the brick factory in Burgundy for a second project later in the year, he created a new series of sculptures. Part of his interest in this project was—as it had been in *My Hands Are My Heart* (1991)—the weight of the clay in his hands, and

OPPOSITE:
Notebook 12, p. 30. Ballpoint pen, graphite, notebook page, and photograph on notebook page, 10¾ × 8¹⁄₁₆" (27.3 × 20.5 cm)

OPPOSITE, INSET:
*Cazuelas (Beginnings)* in progress, 2002

ABOVE:
Detail of Notebook 12, p. 34. Photograph, 2⁷⁄₁₆ × 3¹⁄₈" (6.2 × 8 cm)

BELOW:
*Cazuelas (Beginnings).* 2002 Fired clay, dimensions variable

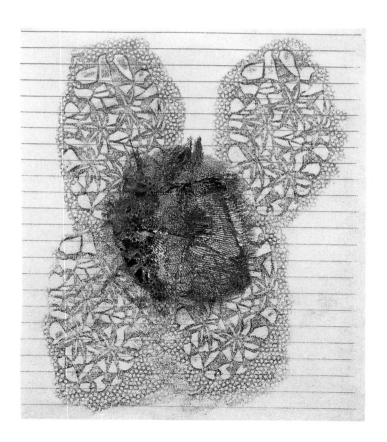

— MOURNING POTS
— BEGINNINGS = PRINCIPIOS, COMIENZOS,

—

Notebook 12, p. 89.
Ballpoint pen and
photograph on notebook
page, 10 3/4 × 8 1/16"
(27.3 × 20.5 cm)

OPPOSITE, TOP ROW AND
BOTTOM LEFT:
Untitled. 2001. Graphite,
powdered pigments,
gouache, and charcoal on
three sheets of paper, each
sheet 5 1/8 × 4 3/8" (13 × 11 cm)

OPPOSITE, BOTTOM RIGHT:
*Pi*. 2002. Fired clay,
6 1/8 × 15 3/16" (15.5 × 38.5 cm)

the way the clay related to his body. No potter's wheel was involved this time, but Orozco pressed his hands and arms, and also a wooden ball, directly into masses of clay, flattening their undersides against the surface of the table. The clay absorbed and blended the two impulses of the organic and the geometric, which Orozco emphasizes in titles that are alternately animal (*Double Tail*) and mathematical (*Pi* and *Tri*). He installed these works on tables typically found in the markets of Paris and exhibited them at Galerie Chantal Crousel. Sixteen of his photographs from Timbuktu hung on the walls, making explicit the connections between the sculpture he had seen in the Malian landscape and that which he had produced upon returning to Europe.

Back in New York for an exhibition at Marian Goodman Gallery in November, Orozco also returned to dryer lint, the material that had formed the fragile substance of his *Lintels* the year before. Here, though, the gritty, organic substance was at something of a remove. Orozco had worked with the printmaker Jacob Samuel to make a series of twelve soft-ground etchings from the lint. The material was difficult to control, and the final results were largely accidental. The dust still looked powdery and tactile, but it swirled across the etching plates' surfaces so that the prints evoked extraterrestrial landscapes. They were bound together into a book titled *Polvo Impreso* (Pressed dust), sometimes referred to simply as the *Lint Book*. At Marian Goodman, they were shown with the photographs from Mali, one kind of landscape speaking to another.

*"From the market place that the tables brought to mind and the bread-like appearance of the clay (which had additionally been cooked, like food) to the mosque, well and cemetery recorded in Mali, Orozco captured that which speaks most resonantly between cultures and times while retaining the specifics of place."*

Jessica Morgan, "Circles in the Sand," *Art Review* (2003–04), p. 78

OPPOSITE:
*Well*. 2002.
Chromogenic color print,
16 × 20" (40.6 × 50.8 cm).
Edition of 5

*Double Tail*. 2002.
Fired clay, 5 1/8 × 27 3/4 × 8 1/4"
(13 × 70.5 × 20.9 cm)

ABOVE, IN FOREGROUND:
*Four and Two Fingers*. 2002.
Fired clay, 5 1/8 × 15 3/8 × 7 1/2"
(13 × 39 × 19 cm)

46.

io 12 02

SO LONG AS THE OLD POND REMAINS A CONTAINER OF A CERTAIN VOLUME OF WATER
QUIETLY REFLECTING THE THING AROUND IT, THERE IS NO LIFE IN IT. TO ASSERT
ITSELF AS REALITY, A SOUND MUST COME OUT OF IT. A FROG JUMPS INTO IT,
THE OLD POND THEN PROVES TO BE DYNAMIC, TO BE FULL OF VITALITY, TO BE
OF SIGNIFICANCE TO US SENTIENT BEINGS. IT BECOMES AN OBJECT OF
INTEREST, OF VALUE.

BUT THERE IS ONE IMPORTANT OBSERVATION WE HAVE TO MAKE, WHICH IS THAT THE
VALUE OF THE OLD POND TO BASHO, THE POET AND SEER (OR MYSTIC),
DID NOT COME FROM ANY PARTICULAR SOURCE OUTSIDE THE POND BUT
FROM THE POND ITSELF. IT MAY BE BETTER TO SAY, THE POND
IS THE VALUE. THE POND DID NOT BECOME SIGNIFICANT TO BASHO
BECAUSE OF HIS FINDING THE VALUE OF IN THE POND'S
RELATIONSHIP TO ANYTHING OUTSIDE THE POND AS A POND.

¡OH! ANCIENT POND!
A FROG LEAPS IN,
THE WATER'S SOUND

               BASHO

O.T. SUZUKI
THE AWAKENING OF ZEN
P. 71 - 72

# 2003: Everyday Altered

IN 2003 VISITORS TO THE ITALIAN PAVILION of the Venice Biennale encountered a large gallery containing a clean-lined architectural structure made out of a light, crisp birch. Three elliptical pillars supported a roof whose elegantly contoured form barely acknowledged gravity. Resting on small balls placed atop each column, the roof seemed to float above the visitors passing through.

This work by Orozco is a kind of shadow—or, as he has put it to Briony Fer, it is an equally impossible "Platonic pavilion."[1] *Shades between Rings of Air* is a replica, to scale, of the sculpture court that the Venetian architect Carlo Scarpa built for the Italian Pavilion in 1952. Orozco's version was installed adjacent to this courtyard and it was possible to spot Scarpa's original while standing inside Orozco's installation. Scarpa had built in concrete, and five decades later it had become something of an overgrown ruin. As Orozco has pointed out, the structure was itself so sculptural that it proved difficult to display sculpture there, and as a result it had been abandoned soon after completion.[2] What Orozco did, then, was recast Scarpa's pavilion as a sculpture. "What interested me," he has said, "was the experience of walking between the two, between the ruin of the dusty, open-air pavilion and the wooden replica inside—one to one, almost like a model, which stood in a white room that was very pristine and clean. It was about the time between the Platonic pavilion and the pavilion eroded by weather. It was a shiny new idea that was immediately eroded and 'accidented' by reality."[3]

OPPOSITE:
Notebook 13, p. 46.
Pen on ink-jet print on
notebook page, 10 3/4 × 8 1/16"
(27.3 × 20.5 cm)

TOP:
*Shade Between Rings of Air*. 2003.
Wood and metal, 9' 2 1/4" ×
26' 2 15/16" × 45' 11 3/16" (280 × 800 ×
1,400 cm). Installation view of
*The 50th International Art
Exhibition: Dreams and Conflicts—
The Dictatorship of the Viewer;*
Venice Biennale, 2003

ABOVE:
Partial view of Carlo Scarpa's
Pensilina, made for the 26th
Venice Biennale (1952), 2003

Il Quotidiano Alterato

Vita vita vita vita vita vita vita vita vita vita vita vita vita vita vita vita vita vita vita vita vita vita vita vita vita vita vita vita vita vita vita vita vita vita vita vita vita vita vita vita vita vita vita vita vita vita vita vita vita vita vita vita vita vita vita vita vita vita vita vita vita vita vita vita vita vita vita vita vita vita vita vita vita crash vita vita vita vita vita vita vita vita vita vita vita vita vita vita vita vita vita vita vita vita vita vita vita vita vita vita vita vita vita vita vita vita vita paura vita vita vita vita vita vita vita vita vita vita vita vita vita vita vita vita vita vita vita vita vita vita vita vita vita vita vita vita vita vita vita vita vita vita vita vita vita vita vita vita vita vita vita vita vita vita vita vita vita vita vita amore! vita vita vita vita vita vita vita vita vita vita vita vita vita vita vita vita vita vita vita vita vita vita vita vita vita vita vita vita vita vita vita vita vita vita vita vita vita vita vita vita vita vita vita vita vita vita vita vita vita vita vita vita vita vita vita vita vita vita vita vita vita vita vita vita vita vita vita vita vita vita vita vita vita vita vita vita vita vita vita vita vita vita vita vita vita vita vita vita vita bomba vita vita vita vita vita vita vita vita vita vita vita vita vita vita bomba vita vita vita vita vita vita vita vita vita vita bomba bomba bomba vita vita bomba bomba bomba bomba bomba bomba bomba bomba bomba bomba bomba bomba bomba vita vita vita vita vita vita vita vita vita vita vita vita vita vita vitta vita vita vita vita vita vita vita vita vita vita vita vita vita vita vita vita vita vita vita vita vita vita vita vita vita vita vita vita vita vita vita vita vita vita vita vita vita vita vita vita vita crash vita vita vita vita vita vita vita vita vita vita vita vita vita vita vita vita vita vita vita vita vita vita vita vita vita vita vita vita vita vita vita vita vita vita vita vita vita vita vita vita vita amore vita vita vita vita vita vita vita vita vita vita vita vita vita vita vita vita vita vita vita vita vita vita vita vita vita vita vita vita vita vita vita vita vita vita vita vita vita vita vita vita vita vita vita vita vita vita vita vita vita vita vita vita vita vita vita vita vita vita vita vita vita vita vita vita vita vita vita vita vita vita vita vita vita vita vita vita vita vita vita vita vita vita vita vita vita vita vita vita vita vita vita vita vita crash vita vita vita vita vita vita vita vita vita vita vita vita vita vita vita vita vita vita vita vita vita vita vita vita vita vita vita vita vita vita vita vita vita vita vita vita vita vita vita vita vita vita vita vita vita vita vita vita vita vita vita vita vita vita vita vita vita vita vita vita vita vita vita vita vita vita vita vita vita vita vita vita vita vita vita vita vita vita vita vita vita vita vita vita vita vita vita vita vita vita paura vita vita vita vita vita vita vita vita vita vita vita vita vita vita vita vita vita vita vita vita vita vita vita vita vita vita vita vita vita vita vita vita vita vita vita vita vita vita vita vita vita vita vita vita vita vita vita vita vita vita vita vita vita vita vita vita amore vita vita vita vita vita vita vita vita vita vita vita vita vita vita vita vita vita vita vita vita viat vita vita vita vita vita vita vita vita vita vita vita vita vita vita vita vita vita paura vita vita vita vita vita vita vita vita vita vita vita vita vita vita vita vita vita vita vita vita vita vita vita vita vita vita vita vita vita vita vita vita vita vita vita vita vita vita vita vita vita vita vita vita vita vita vita vita vita vita vita vita vita vita vita vita vita vita vita vita vita vita vita vita vita vita vita vita crash vita vita vita vita vita vita vita vita vita vita vita vita vita vita vita vita vita vita vita vita vita vita vita vita vita vita vita vita vita vita vita vita vita vita vita vita vita vita vita vita vita vita vitaa vita vita vita vita vita vita vita vita vita vita vita vita morte.

Orozco's sculptural contribution to the Biennale altered and displaced the overlooked in order to bring it to the viewer's attention. His curatorial contribution to the Aperto exhibition continued in this mode. Titled *The Everyday Altered*, it included the works of six artists: Abraham Cruzvillegas, Jimmie Durham, Daniel Guzmán, Jean Luc Moulène, Damián Ortega, and Fernando Ortega. Orozco's statement for the exhibition did not explain his concept so much as literalize it. He submitted a printed page nearly covered with repetitions of the word *vita* — Italian for "life." Orozco disrupted the solid grid of *vita vita vita*, though, irregularly peppering it with variations: *paura* (fear); *bomba bomba bomba* (bomb); crash (in English); and at the end of the last line, *morte* (death). The shock of the everyday altered was most literal in an untitled work by Fernando Ortega, an electric bug zapper that would interrupt the power supply in the exhibition hall every time a fly was electrocuted, causing a brief blackout in the space. None of the other works involved such explicit interruption, but each shared an impulse to jostle the familiar in order to cause a moment in which recognition mingles with misrecognition.

Trinity College in Dublin had also invited Orozco to exhibit that summer. As he had done on a number of occasions, Orozco worked only with objects he found within the gallery. The first of these was a broom, which he used "to clean up a bit." In picking up he also collected bits and pieces of trash that had been left scattered around the room. He inserted a metal ring into the neck of the broomstick, and stretched cotton string from that hole up to the ceiling, over a metal lighting

OPPOSITE:
Notebook 13, p. 92. Ballpoint pen and printed paper on notebook page, 10 3/4 × 8 1/16" (27.3 × 20.5 cm)

ABOVE:
*Project for Shade Between Rings of Air.* 2003. Gouache on four sheets of photographic paper, clockwise from top left: 5 1/8 × 8 1/4" (13 × 21 cm); 6 1/8 × 8 1/4" (15.6 × 21 cm); 5 5/8 × 8 1/4" (14.3 × 21 cm); 6 1/4 × 8 1/4" (15.9 × 21 cm)

track and back down, tying it to one of the bits of detritus he had collected. He repeated this process again and again—linking the broom to a light-bulb box, a coffee cup, a sponge from a used paint roller, and so on—until the weight of the garbage was enough to suspend the broom in mid-air. Orozco has likened the effect of the different weights and balances acting on each other to that of bodies orbiting in a solar system—each keeping the other in check. He titled the work *The Weight of the Sun*: "The idea is that the broom is the representation of the sun. The broom is to clean up, to take away the dust. Taking away the dust brings the light in. Without dust you see the light."

In the fall Orozco showed a set of sculptures, *Spumes*, at Marian Goodman Gallery in New York. He had begun the series a year before, working with Philippe Picoli in a rented space in Brooklyn. The exhibition included about fifty works made from expanding polyurethane foam. The material is often used in construction work: injected in liquid form into the spaces between the walls, it expands into the cracks, usually to act as insulation. In about forty seconds it goes from a dense, heavy liquid to a frothy, bubbly one, doubling or tripling its size and then solidifying. The process is a chemical reaction, and generates a lot of heat. The liquid substance is also quite toxic—it cannot touch bare skin. And while polyurethane foam is a thoroughly industrial material, it was its organic quality that first drew Orozco's attention: "It's a material that works and behaves like an

OPPOSITE:
*The Weight of the Sun*. 2003. Mixed mediums, dimensions variable. Installation view at *Gabriel Orozco: The Weight of the Sun*, The Douglas Hyde Gallery, Trinity College, Dublin, 2003

ABOVE:
*The Weight of the Sun* (details). 2003

*Spume Stream*. 2003.
Polyurethane foam,
10 × 68 × 41"
(25.4 × 172.7 × 104.1 cm)

*Spume 2*. 2003.
Polyurethane foam,
11" × 6'1" × 38"
(27.9 × 183.4 × 96.5 cm)

*Organ Shell*. 2003.
Polyurethane foam,
8 ¹⁄₂ × 39 × 22 ¹⁄₂"
(21.6 × 99 × 57.2 cm)

Installation view of
Marian Goodman Gallery,
New York, 2003

*Multiple Dropping on
Copper Field*. 2003.
Polyurethane foam on
copper screen,
12 × 21 × 20 ¹⁄₂"
(30.5 × 53.3 × 52.1 cm)

organism, like lava or perhaps like the universe as it expands." Orozco devised various means of directing the foam's growth. He made flexible latex hammocks which he referred to as "recipients" and held their edges to guide the foam as it spilled and puffed its way down the mold. He also made structures out of cotton and wire mesh and used these to guide the foam's flow, sometimes interrupting it with balls or other objects. No technique allowed Orozco total control over the material, but its pour was somewhat predictable and could be influenced—by using gravity, for example, or by stretching or slackening the latex hammock in order to increase or decrease the tension, thus stretching or slightly condensing the foam. He was very interested in the time it took for the material to expand, and also in the topography of the final outcome: each sculpture's emergence seemed to chart a particular landscape.

Orozco made *Spumes* in black, gray, and yellow foam. At Marian Goodman, the south gallery was a kind of sci-fi landscape of strange hybrids. Fingerlike droppings of foam on Styrofoam balls or copper screens rested on tables and mobiles

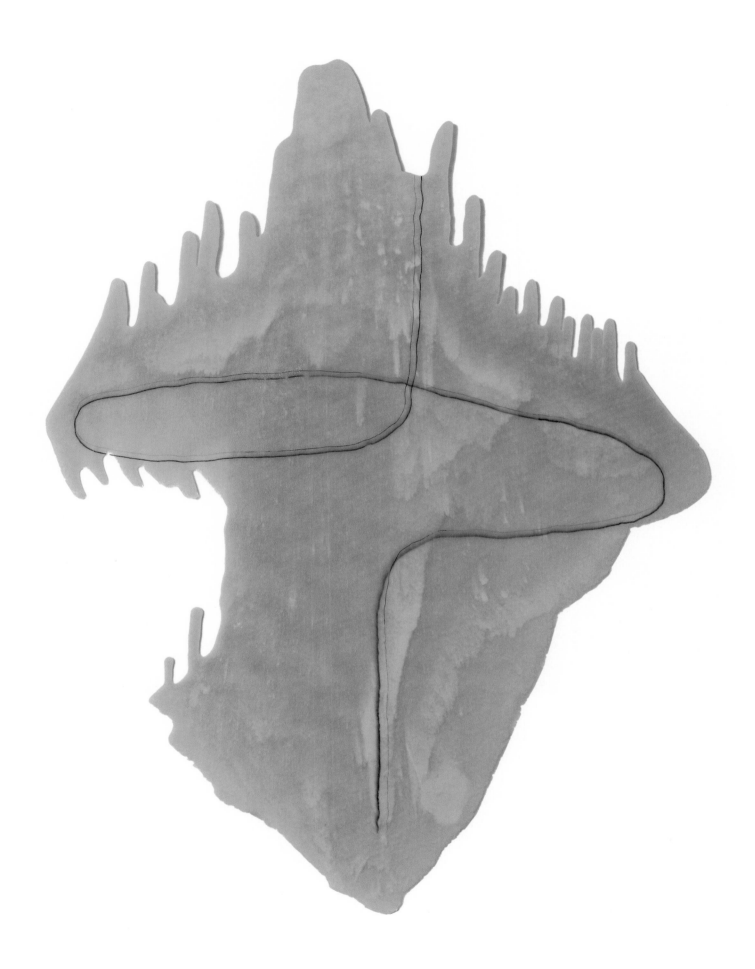

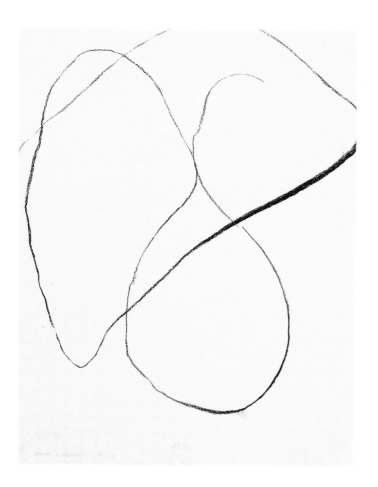

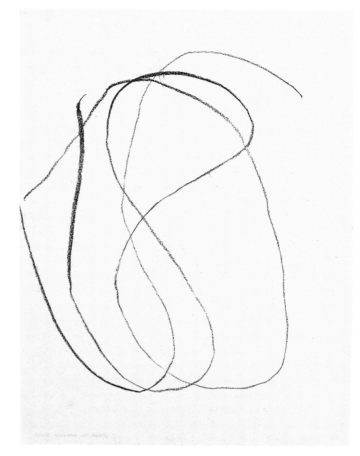

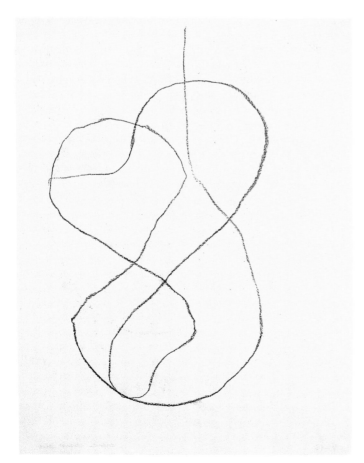

*"In his* Breathing Drawings *(2002), for example, which he has made since 1998, he sets himself an exercise — he closes his eyes and breathes. As he does so, he blindly draws a line on the page. The pressure exerted on the line of chalk varies with his breathing, and at the end of a breath he terminates the line. . . . This is about as* hand-made *and as mechanical, as concentrated and as distracted, as drawing can get. To make a work in the time frame of a few breaths is to make it in an instant. Yet to repeat the exercise will make a drawing that is completely different."*

Briony Fer, "Spirograph: The Circular Ruins of Drawing," in *Gabriel Orozco* (2004), pp. 15–16

OPPOSITE:
*Spume After Trace 2.* 2003. Transfer print on polyurethane foam, 51 × 38 × 1" (129.5 × 96.5 × 2.5 cm)

CLOCKWISE FROM TOP LEFT:
Untitled. 2003. Charcoal on paper, 11 × 8¼" (27.9 × 20.9 cm)

Untitled. 2003. Charcoal on paper, 11 × 8¼" (27.9 × 20.9 cm)

Untitled. 2003. Charcoal on paper, 11 × 8¼" (27.9 × 20.9 cm)

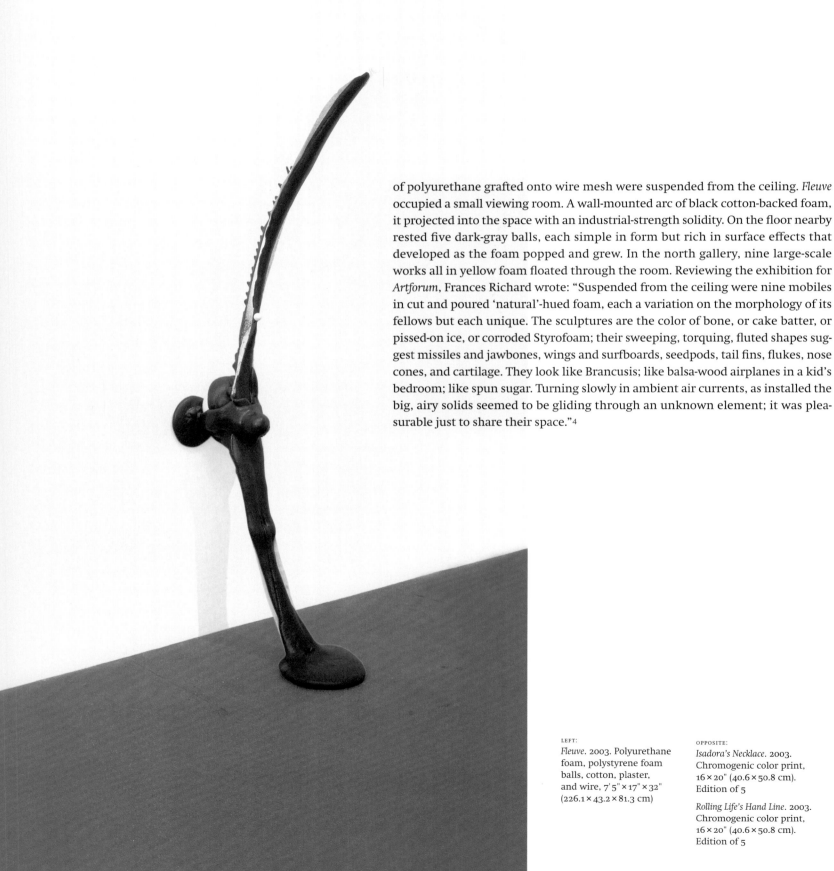

of polyurethane grafted onto wire mesh were suspended from the ceiling. *Fleuve* occupied a small viewing room. A wall-mounted arc of black cotton-backed foam, it projected into the space with an industrial-strength solidity. On the floor nearby rested five dark-gray balls, each simple in form but rich in surface effects that developed as the foam popped and grew. In the north gallery, nine large-scale works all in yellow foam floated through the room. Reviewing the exhibition for *Artforum*, Frances Richard wrote: "Suspended from the ceiling were nine mobiles in cut and poured 'natural'-hued foam, each a variation on the morphology of its fellows but each unique. The sculptures are the color of bone, or cake batter, or pissed-on ice, or corroded Styrofoam; their sweeping, torquing, fluted shapes suggest missiles and jawbones, wings and surfboards, seedpods, tail fins, flukes, nose cones, and cartilage. They look like Brancusis; like balsa-wood airplanes in a kid's bedroom; like spun sugar. Turning slowly in ambient air currents, as installed the big, airy solids seemed to be gliding through an unknown element; it was pleasurable just to share their space."[4]

LEFT:
*Fleuve*. 2003. Polyurethane foam, polystyrene foam balls, cotton, plaster, and wire, 7′5″ × 17″ × 32″ (226.1 × 43.2 × 81.3 cm)

OPPOSITE:
*Isadora's Necklace*. 2003. Chromogenic color print, 16 × 20″ (40.6 × 50.8 cm). Edition of 5

*Rolling Life's Hand Line*. 2003. Chromogenic color print, 16 × 20″ (40.6 × 50.8 cm). Edition of 5

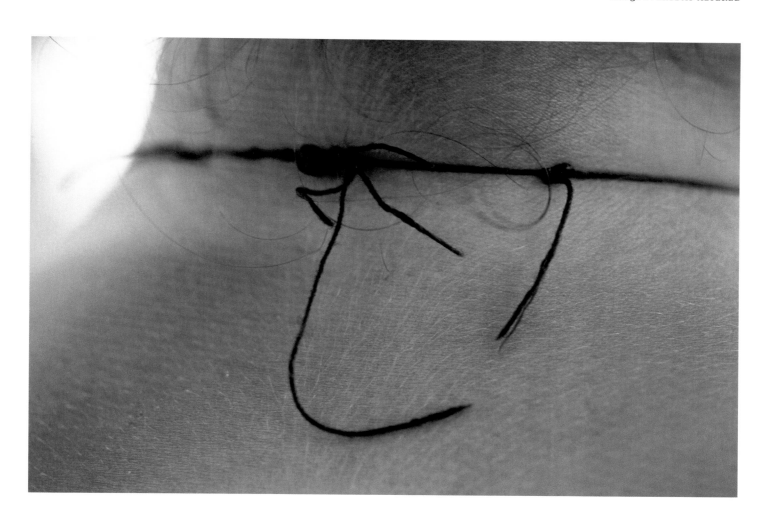

58

RESPONSABLE:                      IRRESPONSABLE:

YIELDING STONE                    MIXIOTE
DS                                MAMAN
VENTILADORES                      DENT DI LION
ELEVADOR                          PINCHED STARS
CUCHARAS                          CARTA BLANCA
MANGUERA                          PENSKE
VESPA
COLOR FLORES
CLINTON
PING POND
BILLAR
LINT

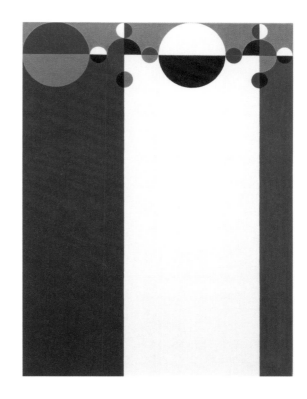

# 2004: Prototypes

**M**ANY OBSERVERS WERE TAKEN ABACK WHEN Orozco's solo exhibition at the Serpentine Gallery in London, which opened in July, featured a selection of paintings on canvas. Not only were these the first paintings the artist had made since the late 1980s, but he had kept them a complete secret for the months he was working on them in Paris. As Rochelle Steiner, organizer of the exhibition, has recalled, "Gabriel was working on something new for the Serpentine show, but I had no idea it would be paintings. We didn't know about them until the last minute. . . . He revealed the first batch of paintings to me just in time so that we could put them on the front and back covers of the catalogue and arrange to ship them from Paris to London. He really wanted them to be a surprise."[1] This return to painting, however unexpected, did not break entirely with Orozco's earlier practice. The circular forms and rotational movements found in these diagrammatic works appear in the drawings he made on currency and airline tickets beginning in 1995, *Light Signs (Korea)*, made for the Kwangju Biennale in 1995, and in the *Atomists* (1996). And yet, materials and material practices matter greatly. "What surprised me about your paintings was not the circular motifs or even the paint," Briony Fer once commented to the artist, "but the canvas. It felt like a risk rather than a return to something."[2] Orozco responded, "People forget that I want to disappoint. I use that word deliberately. I want to disappoint the expectations of the one who waits to be amazed."[3]

Indeed, it has long been the fact of the canvas, rather than the various materials applied to it, that has determined the conventions of painting. Historically, the canvas has functioned as a container for illusionistic space. Most twentieth-century geometric abstract painting articulates this space, studies its limits, and offers up its findings for contemplation. What Orozco most "disappoints" is the assumption that *his* geometric abstract painting would do the same. "I knew they were going to be read as paintings, and I think they are not about painting. They are diagrams. The idea of a diagram has the pretension to explain how things work, how objects behave and how plants grow."[4]

Viewers of Orozco's work are accustomed to seeing diagrams on the most modest of supports—on slips and scraps of graph paper, or in the mutable digital realm. If Orozco is making diagrams, why does he need the formal trappings of actual paintings? For him, the canvas and wood supports with their pairs of parallel edges provide the equivalent of a tabletop for sculpture. The support is conceived not as a container for image but as a container for action. Nonetheless, the painting enterprise can seem well out of character for this artist. As Yve-Alain Bois has put it: "To be a painter you have to have a studio, if not entirely distinct from your living space, at least from your kitchen and bedroom (fumes are toxic): You need to dedicate a space to your artistic practice, a place where your canvases

OPPOSITE:
Notebook 13, p. 58. Ballpoint pen on notebook page, 10 3/4 × 8 1/16" (27.3 × 20.5 cm)

TOP:
*Prototype.* 2004. Synthetic polymer paint on canvas, 19 11/16 × 19 11/16" (50 × 50 cm)

ABOVE:
*Landscape Flag.* 2004. Synthetic polymer paint on canvas, 31 7/8 × 23 5/8" (81 × 60 cm)

can dry, where you can wash your brushes, where you can store your paint; you need to take root. Orozco long ago rebelled against both this sedentary obligation and the notion of an assigned allotment of space. For him, the working space had to be that of his daily life."[5] Indeed, Orozco's mature painting practice began with going over to the house of Philippe Picoli and teaching him how to paint. Picoli had assisted Orozco on many of his most difficult projects, but he was primarily a builder and mechanic. "He happens to live in a wonderful house by Le Corbusier in Paris, built in 1924, that used to be the studio of [Jacques] Lipchitz. So suddenly I go from not having a studio to having a Le Corbusier studio in Paris. But it's his house. It's not really my studio; he lives there."[6] Orozco trained Picoli in a precise technique, following specific rules for the systematic translation of his diagrams into paintings.

One of the paintings in the Serpentine exhibition — titled *The Samurai's Tree* — was especially successful in Orozco's eyes. Its development and final composition best represented the artist's idea of a diagram of a structure in constant evolution. Using a computer and drafting software, Orozco began *The Samurai's Tree* from a single point. He considered this point a center of gravity, the place from which all further development must methodically extend. He drew a circle around the point and divided the circle into quadrants. He then outlined another circle, one that touched the bisecting line of the first at the point of its bisection, and divided the second one into halves and quadrants. He repeated the process, systematically varying the size of the circles until they had grown into a composition that he found complete. With the armature of circles and lines established, he colored in the halves and quadrants red, blue, white, and gold. He proceeded one color at a time, treating the sections of the different circles as if they were squares on an extended chessboard. The color placement was based on the knight's moves — one square front and two to the side, or two squares front and one to the side — again and again, using all four colors until every segment and the background was filled.

*"The most important issue, however, is perhaps not the battle between organic growth and inorganic geometry, but Orozco's stance against the vanishing point, which he sees as the anchor of a painterly way of thinking, a pictorial code, remnant of the past, from which he is intent, if not to wholly cut loose his painting, at least to give it some slack."*

Yve-Alain Bois, "The Tree and the Knight," in *Gabriel Orozco* (2006), p. 282

*The Samurai's Tree*. 2004.
Synthetic polymer paint
on canvas, 47 1/4 × 47 1/4"
(120 × 120 cm)

*Roto Spinal.* 2005.
Synthetic polymer paint
on canvas, 6' 6¾" × 6' 6¾"
(200 × 200 cm)

108 TALLER BOULOGNE JUNIO 2005

TALLER BOULOGNE JUNIO 2005

In 2005 Orozco would use the computer to calculate every possible permutation of colors in *The Samurai's Tree* composition. He titled the group *Samurai Tree Invariants* because the compositional structure remained the same even though the distribution of color transformed its visible appearance. He later realized all the *Invariants* as a series of 672 digital prints and made a video animation that cycled through each and every possibility. As of this writing about 110 paintings have been made.

The show at the Serpentine, in the summer of 2004, was by no means limited to painting. With more than sixty objects in total, it was a wide-ranging survey that included works Orozco had made from the early 1990s on. A number of these—such as *Puddles* (1997–98) *Blackboard Drawings* (1997–98), and the drawings on currency and airline tickets—were important precedents for the paintings. And as Fer has pointed out, it was also possible to read the paintings as retrospective analyses of Orozco's earlier mobile sculpture: "This was made vivid when the canvases were first shown, at the Serpentine in 2004, together with the suspended polyurethane spumes, as if the paintings were asking to be read as notations of the rotational, bodily movements of the sculptures."[7]

The summer of 2004 also brought with it an exhibition at the Hirshhorn Museum and Sculpture Garden in Washington, D.C. This was the largest exhibition of Orozco's work dedicated solely to photography. The presentation featured fifty-five of Orozco's photographs, taken between 1989 and 2003, and highlighted an important strand of continuity in a career marked by constant innovation.

On November 26, Orozco and Gutierrez's son, Simón, was born in Paris.

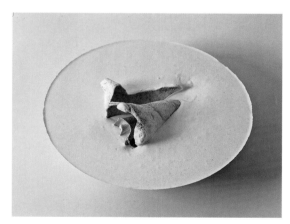

OPPOSITE:
Notebook 14, p. 108.
Graphite and photographs
on notebook page,
10 3/4 × 8 1/16" (27.3 × 20.5 cm)

TOP:
*Simon's Island*. 2005.
Chromogenic color print,
16 × 20" (40.6 × 50.8 cm).
Edition of 6

ABOVE:
*Floating Sinking Shell 2*. 2004.
Plaster and shell, 6 × 12 × 12"
(15.3 × 30.5 × 30.5 cm)

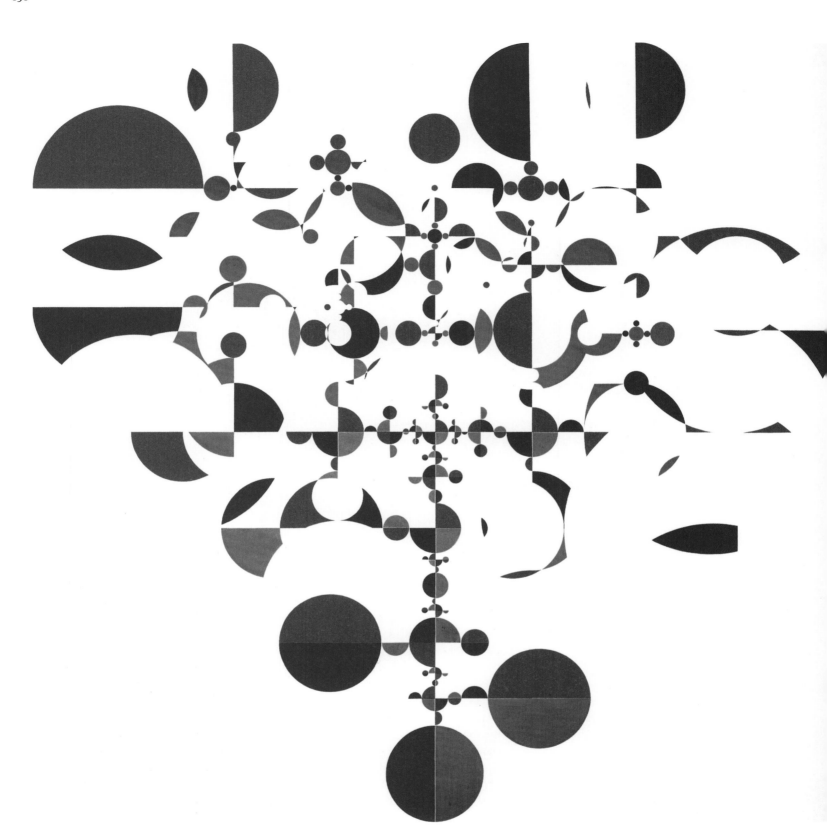

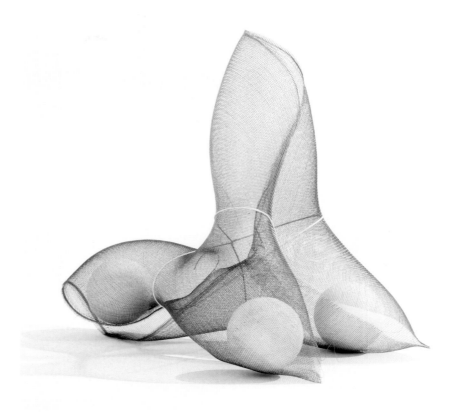

OPPOSITE:
*Kytes Tree*. 2005. Synthetic polymer paint on canvas, 6′6¾″ × 6′6¾″ (200 × 200 cm)

TOP:
*Seed*. 2003. Galvanized steel mesh and polystyrene foam balls, 16¹⁵⁄₁₆ × 18⅛ × 7⅞″ (43 × 46 × 20 cm)

ABOVE:
Installation view of Museo Nacional Centro de Arte Reina Sofía, Palacio de Cristal, Madrid, 2005

# 2005: **Planting Seeds**

IN FEBRUARY THE MUSEO NACIONAL CENTRO DE ARTE REINA SOFÍA mounted an exhibition of Orozco's work at the Palacio de Cristal, a nineteenth-century structure repurposed as an exhibition space affiliated with the museum. The show, coordinated by Marta González Orbegozo, included many of the artist's best-known works: *Ping-Pond Table* (1998), *Horses Running Endlessly* (1995), and *Carambole with Pendulum* (1996), as well as *Shade Between Rings of Air* (2003), exhibited for the first time outside of its original context in Venice. The exhibition marked Orozco's first opportunity to show his work in the city that had played such an important role in his artistic education, nearly twenty years earlier.[1]

The Palacio de Cristal, located in the center of Madrid's Retiro Park, is a building made entirely of glass panels held in place by a wrought-iron armature. The structure resembles a greenhouse, though one executed on a spectacular scale. The unassuming materiality of Orozco's work was positioned in stark contrast to the grand scale of the architecture that housed it. The glass walls of the pavilion also encouraged a dialogue between inside and outside, a setting particularly well suited to the display of *Ping-Pond Table*, with its water lilies, and to *Carambole*, whose red pendulum seemed to swing through the trees. Because of the largely unobstructed view of the park, the temporal component was also vital, if subtle: as the gardens changed over the several months the work was on display, they altered the experience of exhibition within. And although Orozco did not create a new sculpture specifically for the site, the careful selection and installation of objects could be considered a new, site-specific work. Reviewing the exhibition for *Art Nexus*, Santiago Olmo noticed precisely this, writing, "That is why we are so far removed from a traditional museum arrangement: what constitutes the backbone of a full-fledged intervention in the space is the very mise-en-scène. The

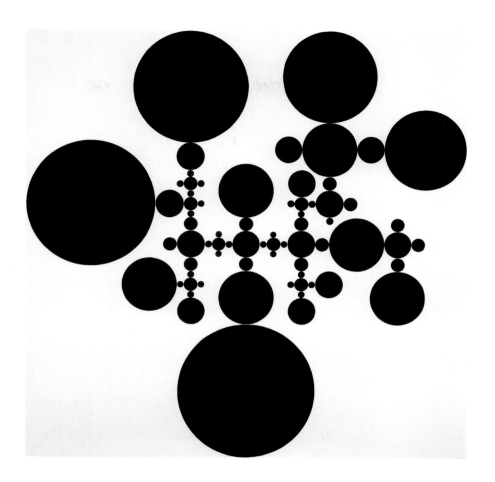

*Go 4 No Borders*. 2005.
Concrete disks, dimensions
variable. Installation view
at Villa Manin Center of
Contemporary Art, Udine,
Italy, 2005

Study for *Go 4 No Borders*.
2005. Digital rendering,
dimensions variable

*The Eye of Go*. 2005.
Synthetic polymer paint
on canvas, 47 1/4 × 47 1/4"
(120 × 120 cm)

*Galaxy Pot*. 2002.
Plaster and gouache,
5 1/2 × 10 1/2 × 10 1/2"
(14 × 26.7 × 26.7 cm)

show is, to be exact, an installation, conceived and planned so that the museum, in a location that is not a museum, resembles something else without it being anything other than a strictly orthodox, yet nonetheless different, art exhibit."[2]

Throughout his career Orozco has consistently annexed the topographical site to his sculptural installations. The space not occupied by sculpture is just as significant to the understanding of Orozco's work as the space that is. *Go 4 No Borders* provides a salient example of this operation. Created for the exhibition *Luna Park*, which opened in June and was organized by Francesco Bonami and Sarah Cosulich Canarutto at the Villa Manin Center of Contemporary Art in Italy, the work consists of three hundred sixty concrete discs dispersed on a grassy lawn. As the title indicates, the work is modeled on the ancient Chinese game of *go*, a strategic two-person game, the basic aim of which is to occupy (with black or white stones) a larger portion of the playing field than that controlled by your opponent. As with Orozco's other modifications of games, the rules as well as the form have been significantly altered. There are now four suits (red and blue playing pieces accompany the standard black and white) and the scale of the game is greatly outsized (the original being a traditional tabletop board game). The most significant alteration is the absence of the board on which the game is typically played. Orozco has moved the field of play to the actual landscape. *Horses Running Endlessly* is the most obvious precursor to *Go 4 No Borders*. Discussing the earlier work, Orozco has said that chess is a war game dependent on conflict and the occupation of territory. The same holds true for *go*. If the board is a diagrammatic representation of land to be occupied, by returning the game to the literal landscape, Orozco makes explicit these preoccupations. Of course, enlarged to an absurdly giant scale, with too many playing pieces and no discernible rules, Orozco's *Go 4 No Borders* undermines any anticipations of territorial control. As with *Horses Running Endlessly, Ping-Pond Table*, or *Carambole with Pendulum*, Orozco removes the game from the system that governs it and leaves the viewer to create his or her own rules of play.

106

Notebook 14, p. 106.
Graphite and photographs on
notebook page, 10¾ × 8¹⁄₁₆"
(27.3 × 20.5 cm)

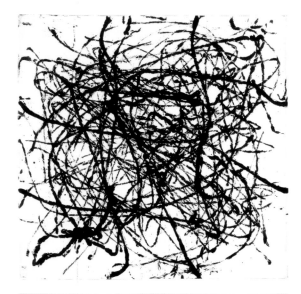

ABOVE, TOP:
*Four Points Expanded.* 2005. Synthetic polymer paint on canvas, 6' 10 11/16" × 6' 10 11/16" (210 × 210 cm)

ABOVE, MIDDLE:
*Estela* in progress at the Fundación Marcelino Botín, Villa Iris, Santander, Spain, 2005

ABOVE:
*Estela.* 2005. Graphite on wall, 59 1/16 × 66 15/16" (150 × 170 cm)

RIGHT:
*Orbit with Six Points of Gravity.* 2005. Synthetic polymer paint on canvas, 14' 11 1/2" × 6' 11 1/16" (456 × 211 cm)

After the Luna Park exhibition opened to the public, a selection of Orozco's paintings was shown at the 51st Venice Biennale. Even to audiences familiar with Orozco's work, these paintings must have seemed like oddities. Gone were the organic materials, the detritus, and the three-dimensionality that had come to characterize much of Orozco's practice. Instead, they had been replaced with the pristine and precise surfaces of *Samurai Trees.* Nonetheless, Orozco's paintings address sculptural concerns. "I try to behave more like a sculptor than a painter," he has said. "The composition of the painting always starts at the center, there is a center point that can function, at the same time, as a gravity point and a vanishing point." The sculptural element stems from Orozco's use of the knight's moves in a chess game as the basis for his color distribution of the painting. "That move is a bizarre invention, unique to chess, that conceptually and physically is a three-dimensional proposition," Orozco has observed. "It is an eccentric behavior on the surface of the bi-dimensional grid. The colors of my paintings are transcurrent between the fields. They are conceptually performing a three-dimensional move." In this way, his paintings acknowledge the vertical axis, traditionally the place for painting, and the horizontal axis, typically occupied by sculpture.

Orozco spent July in Santander, Spain, the city of origin of his wife's family. He had been invited to lead a student workshop at the Fundación Marcelino Botín in Villa Iris. The residency required that an artist spend one month in Santander instructing students and creating new work. After the completion of the workshop, the Fundación Marcelino Botín would mount an exhibition and produce an accompanying catalogue. From start to finish, an artist's involvement could span several months. Orozco accepted the invitation on the condition that the time frame be compressed. Over the course of one month, he would create new

work, plan an exhibition, and produce a catalogue. The new schedule created a sense of urgency and encouraged greater spontaneity, both for Orozco and for his students. It also provided an opportunity for the artist to focus on the temporal component of art-making, or, as he has put it, "finding time for art instead of the space for art." Once again, he arrived empty-handed and over the course of one month created a group of sculptures, paintings, and drawings that were largely improvisational, made with materials lying around the workshop. For instance, Orozco made the black-and-white abstraction *Orbit with Six Points of Gravity* by dipping a tennis ball into acrylic paint and then rolling it on the canvas and created a series of sculptures by simply tying wire mesh with twine. As Orozco wrote in the catalogue documenting the Villa Iris workshop, "A simple gesture can be art or not," and many of the final works were the result of trial and error. Errors, in fact, are a fundamental component of Orozco's process. By allowing his students access to this process, including his "mistakes," Orozco created the room for them to make their own, and along the way to embrace the contingent and accidental aspects of art-making.

Contingency is a crucial factor in *Accelerated Footballs*, which were first shown in September at the reopening of the Museo Experimental El Eco in Mexico City. For this work, Orozco had collected about two hundred fifty soccer balls, both leather and plastic. Each ball was used, weathered, or already deteriorating. These were dispersed on the floor, ready to be kicked, encouraging memories of childhood while calling to mind relics of a now lost civilization. In some cases, Orozco intervened by incising them with the blade of a protractor and removing whole swaths of the skin to created abstract, three-dimensional drawings. Briony Fer, who encountered the work in Orozco's home in Mexico City has described them: "Dirty, warn, frayed and more or less deflated, they lie about the place as if they had grown there. . . . Despite their look of material degradation and abandonment . . . the soccer balls are in fact in the process of being reclaimed. A simple cut can reverse the logic of their decomposition, giving them an uncanny life."[3] The process of reclamation is one that has occupied Orozco throughout his career. It connects *Accelerated Footballs* to works as formally dissimilar as *Recaptured Nature* (also cut and reassembled) and the drawings on devalued banknotes.

The Museo Experimental El Eco was conceived in the early 1950s by artist and architect Mathías Goeritz as an artists' space where painting, sculpture, and performance would commingle to create a complete work of art. As with many utopian spaces, El Eco, which first opened to the public on September 7, 1953, closed one year later and eventually fell into ruin. It was only after an extensive renovation undertaken by Universidad Nacional Autonóma de México's Department of Architecture that the Museo Experimental El Eco opened to the public a second time, in 2005. For the inaugural exhibition, Guillermo Santamarina, an early collaborator of Orozco's, had invited the artist to create a work for the space. Orozco decided to show the *Accelerated Footballs* on the outdoor patio of El Eco, which seemed like a natural home for the sculpture. Single-family homes in Mexico City often contain a courtyard or patio, where a soccer ball can often be found. *Accelerated Footballs* lifted the everyday into the context of art.

RIGHT:
*Accelerated Footballs*. 2005. One hundred sixty-five modified soccer balls, dimensions variable

P. 206:
*Helicopter*. 2005. Chromogenic color print, 16 × 20" (40.6 × 50.8 cm). Edition of 6

*Comet*. 2005. Chromogenic color print, 16 × 20" (40.6 × 50.8 cm). Edition of 6

P. 207:
*Mop*. 2005. Chromogenic color print, 16 × 20" (40.6 × 50.8 cm). Edition of 5

*Stuck Stones*. 2005. Chromogenic color print, 16 × 20 (40.6 × 50.8 cm). Edition of 6

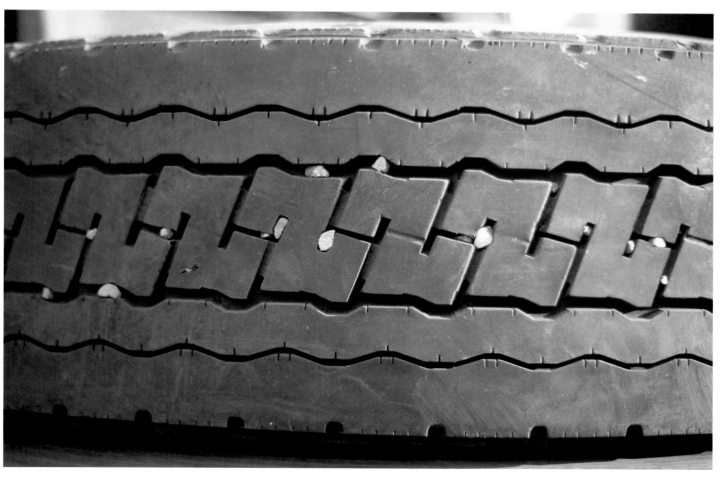

*Working Tables, 2000–2005.*
2005. Mixed mediums,
including unfired clay, straw,
egg container, bottle caps,
wire mesh screen, string,
stones, shells, plaster, bark,
polystyrene foam, painted
wood elements, and pizza
dough, dimensions variable

Wanting to foster a sense of collaboration that had been a guiding mandate of the historical Eco, Orozco invited Damián Ortega and Carlos Amorales to take part in the exhibition. Ortega embraced this invitation by exhibiting his large-scale sculpture *A critical state of philosophy. Black Kites* (2004). The work was a creative reimagining of Orozco's by then iconic *Black Kites* (1997). Rather than use an actual human skull, as Orozco had, Ortega created a much larger "skull" out of wood, wire, and paper. The overall effect was that of a colossal and quite elaborate kite. Airy and immaterial rather than dusty and dense, Ortega presented a formal inversion of Orozco's earlier work.

One month later a solo exhibition opened at Marian Goodman Gallery in New York. The exhibition was divided into two parts. On view in the north gallery were Orozco's paintings, including examples of the ongoing series *Samurai Tree Invariants* and new, larger-format works like *Kytes Tree* and *Roto Spinal*. Unlike the *Samurai Tree* paintings, all of which feature the same design schema, the compositional structure of the "variants," as Orozco calls them, is unique to each painting. The composition of a work like *Kytes Tree*, for instance, combines two organizing principles. The first of these adheres loosely to that which Orozco developed for the *Samurai Tree Invariants*. The composition began with a circle positioned at the center of the canvas that was then divided into quadrants along its vertical and horizontal axes. Subsequent circles were abutted along the first at the four points where the bisecting lines met the perimeter. Moving out from the center, Orozco repeated the process, varying the size of the circles using a formula based on the size of the first. Small circles positioned along the vertical axis form a barely perceptible "spine," which stabilizes the composition. The second organizing principle disrupts the visual equilibrium created by the first. It consists of a series of concentric circles that originate at several points across the surface of the canvas and grow outward from those points, intersecting with their neighbors. The pattern floating on the white background is formed by applying color to areas where various circles intersect. As a result, the conceptual structure that holds the colors in place becomes difficult to discern. Orozco likens these large canvases to earlier works: "Like the paper kites on tree branches in *Vitral* or the black diamonds in graphite floating on the skull, gravity and the void seem to conflate and generate this series of dynamic geometric structures."

For the south gallery, Orozco presented a new set of *Working Tables* and, alongside them, exhibited many small-scale sculptures made from materials like plaster, wire mesh, plasticine, and clay. On view were objects like *Containers* (2001), a series of four found pieces of polystyrene packaging that the artist filled with lint, plasticine, butterfly wings, and bottle caps; *Galaxy Pot* (2002), plaster casts of nesting bowls covered with a gouache patina that resembles a night sky filled with celestial bodies; and *Carbonized Torso* (2005), an anthropomorphic solid mass of carbonized clay. In short, this feast of eccentric objects provided a sharp counterpoint to the elegant, clean-lined canvasses. The work on view at Marian Goodman thus represented the complicated trajectory of Orozco's career: moving fluidly between divergent poles while negotiating a treacherous formal and conceptual terrain. As Holland Cotter wrote in his review of the show, it is "an art of paradox, elusive and empty-full."[4]

*"Thus the 'collection' of Orozco's work tables records first of all the diversity and heterogeneity of his conception of sculptural procedures and materials, and the inevitable hybridity of sculpture's object status in the present: in fact, the 'work' on the* Working Table *in many cases is neither an object nor a work. It might be a sketch, a model, and more often than not it is a model for a sculpture that will never be made. It might be called material in transition toward becoming an object; it might be an object evolving in its becoming a work, stages of an object's sculptural abilities; it is a project of sculpture in production and in simultaneous negation."*

Benjamin H. D. Buchloh, "Gabriel Orozco: Sculpture as Recollection," in *Gabriel Orozco* (2006), p. 163

TOP:
*Hand Pressing Five Balls into a Mass, After a Drawing.* 2002. Graphite on clay, 3½ × 6½ × 5¼" (8.9 × 16.5 × 13.3 cm)

ABOVE:
*Chunk.* 2005. Plaster, asphalt, concrete, and stones, 8½ × 8 × 4" (21.6 × 20.3 × 10.2 cm)

## 2006: The Whale and the House

**F**OR SEVERAL YEARS OROZCO HAD BEEN BASED, effectively, in three cities: Mexico City, New York (since 1992), and Paris (since 1998). "We were moving between the three," Orozco has said. "And there are three different cultures, three different languages, three different everything." More than that, these three sites were "like states of thinking, different types of thinking."[1] In 2006, after nearly a year of construction, Orozco completed Observatory House. Located on the beach, along the Pacific Coast of Mexico, the structure is a twenty minute drive from the nearest town, Puerto Escondido, and its airport. This remote location lends itself to yet another type of thinking: the slow and contemplative kind, responsive to its immediate surroundings, and inspired by the vastness of the landscape beyond.

The idea for the beach house came from Orozco's 1996 visit to the eighteenth-century Jantar Mantar observatory complex in New Delhi, India. The complex functioned as an astronomical instrument used to tell time and track the movements of stars and planets. The site fascinated Orozco. Particularly interesting was an area of the complex called Jai Prakash, which consists of two cruciform structures positioned alongside one another. Nearly identical, the defining feature of each building is the concave hemispherical basin that stretches from the rim located on the roof to the base of the bowl, which is submerged below ground. This feature serves as a complex sundial, its surface incised with various markings corresponding to the movement of the sun and stars. As Orozco recalled, "You are standing on a big flat plane looking down into this half of a sphere with all these measurements, and you could go down into it. And, I thought that this could be a great little house, and if this basin was filled with water it would be a beautiful

OPPOSITE:
*Mobile Matrix*. 2006. Graphite on gray whale skeleton, 6' 5 3/16" × 35' 8 3/4" × 8' 8 3/4" (196 × 1,089 × 266 cm). Installation view at Biblioteca Vasconcelos, Mexico City, 2006

ABOVE:
View of Observatory House, Oaxaca, Mexico, 2006

swimming pool. It was a crazy idea but anyway I made a little drawing of it in my notebook and I left. And it stayed in my mind for almost ten years." When Orozco visited India a second time two years later, he returned to Jantar Mantar. The visit reaffirmed his convictions. He took some measurements at the site and began to think seriously about finding a plot of land for his structure. The area of land he settled on was one with which he had been long acquainted—from the time he had been in high school, Orozco would come here to camp—and the familiarity of the landscape appealed to him.

Like Jai Prakash, which consists of hollowed out hemispheres, Orozco's one-story building has a cruciform footprint. The core of the building is a centrally positioned, hemispherical swimming pool. Three bedrooms and a kitchen radiate out in each of the four directions. While Observatory House is architecturally extraordinary, it is not extravagant. It is modestly scaled, tucked into the land so as to be imperceptible from most vantage points, and equipped with only bare necessities—a quiet place, exposed to nature. "The house, in itself, is an instrument somehow. . . . It's an observatory house. When I go there I am grabbing things outside, I am working with real objects, I am taking photographs, swimming and walking. It's all very exposed. . . . It's not a conventional vacation house. It's a platform for observation."

Perhaps Orozco's constant proximity to the ocean during the construction of Observatory House led to his next ambitious work, *Mobile Matrix*. A gray whale skeleton covered with graphite circles, it hangs in the Biblioteca Vasconcelos in Mexico City. The work was a public commission sponsored by the National Institute of Fine Arts and the Ministry of Culture in Mexico. While the library was still under construction, Orozco was asked if he would be interested in creating an artwork for the building. Before agreeing, he visited the library as construction was nearing completion. "Walking in, I liked it very much. It's an interesting, open space with all these hanging bookshelves. It's quite an impressive, monumental library. I had a couple of ideas, and one of these ideas was to have the skeleton of a whale in the center. . . . It came to me like a very clear image of this floating whale in the center of the bookshelves and the library. So that's what I proposed."[2]

For help realizing the project, Orozco approached his longtime friend Marco Barrera Bassols, an anthropologist and former director of the Natural History Museum in Mexico City. As Barrera has recalled, Orozco asked, "Is there any way I can get a hold of a whale skeleton in Mexico?"[3] Barrera assembled a team of four people, and in February, together with Orozco, they headed to the Isla Arena in Baja California Sur to find their specimen. According to Barrera, this area "constitutes a sanctuary for the gray whale . . . gray whales mate, give birth, and raise their young: some of them are beached and die there."[4] Because the site is a wildlife reserve, Orozco and his team needed to obtain permission to go to the island and extract a whale skeleton from the sand. Once they secured the authorization, they went about their work, and out of the seven skeletons they found they selected the one that was most intact. They excavated it from the sand, removed as much skin from the bones as was possible, and cataloged and tagged all of its one hundred sixty-nine pieces. The skeleton was then sent to a facility in Guerrero Negro for additional cleaning. Once this process was complete, the bones made their way to the central train station in Mexico City, temporarily out of use. There they were classified, reassembled, and fitted for the metal armature on which they would be suspended.

LEFT:
Observatory House, Oaxaca,
Mexico, in progress, 2005–06

OPPOSITE, TOP:
*Whale Skull.* 2006.
Chromogenic color print,
20 × 16" (50.8 × 40.6 cm).
Edition of 5

OPPOSITE, BOTTOM:
*Whale in the Sand.* 2006.
Chromogenic color print,
16 × 20" (40.6 × 50.8 cm).
Edition of 5

After studying the bones for weeks, Orozco determined to intervene with a drawing. This gesture would be similar to *Black Kites* (1997) but realized on a maximal scale. It was important for Orozco that the drawing depended on the skeleton itself. "What I decided to express in the drawing was the structure of this machine, how the forms of these bones are related to the movement and functionality of this structure. I chose some points of movement in the whale, and with very big compasses, started to draw circles."[5] These points were marked with dark, solid circles. Like the bull's eye of a target, the circles were then surrounded by a seemingly endless series of concentric rings. As they move further out from the center, the rings collide with and overlap each other, becoming more and more illegible. The finished drawing creates a dizzying effect of movement. It was completed with the help of approximately twenty assistants who worked tirelessly to create the graphite rings and circles which envelop the mammoth beast (in total, six thousand mechanical pencil leads were used for the drawing). When the library opened to the public on May 16, the sculpture was suspended in the central nave of the building. The drawing and its whale skeleton support seemed strangely at home in the architectural scaffolding of the library's interior.

Later in the year Orozco created a second whale sculpture, titled *Dark Wave*, which he exhibited at his first solo exhibition in London's White Cube gallery. The show was called *Twelve Paintings and a Drawing* and was on view at the gallery's newly opened Mason's Yard space beginning in late September. The "drawing" referred to in the exhibition's title was *Dark Wave*. Like *Mobile Matrix*, *Dark Wave* was a whale skeleton covered in graphite, but in almost all aspects the later work was an inverse of the earlier one. Whereas *Mobile Matrix* was predominantly bone-colored, the second incarnation was dark overall. Orozco reversed the procedure

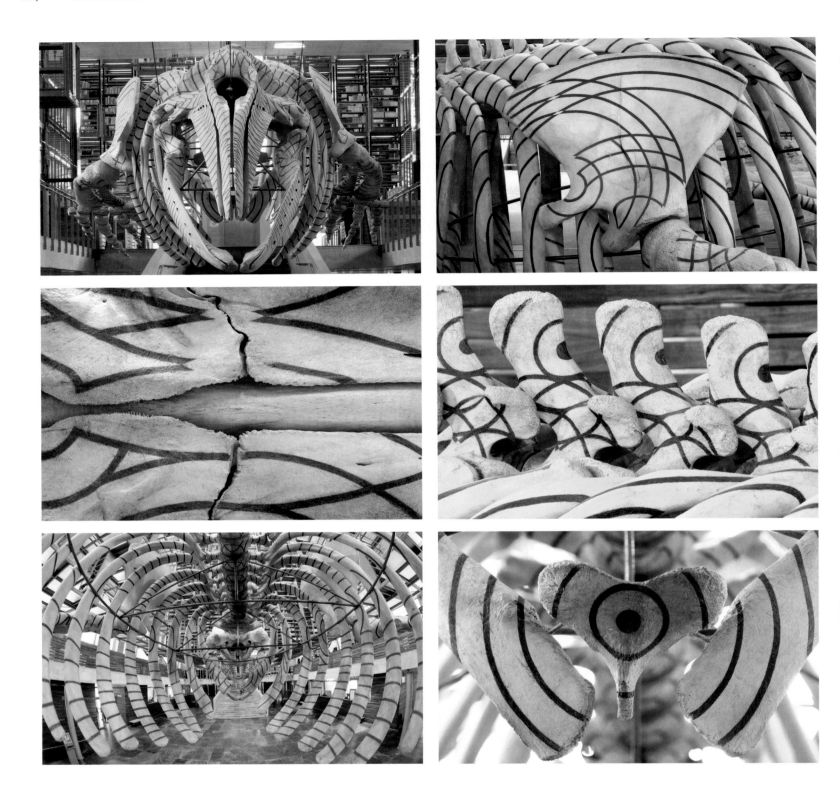

*Mobile Matrix* (details). 2006

"A commission was the only way to make this piece, because by making it for the library it remains in the hands of the state; it's national property from start to finish. Making it is a sort of rescue; there's something political and ecological about it, something to do with national-culture symbolism as well, like the serpent and the eagle, because since the whale belongs to the nation, it can be a symbol of another sort."

Gabriel Orozco, interview by Carmen Boullosa, *Bomb Magazine* (2007), p. 73

TOP AND ABOVE:
*Mobile Matrix* in progress.
Views in train station,
Mexico City, 2006

P. 216:
*Mobile Matrix*. 2006. Graphite on gray whale skeleton, 6' 5 3/16 × 35' 8 3/4 × 8' 8 3/4" (196 × 1,089 × 266 cm). Installation view at Biblioteca Vasconcelos, Mexico City, 2006

P. 217:
Notebook 15, p. 21. Ballpoint pen, graphite, notebook pages, and photograph on notebook page, 10 3/4 × 8 1/16" (27.3 × 20.5 cm)

and left the circles and rings unmarked and instead filled the space between them with graphite. As he has said, "It's a kind of mirror image of the original."[6] The most significant distinction between the two works, however, is hardly visible to the eye: unlike *Mobile Matrix*, which is a drawing on bone, the skeleton used for *Dark Wave* is, in fact, a cast. Made of resin and calcium carbonate, the form was fabricated in Spain and modeled on a blue whale skeleton that had washed up on Spanish shores many years prior and was housed in a museum in Huelva.

As with nearly all examples of Orozco's sculpture, the context in which a work is shown plays an important role in both in the artist's conception and the viewer's understanding of it. As if to underscore this point, Orozco has explained, "*Mobile Matrix* was made for that particular library. It's the national library. . . . It's public and noisy and there are bookshelves. It's a side piece; it's not the main objective to go to the library. You don't go to see the whale, you go to look for books and then you see a whale. *Dark Wave* is meant to be shown in a white cube, like a gallery, where it's quiet. You go to see that whale, it's the focus."[7] Indeed, the drawings on both skeletons reinforce this notion. *Mobile Matrix*, hanging in the visually active and vast interior of the library, almost disappears. Rather than stand apart from its surroundings, it melds into them. Visitors to the library, having read about the whale in newspapers as work progressed, were underwhelmed by the size when they first encountered the sculpture. "They thought it was too small! . . . It's like the *Statue of Liberty*. People think it's really big, because you see it in the movies and all that. But when you arrive, it's actually quite small."[8] In turn, the nearly black surface of *Dark Wave* stands in stark contrast to the unadulterated white of gallery walls. It fills even a large gallery space, as it filled the space in London. Reviewing the White Cube installation in the *Guardian*, Adrian Searle noted, "As if to prove how big it is, the gallery is currently occupied by the skeleton of a rorqual whale, more than 14 m of it, the bones suspended from the ceiling."[9] Like Observatory House, both whale sculptures were the result of months of careful planning and execution; they provide a strong counterpoint to the often highly provisional work Orozco has made throughout his career.

The year concluded with two important exhibitions of Orozco's work, one at the Ludwig Museum in Cologne, organized by Kasper König with Paola Malavassi, the other at the Museo del Palacio de Bellas Artes in Mexico City, organized by Mercedes Iturbe with Patrick Charpenel. Vastly different from one another in scale and in scope, both opened in November. For the exhibition in Cologne,

SECUENCIA DE
AROS CETACEOS

A. OSEOAROSCETACEOS

OSEOANILLOSCETACEOS

~~NAXA DE~~

OSEOAROSCETACEOS

PRIMUM MOBILE
EMPYREAN

BALLENA EMPÍRICA

AROS CETACEOS

MÁTRIX

ESPÍRITU

JUNIO 2006

TURBULENCIA ÓSEA
TURBULENCIA ÓSEA CETACEA

ANILLOS CETACEOS

AROS CETACEOS

ANILLOS NAVEGANTE

MÁTRIX MOVIL

ESPIRITU

MÁTRIX MÓVIL

he showed just one work in 672 parts. That work, *Samurai Tree Invariants*, was an installation of digital prints illustrating every possible permutation of the *Samurai Tree* schema. If Orozco had likened his paintings to diagrams, the prints were themselves diagrams for the paintings, the majority of which were not yet realized. Installed in a grid on all four walls of the gallery, these diagrams resisted any sort of obvious legibility that could be expected of a diagram. Instead, their sheer quantity was overwhelming to the eyes and created a complex matrix of computer-generated patterns that could be read as apocalyptic wallpaper for the twenty-first century.

The exhibition at the Palacio de Bellas Artes took place in a grand Art Nouveau–style building in the center of Mexico City. The venue, which rarely showcases contemporary art and whose galleries are named after artists like Diego Rivera and David Alfaro Siqueiros, pointed to the significance Orozco had assumed in his native country. It was a large-scale retrospective, with an extensive checklist that included many of Orozco's sculptures, photographs, drawings, and paintings, even though some of his major early works were missing. The centerpiece of the exhibition, shown in the Sala Nacional, was a new set of working tables, which Orozco had assembled for the occasion. *Working Tables, 1991–2006, Mexico* were large not only in terms of the quantity of small objects included but also in the temporal span they represented. The tables provided a microcosmic retrospective glance at Orozco's career within the larger macrocosmic context of a retrospective exhibition. As such they functioned similarly to the artist's notebooks, also on view for the first time. Since 1992 Orozco has been fastidiously keeping notebooks — hardbound, unlined books whose pages he numbers and fills with writing, drawing, and collage. By the time of the exhibition, these books

"Orozco says he is describing the topography of the object. I think *Dark Wave* describes something rather different—the topography of a relationship, between skeleton and body, body and water, the body of the artist and the body of another species. It is more than mapping. The drawing does more than decorate the forms on which it has been transcribed: it intersects with the whale."

Adrian Searle, "Lovely Bones," *Guardian* (2006)

*Dark Wave.* 2006. Calcium carbonate and resin with graphite, 9' 1 1/16" × 12' 10 15/16" × 45' 1 5/16" (304 × 392 × 1,375 cm). Installation view at *Gabriel Orozco: Twelve Paintings and a Drawing*, White Cube, London, 2006

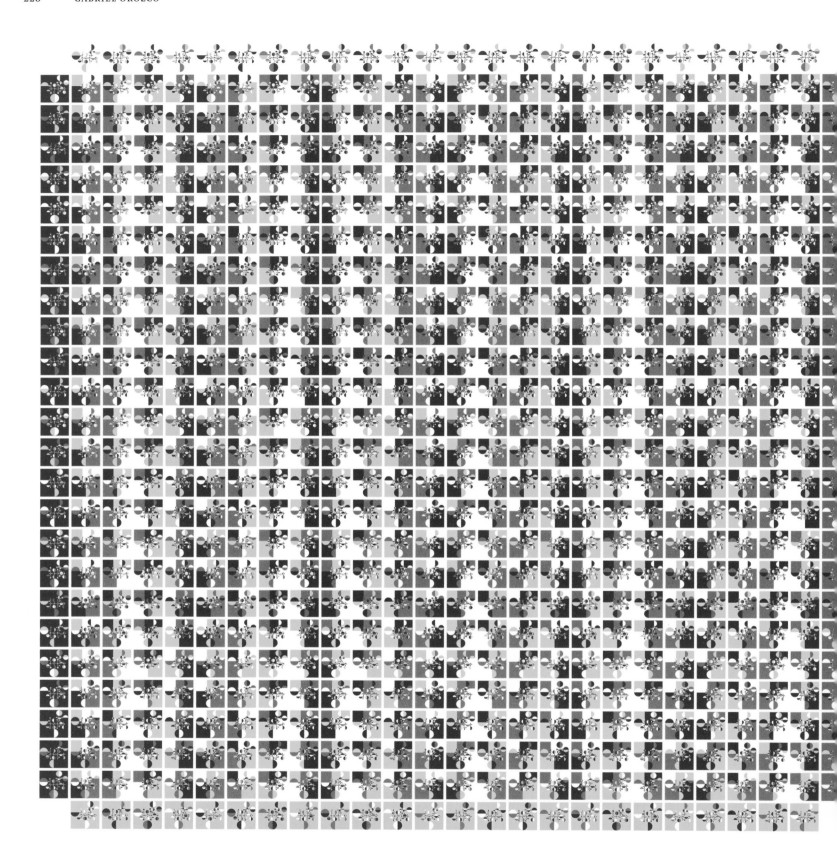

*Samurai Tree Invariants.* 2006.
Six hundred seventy-two
digital prints with digital
files, each print 21⁷/₁₆ × 21⁷/₁₆"
(54.5 × 54.5 cm)

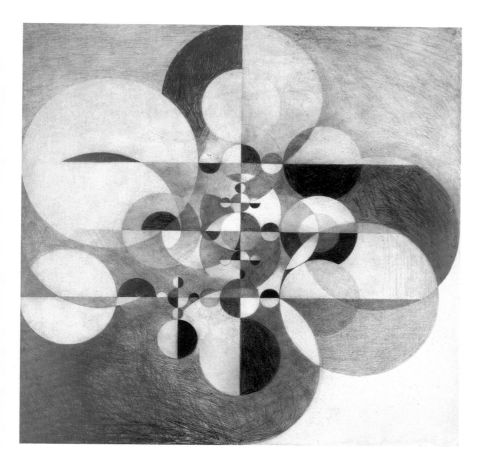

*Solar Graphite*. 2006.
Graphite and plaster on
wood, 21⁷/₈ × 21⁷/₈"
(55.5 × 55.5 cm)

had swelled to a volume of fifteen, all of which were on display, left open to particular pages. The artist likens the books—which include elements such as photographs, money, exhibition announcements—to realia, a term used to describe objects housed in libraries. As he has explained, "I call the notebooks realia, and think that maybe the tables should be considered realia as well. Maybe that is a new and nice way to think about them, as a kind of fact, a real fact presented in a kind of neutral way. So, you see, they are not works of art properly, they are just works in process, they are real in time." Like the tables, many pages of the notebooks reveal plans for Orozco's best-known works, as well as those for works not yet realized. Flipping through the pages, unexpected connections between seemingly unrelated passages emerge, as they do between the objects on the tables. In the context of the exhibition, the notebooks and the tables offered the visitor a rare glimpse into the artist's private working process.

LEFT:
*Working Tables, 1991–2006,
Mexico*. 2006. Installation
with four tables and
various objects of different
materials, dimensions
variable

ABOVE:
Installation view of
*Gabriel Orozco: The Samurai Tree
Invariants*, Museum Ludwig,
Cologne, 2006

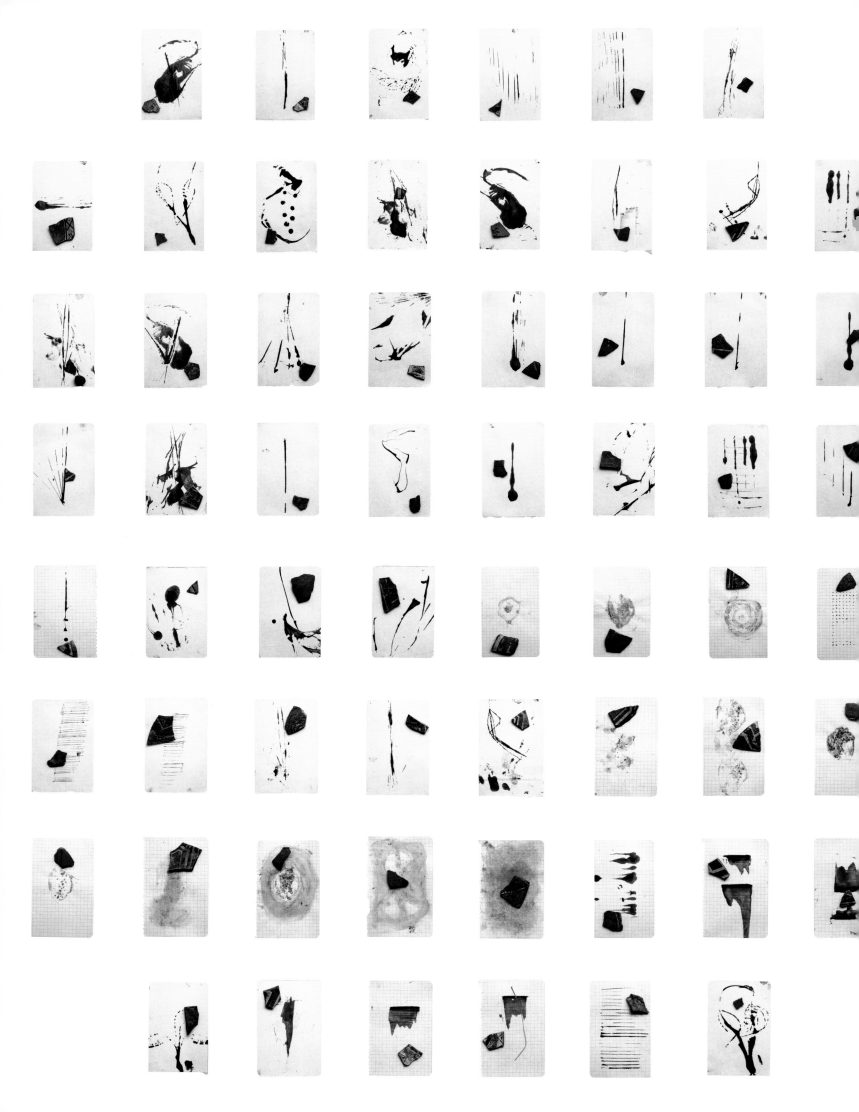

# 2007: Imprints

ABOVE:
*Home.* 2007. Chromogenic color print, 16 × 20"
(40.6 × 50.8 cm).
Edition of 5

OPPOSITE:
Untitled. 2007. Ink on paper with pottery shards, sixty sheets, each 5 1/2 × 3 3/8" (14 × 8.6 cm)

P. 224:
*Drawing.* 2007.
Chromogenic color print, 16 × 20" (40.6 × 50.8 cm).
Edition of 5

*Oil Beetle.* 2007.
Chromogenic color print, 16 × 20" (40.6 × 50.8 cm).
Edition of 5

P. 225:
*Bus Stop.* 2007.
Chromogenic color print, 16 × 20" (40.6 × 50.8 cm).
Edition of 5

*Inner Tire Garden.* 2007.
Chromogenic color print, 16 × 20" (40.6 × 50.8 cm).
Edition of 5

**A**FTER HAVING SPENT MORE THAN TWO YEARS primarily in Mexico, Orozco and his family went to Bonn, Germany, where they would stay for approximately five months. His wife, Maria Gutierrez, who completed her PhD in anthropology, was working at the United Nations Climate Change Secretariat, whose offices are located in the former West German capital. Orozco interrupted this stay only with occasional visits to Paris and one to Ecuador.

That April David de Rothschild, a friend of Orozco's, invited the artist to join him on an expedition to explore the Ecuadorian rainforests ravaged by the oil industry. Along with Orozco, Rothschild invited photographers Oliver Chanarin and Adam Broomberg, filmmaker Dustin Lynn, and ethnobotanist Maria Fadiman "as a test of what artists could accomplish when brought face to face with ecological disaster."[1] After traveling throughout the Amazon, the group ended up in an Achuar Nation settlement in the village of Sharamentsa. There Orozco created a series of drawings that eventually became an installation reminiscent of the *Working Tables*. Borrowing a small notebook from Rothschild and using dried twigs as brushes, Orozco stained the paper with an ink that the people of Sharamentsa traditionally used as body paint. A group of children watched him work. He asked the children to grab handy pieces of clay to hold the paper in place while the ink dried. They brought him the broken bits of pottery and placed one piece per paper. As Orozco has recalled, "The moment I put the paper on the table, they tried to be the fastest to put the piece of pottery on top of it. Probably they liked that I was doing my own thing and they could check me out, instead of me looking at how they work the land or how they do their own things."[2] Admiring the pieces of red-stained paper weighed down by red pottery shards, Orozco decided

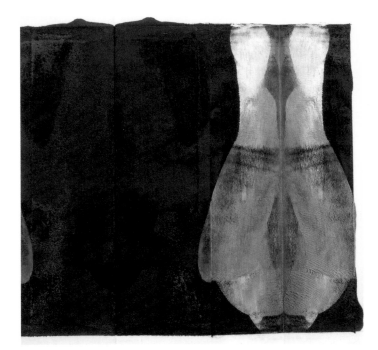

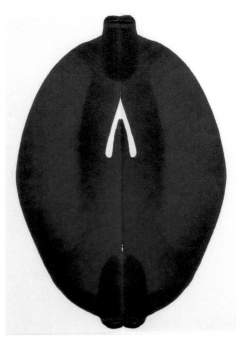

*"Orozco's technique makes one think of Rorschach blots, and the abstract figures do invite contemplative and perhaps revealing free associations. If we take the test, the standard Freudian response is not long in coming. Sex is everywhere. From the bow of the legs to the curve of the hips, from the folds of the female sex to languid penises, the shapes of 'Dépliages' cannot help but appear as abstract and highly stylized bodily portraiture."*

Aaron Schuster, "Gabriel Orozco," *Frieze* (2008), p. 195

CLOCKWISE FROM TOP LEFT:
*BONN180820072110.* 2007.
Oil on folded and unfolded paper,
9 3/4 × 9 11/16" (24.7 × 24.6 cm)

*PARIS010820071600.* 2007.
Oil on folded and unfolded paper,
9 13/16 × 9 13/16" (25 × 25 cm)

*BONN160820071630.* 2007.
Oil on folded and unfolded paper,
9 13/16 × 9 13/16" (25 × 25 cm)

*PARIS050820071800.* 2007.
Oil on folded and unfolded paper,
9 13/16 × 9 13/16" (25 × 25 cm)

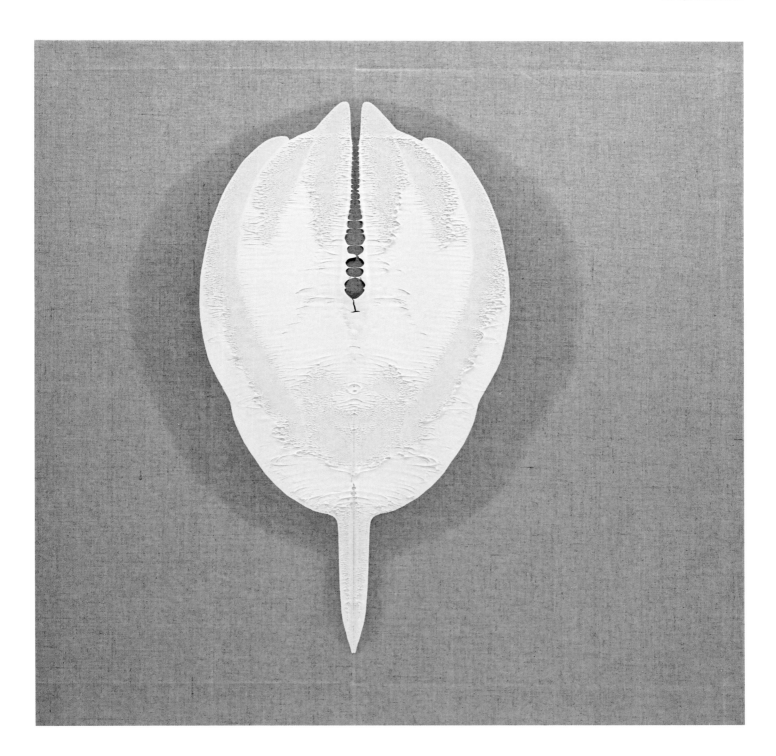

*Dépliage, White 4*. 2007.
Oil on canvas, 26 × 26"
(66 × 66 cm)

that the drawings should remain in this configuration. The tabletop installation was exhibited at Marian Goodman Gallery the following year.

Orozco also returned from Ecuador with several new photographs. As usual his goals were not journalistic. In works such as *Oil Beetle* and *Inner Tire Garden*, the viewpoint is close and the spirit is intimate.

Back in Bonn, Orozco continued a series of works on paper that he had begun during short trips to Paris earlier in the year. The *Dépliages*, as they are titled, exist somewhere on the continuum between drawing, painting, and sculpture. Orozco would begin with a piece of white paper onto which he would drop a bit of oil paint straight from the tube. Next he would fold the paper, sometimes once but often several times, and, using his hands or a spatula, smooth out the paint, now trapped within the folds of the paper. He would then unfold the paper to reveal the image. The process of folding is inherently sculptural: the flat sheet of paper becomes three-dimensional. As Orozco has said, "The moment you fold the paper

ABOVE:
Views of *Head*. 2007. Bronze, 7 × 9 × 7" (17.8 × 22.9 × 17.8 cm). Edition of 7

RIGHT:
*Face Imprint*. 2007. Black makeup, 7 ¹¹/₁₆ × 5 ¹³/₁₆" (19.6 × 14.7 cm). Edition of 3

to become an envelope, it is an object, but then when you unfold it, it becomes an image, hidden in the envelope. There is a circular movement between an object and a picture, folded and unfolded."[3] While the resulting images might evoke Rorschach tests, the imagery is not revelatory, nor is it meant to be. Rather it is a remnant or trace of an encounter between body (Orozco's) and material. The paint registers the pressure the artist has applied, abstractly mapping the movements that generate the stains. In this way the work harkens back not only to his red terracotta sculptures of 2002, which were inspired by a trip to Mali, but even further to early works such as *My Hands Are My Heart* (1991) and *Yielding Stone* (1992). With the *Dépliages*, there is also an important temporal component. Because Orozco used oil paint the image continues to change long after it has been completed, as the oil soaks further toward the edges of the paper, creating a ghostly aura around the central image. The temporal component is also explicit in the title of each work, which generally records the place where it was made followed by the date and the time, as in *BONN160820071630* or *PARIS010820071600*. The *Dépliages* thus function as a type of diary marking Orozco's movements over time and through different cities.

Orozco first showed the *Dépliages* in an exhibition at Galerie Chantal Crousel that opened in September. Also on view was a new group of black terracotta sculptures—a series he had begun three years prior and had been working on intermittently at the ceramic workshop in Burgundy, where he first had worked in 2002. Like the *Dépliages* on view, these new sculptures concern themselves with the play between Orozco's body and the mass of clay. To create the forms, Orozco pressed his palms and fingers, or sometimes his elbows and knees, against the clay, rolling and unrolling it, occasionally aided by an old wooden ball. During the

*Pelvis.* 2007. Bronze,
9 3/4 × 12 1/4 × 6 1/2"
(24.8 × 31.1 × 16.5 cm).
Edition of 7

*"It's not the diversity of genres he has explored over
time that surprises me as much as the variety
of directions he takes, occasionally leaving behind
some enigma that happily forces us to delve back into
his earlier work when some new piece sheds light on
his initial agenda."*

Christine Macel, "Gabriel Orozco: Space-Time-
Matter, from One Instant to the Next," in
*Time Taken: Time at Work in the Work of Art* (2008),
pp. 108–09

firing process, ashes were thrown on the sculptures, producing a deep black surface. As much as these works record the processes of their making, they are also
formally evocative of body parts. Acknowledging this, Orozco titles them accordingly: *Torso*, *Pelvis*, or *Head*, for instance. (He later cast *Pelvis* and *Head* in bronze.)

The show also included four new *Samurai Tree* paintings as well as a new video,
*Samurai Tree Animation*, which again showed all six hundred seventy-two possible
*Samurai Tree* permutations, but this time with three-dimensional graphics. It is as
though the video served as a reminder not only to the gallery's visitors but also to
Orozco of the vastness of the enterprise.

Continuing with what could be considered the exhibition's meditation on
time, Orozco decided to remake an ephemeral work from 1993, conceived and
executed in the weeks leading up to his first exhibition at the gallery. The work,
alternatively titled *Face Imprint* or *Corner Face*, was originally realized in Chantal
Crousel's home, where Orozco stayed while constructing *La DS* (1993). For the 1993
version, Orozco had applied black acrylic paint to his face and then pressed his
face against a corner of the room. In 2007, he recreated the work in the gallery,
this time using a greasy face paint. As Orozco has pointed out, *Face Imprint* can be
related to *La DS*. Despite their material differences, both works are, among other
things, explorations of symmetry. Taken together, a parallel is drawn between
the body and the machine. But, in the context of the current exhibition, the work
also signaled the consistency of Orozco's enterprise; both formally and conceptually, *Face Imprint* was congruent with the recently made works on view.

Around this time, Orozco and his family returned to New York. The Museum of
Modern Art had proposed a twenty-year retrospective exhibition of his work and
he was eager to begin the planning for it.

# 2008: The Obituary Collector

**I**N NEW YORK OROZCO BEGAN TO PREPARE a new series of works for his forth-coming exhibition at Marian Goodman Gallery, which would open in May. Orozco had long been fascinated by obituary headlines and had begun to casu-ally collect them in the early 1990s. To Orozco, it seemed quite astonishing that a person's life can be summed up with these pithy phrases, his or her life's achieve-ments distilled to a few words. He decided that these headlines would be the sub-ject of his next project, and began to expand his archive of them. With assistance and over the course of several months he scoured current and past issues of the *Times*, collecting any headline that seemed particularly intriguing.

Most *New York Times* obituary headlines follow a standard format, which begins with a person's name, followed by his or her age at death and the sum-mary phrase. For example, a headline could read: "John Doe, 82, Unknown Man of Unknown Origins." Orozco decided to reproduce a collection of select obituary headlines on large sheets of Japanese paper, but rather than reprint the entire headline he excised only the qualifying phrase. Each sheet contained exactly twenty-seven such phrases printed on an off-white ground so that each one's size proportionally reflects the size of the headline as it originally appeared in the paper, as if to suggest that certain lives were more significant than others. At first glance, the texts appear remarkably familiar although their source is not at

Installation view of *Obits* at
Marian Goodman Gallery,
New York, 2008

INSET:
*Obit: 'Bleak, Explosive Playwright'*.
2008. Ink-jet print on
Japanese paper, 6' 11" × 43 ¾"
(210.8 × 111.1 cm).
Edition of 3

Bleak, Explosive Playwright

Executive Who Oversaw Apache Copters

Ex-Chief of Soap Maker

Much More Than Just a Hall of Famer

Statistics Authority

Impersonator of Screen Divas

Had Style in and Out of the Ring

a Voice of Cheer and Cheese

Wrote Patriotic Chinese Music

Irish Actor With Powerful Style

a Comedian Known for Unorthodox Skits

Trumpeter and Symbol of New Orleans

One of Highest-Paid Portraitists

Expert On Psychology of Prostitutes

Deviser of Two-Way Radios

Legal Giant in a City of Lawyers

World Authority on Art of Tibet

Author of Many Suspense Novels

Philosopher, Author and Friend of Popes

Expert on Sun's Ingredients

the Maker Of Corgi Toy Cars

Dumbo's Creator

Defied Army and Kept His Land

Famed Rainmaker in Drought

Art Dealer In Big Pollock Sale

Microbiologist and Expert on African Swine Fever

Champion Archer Who Shot for Errol Flynn

*Tuttifruti.* 2008.
Tempera and gold leaf on
canvas, 6' 6 ¾" × 6' 6 ¾"
(200 × 200 cm)

ABOVE, LEFT TO RIGHT:

*Tronco 3.* 2008. Tempera and gold leaf on wood, 35⁷⁄₈ × 11⁵⁄₈ × 5⁷⁄₈" (90 × 29.5 × 15 cm)

*Tronco Verde.* 2008. Tempera and gold leaf on wood, 35⁷⁄₈ × 8¼ × 5½" (91.1 × 21 × 14 cm)

*Tronco 2.* 2008. Tempera and gold leaf on wood, 35 × 11 × 5⁷⁄₈" (88.9 × 27.9 × 14.9 cm)

all obvious. The viewer then reads a long succession of phrases — "Who Wrote of Trips At Sea/Battled to Improve Varied Laws/Devised a Convention Used in Bridge Games/Pastor Who Pressed for Social Harmony/Expert on Young/Princess Founded Convent in U.S," and so on, and eventually recognizes them as obituaries, reproduced in the newspaper's characteristic fonts. Sixteen sheets covered all four walls of the north gallery. Orozco titled each work in the series *Obit*. On the one hand, the title is entirely self-evident but, also a mere consonant away from the word "orbit". Considering Orozco's fascination with astronomy and his penchant for word play, this slippage was not accidental. By indirectly evoking orbits — with their allusions to both the solar system and the life cycle — alongside the earthly obituaries, Orozco softens the line between the cosmic and the everyday, where nothing more than a gathering of newspaper clippings evolves into a meditation on life.

The south gallery of Marian Goodman featured a new selection of paintings. With their profusion of spiraling circles they depicted another kind of orbit. One work in particular broke with expectations. The painting *Tuttifruti* diverged from Orozco's until now standard palette, and featured green, orange, and black alongside the requisite red, blue, gold and white. Perhaps the biggest surprises were the *Troncos*. Positioned on a large tablelike platform in the center of the gallery, these objects were a hybrid between painting and sculpture. Like the vast majority of the *Samurai Tree Invariants*, the *Troncos* have wooden supports. Unlike the paintings, the wood used for each *Tronco* is a stout block, one side of which is covered in gold leaf and painted, and the remaining sides of which are raw wood.

ABOVE:
*Graphite Sequence*. 2008.
Graphite and plaster
on three canvases, each
15 3/4 × 15 3/4" (40 × 40 cm)

OPPOSITE:
*Shower Head*. 2008.
Chromogenic color print,
16 × 20" (40.6 × 50.8 cm).
Edition of 5

*Bubble on Stone*. 2008.
Chromogenic color print,
16 × 20" (40.6 × 50.8 cm).
Edition of 5

Early in the year and concurrent to his preparation for the exhibition at Marian Goodman, Orozco began meeting regularly with curator Ann Temkin, to discuss the forthcoming exhibition at The Museum of Modern Art. The show was scheduled to open in New York in December 2009, after which it would travel to the Kunstmuseum in Basel, Switzerland; the Musée National d'Art Moderne, Centre Georges Pompidou, in Paris; and Tate Modern in London. From the beginning, Orozco and Temkin, in conversation with Bernhard Bürgi in Basel, Christine Macel in Paris, and Jessica Morgan in London, knew they wanted to present the artist's career in an unconventional way. With a nod to Orozco's constant travels and to the heterogeneity of his oeuvre, they decided that the exhibition should vary at each venue. While there would be a core group of works installed in every city, if a museumgoer visited all four sites the effect would be akin to seeing four different exhibitions. This strategy also reflects Orozco's interest in site-specificity and its effect on his work. As he has said, the character of a city has a tremendous impact on the tone of the work he produces. Thus, the selection of objects and the installation at each of the four venues would respond to the particularities of each setting.

Although planning the exhibition took a great deal of Orozco's attention, he also produced a new series of works at the studio in Mexico City, directed by Christian Macia, who had first worked together with Orozco on *Mobile Matrix* (2006). Titled *Grafitos*, these merge painting and drawing while also alluding to sculpture. Each begins with a canvas or wood panel primed with plaster. Its surface is then covered with a thick layer of graphite. Using a metal-tipped compass, with one point positioned in the exact center of the board, the artist creates circles, half-circles, and arcs by scratching away at the layers of graphite to reveal the white plaster beneath. Moving outward from the central point, the process is repeated until the composition is complete. As Orozco has pointed out, the experience as well as the result is not unlike drawing on bone — a process he engaged in the creation of *Black Kites* (1997) and, later, *Mobile Matrix*. Due to the shiny metallic finish and the thick supports, the finished *Grafitos* become resolutely object-like.

The year began in New York but ended in Mexico City, where kurimanzutto inaugurated its new, permanent exhibition space. From the time of its founding in 1999, the gallery had lacked a fixed location. In the nine years since the opening of the exhibition *Market Economics* at the Mercado de Medellín, Mónica Manzutto and José Kuri had organized exhibitions in places as unlikely as Mexico City's airport, a carpet store, a subterranean parking lot, and a movie theater. Any location fell within the realm of possibility as long as it suited the work on view. For years the gallery had been described as "nomadic," and its sensibilities echoed those of the artists it represented, including Damián Ortega, Daniel Guzmán, Gabriel Kuri, Dr. Lakra (Jerónimo López Ramírez), Rirkrit Tiravanija, Monika Sosnowska, Minerva Cuevas, and Jimmie Durham. After years of operating from a small office in the same complex where Manzutto and Kuri had an apartment, they decided that it was time to concentrate the gallery's activities in one building. After the months of renovation necessary to transform a 1949 timber yard into a gallery, the space opened in late November with a group exhibition featuring twenty-two artists. Works by gallery artists commingled with those of invited guests like Pawel Althamer, Thomas Hirschhorn, and Wilhelm Sasnal, among others. The installation paid tribute to the gallery's history and particularly to the show at the Mercado de Medellín. In that first exhibition, artworks were sold from a stall in the market. At the new gallery, the art was placed on industrial shelving units, approximately thirty in all. Even in the airy architecture of the newly opened gallery, the overall effect of the installation brought to mind the interior of a storage facility or a mysterious archive that held such oddities as cases of eggs (Tiravanija), old and dusty photographs (Dr. Lakra), and empty ink containers (Orozco).

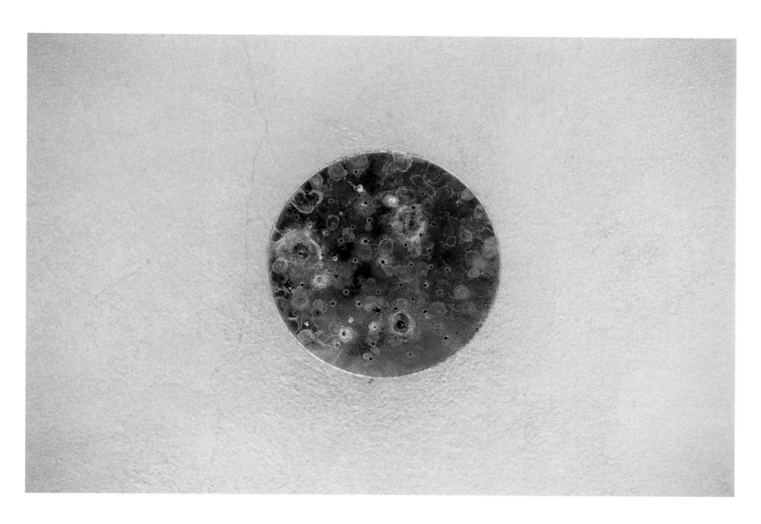

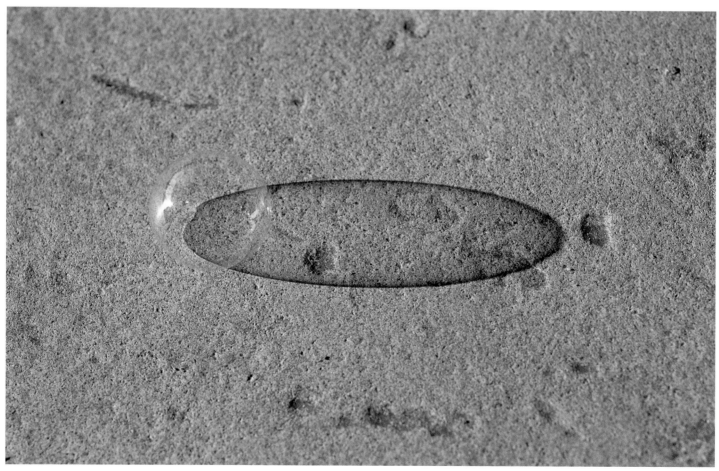

*Barked Nopal.* 2009. Cactus
on wood base, 8′ 9 9/16″ ×
6′ 4 3/4″ × 41 3/16″ (260.5 ×
195 × 105 cm)

OPPOSITE:
Installation view at
kurimanzutto, Mexico City,
2009

*Christ.* 2009. Cactus on wood
base, 46 7/8 × 28 3/8 × 13 3/4″
(119 × 72 × 34.9 cm)

## 2009: **Reconstructing Cacti**

**P**REPARATION FOR A SOLO SHOW at kurimanzutto in Mexico City took Orozco on expeditions across his native country to different deserts and the natural reserves and biospheres in Puebla, San Luis Potosí, Querétaro, and Oaxaca. At these various locations Orozco gathered examples of dry indigenous plant life including various cacti and mango trees. He would use these materials as the basis for a new group of sculptures. Installed in the gallery in late April, they transformed the room into an arid landscape. Punctuating the open space at regular intervals were large-scale works made from cacti. The plants had shed their spiky skin, revealing the coral-like texture of the interior core. These gnarled and perforated stems were then propped up by scaffolding made of two-by-fours. Orozco's decision to use this construction material was in part pragmatic as the cacti would not stand unsupported. The lumber's rectilinear form contrasted with the organic and aged found vegetation. A confluence of nature and culture, the finished sculptures are reminiscent of two very early installations of Orozco's: *Scaffolding for Our Modern Ruins* from 1988 and *Chapel*, the 1989 installation at the Museo del Ex-Convento del Desierto de los Leones.

Also on view were a series of smaller works like *Eyes Under Elephant Foot*. Orozco used the Beaucarnea recurvata, commonly known as "*pata de elefante*" or elephant's foot because of its enlarged base, and inserted glass eyes into its porous hollows, creating an object evocative of Surrealist sculpture. Following the example of the *Troncos* (2008), Orozco used the trunk of a mango tree as the support for another group of sculptures, including *Lighted Tumbleweed* and *Drops on Trunk*. For the former, he covered the base with gold leaf and positioned a rather delicate tumbleweed on its surface. The latter featured the artist's signature circular pattern scratched into a thick application of graphite.

The gallery also housed a new and atypically large painting that Orozco titled *Corporal Coordinates with Bands of Color*. Measuring nearly eight feet in height, this was a work on wood panel that had been covered with gold leaf and featured Orozco's circular motifs in blue, white, and red. However, unlike in other paintings, the arrangement and distribution of the circles generated an anthropomorphic design that mapped the points of movement in the human anatomy. The painting was also inspired by Orozco's longtime interest in the Hindu concept of the seven chakras, or points of energy that emanate from the body along its vertical axis. This nod to figuration is extremely unusual for Orozco, even if it is a figuration that is wholly diagrammatic.

Shortly after the show opened, Orozco was back in New York, primarily to work on the catalogue for his upcoming museum exhibition. He then spent the summer at Observatory House in Oaxaca, Mexico, and in Burgundy making new ceramics. Orozco briefly visited London and Paris to meet with the curators of the traveling exhibition. He would return to New York in September and continue to work on the installation design for The Museum of Modern Art.

TOP LEFT:
*Corporal Coordinates with Bands of Color*. 2009. Tempera, gold leaf, and plaster on wood, 7' 11 $^{11}/_{16}$" × 34 $^{7}/_{16}$" × 9 $^{13}/_{16}$" (243 × 87.5 × 25 cm)

LEFT:
*Drops on Trunk*. 2009. Graphite and plaster on mango tree trunk, 22 $^{1}/_{4}$ × 23 $^{1}/_{16}$ × 21 $^{5}/_{8}$" (56.5 × 58.5 × 55 cm)

ABOVE:
*Fertile Structure*. 2008. Graphite and plaster on wood, 19 $^{1}/_{2}$ × 19 $^{1}/_{2}$" (49.5 × 49.5 cm)

P. 240:
*Plastic Bag with Water*. 2009. Chromogenic color print, 16 × 20" (40.6 × 50.8 cm). Edition of 5

*Winter Hoop*. 2009. Chromogenic color print, 16 × 20" (40.6 × 50.8 cm). Edition of 5

P. 241:
*Windshield Altar with Bullet Hole*. 2009. Chromogenic color print, 16 × 20" (40.6 × 50.8 cm). Edition of 5

*Great Headlight*. 2009. Chromogenic color print, 16 × 20" (40.6 × 50.8 cm). Edition of 5

*Eyes under Elephant Foot.* 2009.
Beaucarnea trunk and glass
eyes, 57⅞ × 56⅞ × 55⅛"
(147 × 144.5 × 140 cm)

# Endnotes

**Open Studio**
**Ann Temkin**

1  Daniel Buren, "The Function of the Studio," trans. Thomas Repensek, *October* 10 (Autumn 1979): 51.

2  Ibid.

3  Lawrence Alloway, "Robert Smithson's Development," *Artforum* 11, no. 3 (November 1972): 52–61.

4  Gabriel Orozco, unpublished interview by the author, March 27, 2009. Orozco's notebooks have been a central part of his practice since the beginning; see Briony Fer's essay, "Constellations in Dust: Notes on the Notebooks," in the present volume.

5  Gabriel Orozco, "Benjamin Buchloh Interviews Gabriel Orozco in New York," in *Gabriel Orozco: Clinton Is Innocent* (Paris: Musée d'Art Moderne de la Ville de Paris, 1998), p. 59.

6  Maurizio Cattelan, *Untitled (Torno Subito)*, Galleria Neon, Bologna, 1989.

7  For a more in-depth discussion of relational aesthetics, see the exhibition catalogue *theanyspacewhatever* (New York: The Solomon R. Guggenheim Foundation, 2008).

8  *Working Tables, 1993–2000* (2000) is in the collection of Musée national d'art moderne, Centre Georges Pompidou, Paris; *Working Tables, 2000–2005* (2005) is in the collection of The Museum of Modern Art, New York; *Working Tables, 1991–2006, Mexico* (2006) is in the collection of Kunstmuseum Basel.

9  Hesse, quoted in Lucy R. Lippard, *Eva Hesse* (New York: New York University Press, 1976), p. 105.

10  Briony Fer, "Gabriel Orozco," in *Part Object, Part Sculpture*, ed. Helen Molesworth (Columbus: Wexner Center for the Arts, The Ohio State University; University Park: The Pennsylvania State University Press, 2005), p. 247.

11  The *Samurai Tree Invariants* are all illustrated in *Gabriel Orozco: The Samurai Tree Invariants* (Cologne: Verlag der Buchhandlung Walther König, 2006).

12  Philippe Picoli had worked as an assistant for the artist Absalon, whose family owned this building. After Absalon's death in 1993, the family asked Picoli to live and work in the building in exchange for undertaking its restoration and its ongoing maintenance.

13  Orozco, interview by the author, March 27, 2009.

14  László Moholy-Nagy, "The New Vision" (1928), trans. Daphne M. Hoffmann, in *The New Vision and Abstract of an Artist* (New York: Wittenborn, Schultz, 1947), pp. 79–80.

15  Orozco does not sign the paintings. When one is sold it is accompanied by a signed certificate, which also lists the names of those who painted it.

**Constellations in Dust: Notes on the Notebooks**
**Briony Fer**

1  Gabriel Orozco, Notebook 2, pp. 1–2.

2  Jorge Luis Borges, *The Total Library: Non-Fiction, 1922–1986* (Harmondsworth, England: Penguin, 1999), p. 216.

3  Jorge Luis Borges, *Labyrinths* (Harmondsworth, England: Penguin, 1999), p. 85.

4  Pages from the notebooks were reproduced and published for the first time in the exhibition catalogue *Gabriel Orozco: Photogravity*, Philadelphia Museum of Art, organized by Ann Temkin.

5  See, for example, Paule Thevenin, "The Search for a Lost World," in Jacques Derrida and Paule Thevenin, *The Secret Art of Antonin Artaud* (Cambridge, Mass.: The MIT Press, 1998); Yve-Alain Bois, "Pichenette," in *Ellsworth Kelly, Tablet: 1949–1973* (New York: The Drawing Center, 2002); Benjamin H. D. Buchloh, "Gerhard Richter's 'Atlas': The Anomic Archive," *October* 88 (Spring 1999) (for a discussion of Hannah Hoch's scrapbooks); and James Meyer, "Second Degree," in Mel Bochner, *Working Drawings and Other Visible Things on Paper Not Necessarily Meant to Be Viewed as Art* (Geneva: Cabinet des estampes du Musée d'art et d'histoire, 1997). *Jasper Johns Writings, Sketchbook Notes, Interviews*, edited by Kirk Varnedoe, was published in conjunction with the major retrospective of Johns's work held at The Museum of Modern Art in 1997.

6  Gabriel Orozco, Notebook 1, p. 63.

7  Gabriel Orozco, Notebook 2, p. 86. The exhibition was organized by Catherine de Zegher at the Kanaal Art Foundation, Kortrijk, Belgium, in 1993.

8  Gabriel Orozco, Notebook 12.

9  Gabriel Orozco, Notebook 8, p. 51.

10  Gabriel Orozco, Notebook 6, pp. 66–67.

11  Gabriel Orozco, Notebook 14, p. 88.

12  Paul Valéry, cited in *Stéphane Mallarmé: Collected Poems* (Berkeley and Los Angeles: University of California Press, 1995), p. 266.

**Sculpture Between Nation-State and Global Commodity Production**
**Benjamin H. D. Buchloh**

1  I am not suggesting that there is currently not any sculptural production to be encountered; in fact, there has been a proliferation of sculpture in a variety of mediums. The gamut ranges from Rachel Whiteread to Damien Hirst, from Felix Gonzalez–Torres to Robert Gober, from Isa Genzken to Rachel Harrison. What I am suggesting, by contrast, is the fact that only work such as Orozco's (or that of Thomas Hirschhorn in Europe) has fundamentally challenged the traditional iconographies, materials, and procedures of sculptural production, and, most importantly, that the work has contested the very credibility of sculpture's proper object status and the condition of object production.

2  The psychoanalytic definition of the "part object," as given by Melanie Klein, suggests that all human-object relationships operative in later social contexts are determined to a considerable extent by the subject's initial interaction with the libidinally charged zones of the human body. Melanie Klein, "Love, Guilt and Reparation," in Klein and Joan Riviere, *Love, Hate and Reparation* (London: Hogarth Press, 1937), p. 91. For an excellent discussion of this phenomenon in sculptural production of the twentieth century, see the various essays in Helen Molesworth's important exhibition catalogue *Part Object, Part Sculpture* (Columbus: Wexner Center for the Arts, The Ohio State University; University Park: The Pennsylvania State University Press, 2005).

3  Damián Ortega, in his splendid cartoon commentary on Orozco's work, defines Mexico in the following terms: "We're a country of 100 million inhabitants, forty of those are poor, and twenty live in conditions of extreme poverty . . . . illiteracy, immigration problems, pollution, drug smuggling, kidnappings, guerilla warfare, unplanned births, our disappointing performance at the world soccer championships . . . " Ortega, "El pájaro: Para principiantes," in Alma Ruiz, ed., *Gabriel Orozco* (Los Angeles: The Museum of Contemporary Art, 2000), n.p.

4   An extraordinary example of this conflict between the claim to a purely self-reflexive modernist type of sculpture, as it was undoubtedly made by Carl Andre, and the irrepressibility of a mnemonic dimension of sculptural materials and forms is evident in Eva Hesse's notorious claim, upon seeing Andre's sculpture for the first time, that these were the floors of the gas chambers at Auschwitz.

5   Benedict Anderson, *Imagined Communities: Reflections on the Origin and Spread of Nationalism* (London: Verso, 1991).

### Chronology

#### 1981–1991: Early Years

1   Gabriel Kuri, "Gabriel Orozco: By Way of Introduction," in *Gabriel Orozco* (Los Angeles: The Museum of Contemporary Art; Mexico City: Museo Internacional Rufino Tamayo; Monterrey, Mexico: Museo de Arte Contemporáneo de Monterrey, 2000), p. 38.

2   Gabriel Orozco, unpublished interview by Paulina Pobocha, May 14–June 4, 2008. Unless otherwise noted, all subsequent quotations by Orozco are from this series of interviews conducted in preparation for this publication and the exhibition it accompanies.

3   Gabriel Orozco, interview by Guillermo Santamarina, "Gabriel Orozco in Conversation with Guillermo Santamarina, Mexico City, August 2004," in *Gabriel Orozco* (Madrid: Museo Nacional Centro de Arte Reina Sofía, 2005), p. 136.

4   Abraham Cruzvillegas, "G.O. Untitled Workshop," in *Gabriel Orozco* (Los Angeles: The Museum of Contemporary Art; Mexico City: Museo Internacional Rufino Tamayo; Monterrey, Mexico: Museo de Arte Contemporáneo de Monterrey, 2000), p. 183.

#### 1992: Migrations

1   M. Catherine de Zegher and Benjamin H. D. Buchloh, "Ver América: A Written Exchange," in *America: Bride of the Sun* (Antwerp: Royal Museum of Fine Arts, 1992), p. 226.

2   The lecture took place at Museo Internacional Rufino Tamayo, Mexico City, January 30, 2001.

3   Jean Fisher, "The 'Bride' Stripped Bare. Even So . . ." *Artforum* 31, no. 3 (November 1992): 100.

4   James Meyer, "Nomads," *Parkett*, no. 49 (May 1997): 205.

#### 1993: First Was the Spitting

1   Kostas Gounis, John Jeffries, and France Morin, "In Transit: January 15–April 11, 1993," exh. brochure (New York: New Museum of Contemporary Art, 1993), p. 1.

2   *First Was the Spitting I–IV* is a four-part work. Each sheet is numbered on the verso. Only sheets two, three, and four have visible toothpaste residue.

3   Francesco Bonami, "Back in Five Minutes," *Parkett*, no. 48 (December 1996): 41.

4   Francesco Bonami, "Sudden Death: Roughs, Fairways and the Game of Awareness," in *Gabriel Orozco: Clinton Is Innocent* (Paris: Musée d'Art Moderne de la Ville de Paris, 1998), p. 23.

#### 1994: Portable Puddle

1   Benjamin H. D. Buchloh, "Cosmic Reification: Gabriel Orozco's Photographs," in *Gabriel Orozco* (London: Serpentine Gallery, 2004), p. 75.

2   James Lingwood, "Different Times," in *The Epic and the Everyday: Contemporary Photographic Art* (London: The South Bank Centre at the Hayward Gallery, 1994).

3   Dan Cameron, "Gabriel Orozco: Marian Goodman Gallery," *Artforum* 33, no. 3 (November 1994): 84.

#### 1995: Bubble Maker

1   Benjamin H. D. Buchloh, "Gabriel Orozco: The Sculpture of Everyday Life," in *Gabriel Orozco* (Los Angeles: The Museum of Contemporary Art; Mexico City: Museo Internacional Rufino Tamayo; Monterrey, Mexico: Museo de Arte Contemporáneo de Monterrey, 2000), p. 88.

2   Bonami, "Sudden Death," p. 19.

3   Ibid., p. 17.

#### 1996: Player for an Empty Club

1   Briony Fer, "Sculpture's Orbit: The Art of Gabriel Orozco," *Artforum* 45, no. 3 (November 2006): 264.

2   Gabriel Orozco, "Benjamin Buchloh Interviews Gabriel Orozco in New York," in *Gabriel Orozco: Clinton Is Innocent* (Paris: Musée d'Art Moderne de la Ville de Paris, 1998), pp. 117, 119.

3   Orozco, quoted in Briony Fer, "Crazy about Saturn: Gabriel Orozco Interviewed by Briony Fer," in *Gabriel Orozco* (Mexico City: Museo del Palacio de Bellas Artes/Turner, 2006), p. 65.

#### 1997: Emptying the Mind

1   Orozco, "Benjamin Buchloh Interviews Gabriel Orozco," p. 99.

2   Letter between Kasper König and Gabriel Orozco, February 15 and February 18, 1997, http://www.lwl.org/skulptur-projekte-download/muenster/97/orozco/k.htm.

3   Orozco, quoted in Daniel Birnbaum, "A Thousand Words: Gabriel Orozco Talks about His Recent Films," *Artforum* 36, no. 10 (Summer 1998): 115.

4   Orozco, "Benjamin Buchloh Interviews Gabriel Orozco," p. 91.

5   Ibid.

6   Orozco, quoted in Fer, "Crazy about Saturn," p. 113.

#### 2000: The Prodigal Sun

1   Damián Ortega, "El pájaro: Para principiantes," in *Gabriel Orozco* (Los Angeles: The Museum of Contemporary Art; Mexico City: Museo Internacional Rufino Tamayo; Monterrey, Mexico: Museo de Arte Contemporáneo de Monterrey, 2000), p. 106.

#### 2001: Fear Not

1   Peter Schjeldahl, "Exquisite Debris: The Transforming Eye of Gabriel Orozco," *New Yorker*, December 3, 2001, p. 103.

#### 2002: Down to Earth

1   Buchloh, "Cosmic Reification," p. 80.

2   Orozco, quoted in Fer, "Crazy about Saturn," p. 120.

#### 2003: Everyday Altered

1   Orozco, quoted in Fer, "Crazy about Saturn," p. 127.

2   Ibid.

3   Ibid.

4   Frances Richard, "Gabriel Orozco: Marian Goodman Gallery," *Artforum* 42, no. 5 (January 2004): 152.

#### 2004: Prototypes

1   E-mail correspondence with The Museum of Modern Art, July 27, 2009.

2   Fer, "Crazy about Saturn," p. 109.

3   Orozco, quoted in ibid.

4   Ibid., p. 113.

5   Yve-Alain Bois, "The Tree and the Night," in *Gabriel Orozco* (Mexico City: Museo del Palacio de Bellas Artes/Turner, 2006), p. 255.

6   Gabriel Orozco, interview by Wesley Miller, "Samurai Tree," Art:21 Blog (November 6, 2008), http://blog.art21.org/2008/11/06/gabriel-orozco-samurai-tree.

7   Fer, "Sculpture's Orbit," p. 267.

#### 2005: Planting Seeds

1   Though Orozco's work had been included in group exhibitions on view in Madrid, he did not have a solo exhibition in the city until 2005.

2   Santiago Olmo, "Gabriel Orozco," *Art Nexus* 3, no. 57 (June–August 2005): 136.

3   Fer, "Sculpture's Orbit," p. 263.

4   Holland Cotter, "Gabriel Orozco: Marian Goodman," *New York Times*, November 11, 2005.

#### 2006: The Whale and the House

1   Gabriel Orozco, unpublished interview by Ann Temkin, March 27, 2009.

2   Gabriel Orozco, interview by Wesley Miller, "Samurai Tree," Art:21 Blog (September 18, 2008), http://blog.art21.org/2008/09/18/gabriel-orozco-mobile-matrix.

3   Marco Barrera Bassols, "The Epic of the Mátrix Móvil," in *Biblioteca Vasconcelos Library*, trans. Gregory Dechant (Mexico City: Consejo Nacional para la Cultura y las Artes Dirreción General de Publicaciones, 2006), p. 128.

4   Ibid., pp. 130–31.

5   Orozco, interview by Miller, "Samurai Tree."

6   Ibid.

7   Ibid.

8   Ibid.

9   Adrian Searle, "Lovely Bones," *Guardian* (London), September 28, 2006.

#### 2007: Imprints

1   Kevin Conley, "Art of Darkness," *Men's Vogue*, September 2007, p. 248.

2   Ibid., p. 263.

3   Gabriel Orozco, press release for the exhibition.

# List of Illustrations

This alphabetical list contains all works of art illustrated throughout this volume. An asterisk (*) indicates a work included on the checklist for the exhibition at Tate Modern at the time of publication, September 2009. A double asterisk (**) indicates a work on the checklist not illustrated here. For editioned works that are included in the exhibition, the collection information refers to the lender to the exhibition; for editioned works that are not included in the exhibition, no collection information is included. Unless otherwise noted, all of the photographs listed below are courtesy of Marian Goodman Gallery, New York; Galerie Chantal Crousel, Paris; and kurimanzutto, Mexico City. For dimensions, height precedes width precedes depth.

## Works by Gabriel Orozco

### A

* *Accelerated Footballs*. 2005. One hundred sixty-five modified soccer balls, dimensions variable
Museo Universitario Arte Contemporáneo, UNAM
Pp. 204–05

* *Atomist: Complete Concentration*. 1996. Gouache and graphite on newspaper clipping, 7 × 5 1/8" (17.8 × 13 cm)
Courtesy of Marian Goodman Gallery, New York
P. 112

* *Atomist: Crews Battle*. 1996. Gouache and ink on color electrostatic print, 6 1/4 × 8 3/4" (15.9 × 22.2 cm)
Courtesy of Marian Goodman Gallery, New York
P. 116

* *Atomist: Heavy Whipping*. 1996. Gouache and ink on newspaper clipping, 6 3/8 × 6 3/4" (16.2 × 17.2 cm)
Courtesy of Marian Goodman Gallery, New York
P. 116

** *Atomist: Jump Over*. 1996. Gouache and ink on electrostatic print, 8 × 6 3/4" (20.3 × 17.2 cm)
Courtesy of Marian Goodman Gallery, New York

* *Atomist: Making Strides*. 1996. Gouache and ink on newspaper clipping, 8 1/4 × 8 1/4" (20.9 × 20.9 cm)
Courtesy of Marian Goodman Gallery, New York
P. 116

*Atomists: Asprilla*. 1996. Ink-jet print, 6' 6 3/4" × 9' 7" (200 × 292.1 cm). Edition of 3
P. 116

### B

*Ball on Water*. 1994. Silver dye bleach print, 16 × 20" (40.6 × 50.8 cm). Edition of 5
P. 97

*Barked Nopal*. 2009. Cactus on wood base, 8' 6 9/16" × 6' 4 3/4" × 41 3/16" (260.5 × 195 × 105 cm)
Courtesy of kurimanzutto, Mexico City
P. 236

* *Black Kites*. 1997. Graphite on skull, 8 1/2 × 5 × 6 1/4" (21.6 × 12.7 × 15.9 cm)
Philadelphia Museum of Art. Gift (by exchange) of Mr. and Mrs. James P. Magill, 1997
Pp. 37, 42, 124, 125

*Blackboard Drawings 1–10*. 1997–98. Screenprint on blackboard, eraser, chalk, and aluminum, 39 15/16" × 62 3/16" (101.5 × 158 cm). Each version, edition of 2
P. 136

*BONN160820071630*. 2007. Oil on folded and unfolded paper, 9 13/16 × 9 13/16" (25 × 25 cm)
Courtesy of Galerie Chantal Crousel, Paris
P. 226

*BONN180820072110*. 2007. Oil on folded and unfolded paper, 9 3/4 × 9 11/16" (24.7 × 24.6 cm)
Fonds régional d'art contemporain, Picardie, France
P. 226

* *Breath on Piano*. 1993. Chromogenic color print, 16 × 20" (40.6 × 50.8 cm). Edition of 5
Pp. 36, 76

*Broken Landscape*. 1985. Color slide
Collection of the artist
P. 45

*Bubble on Stone*. 2008. Chromogenic color print, 16 × 20" (40.6 × 50.8 cm). Edition of 5
P. 235

*Bus Stop*. 2007. Chromogenic color print, 16 × 20" (40.6 × 50.8 cm). Edition of 5
P. 225

*Butterfly Effect 9*. 1998. Cut-and-pasted printed paper, 11 7/8 × 9 1/4" (30.2 × 23.5 cm)
Collection of Patricia and Morris Orden, New York
P. 152

*Butterfly Effect 11*. 1998. Cut-and-pasted printed paper, 11 7/8 × 9 1/4" (30.2 × 23.5 cm)
Private collection
P. 152

### C

* *Carambole with Pendulum*. 1996. Modified billiard table and billiard balls, 35" × 10' 1 3/4" × 7' 6" (88.9 × 309.2 × 228.6 cm). One of three versions
Pp. 113, 115

*Carta Blanca*. 1999. Beer labels on metal cans and sand, dimensions variable
Marieluise Hessel Collection, Hessel Museum of Art, Center for Curatorial Studies, Bard College, Annandale-on-Hudson, New York
P. 147

* *Cats and Watermelons*. 1992. Chromogenic color print, 16 × 20" (40.6 × 50.8 cm). Edition of 5
P. 66

*Cazuelas (Beginnings)*. 2002. Fired clay, dimensions variable
Kunsthaus Zürich
Pp. 174, 175

*Cemetery (View I)*. 2002. Chromogenic color print, 16 × 20" (40.6 × 50.8 cm), edition of 5; chromogenic color print mounted on Sintra board, 33 3/4 × 46 3/4" (85.7 × 118.7 cm), edition of 3
P. 172

*Cemetery (View V)*. 2002. Chromogenic color print, 16 × 20" (40.6 × 50.8 cm), edition of 5; chromogenic color print mounted on Sintra board, 33 3/4 × 46 3/4" (85.7 × 118.7 cm), edition of 3
P. 171

*Chair with Cane*. 1990. Silver dye bleach print, 20 × 16" (50.8 × 40.6 cm). Edition of 5
P. 12

*Chapel*. 1989. Taxidermied elephant head and tree trunks, dimensions variable. Temporary installation
P. 51

*Christ*. 2009. Cactus on wood base, 46 7/8 × 28 3/8 × 13 3/4" (119 × 72 × 34.9 cm)
Courtesy of kurimanzutto, Mexico City
P. 237

*Chunk*. 2005. Plaster, asphalt, concrete, and stones, 8 1/2 × 8 × 4" (21.6 × 20.3 × 10.2 cm)
Courtesy of Marian Goodman Gallery, New York
P. 209

*Clinton Is Innocent*. 1998. Synthetic polymer paint on wall, dimensions variable. Temporary installation
P. 134

*Clinton Is Innocent*. 1998. Ink-jet on newspaper clipping, 11 3/4 × 8 1/2" (29.8 × 21.6 cm)
Courtesy of Marian Goodman Gallery, New York
P. 135

*Coins in Window*. 1994. Silver dye bleach print, 16 × 20" (40.6 × 50.8 cm). Edition of 5
P. 97

*Color Travels through Flowers*. 1998. Dye on paper, dimensions variable
Courtesy of Marian Goodman Gallery, New York, and Galerie Chantal Crousel, Paris
Pp. 138–39

*Columpio*. 1997. Silver dye bleach print, 16 × 20" (40.6 × 50.8 cm). Edition of 5
P. 133

*Comet*. 2005. Chromogenic color print, 16 × 20" (40.6 × 50.8 cm). Edition of 6
P. 206

*Common Dream*. 1996. Silver dye bleach print, 16 × 20" (40.6 × 50.8 cm). Edition of 5
P. 120

*Concha con Conchas*. 1999. Steel and shells, 33 × 28 1/2 × 37" (83.8 × 72.4 × 94 cm)
Collection of Anita and Burton Reiner, Bethesda, Maryland
P. 146

*Corporal Coordinates with Bands of Color*. 2009. Tempera, gold leaf, and plaster on wood, 7' 11 11/16" × 34 7/16" × 9 13/16" (243 × 87.5 × 25 cm)
Collection of Alejandra and Alberto Fernández
P. 238

* *Crazy Tourist*. 1991. Chromogenic color print, 16 × 20" (40.6 × 50.8 cm). Edition of 5
P. 58

**D**

*Dandelions.* 1998. Fabric, paper, and steel, approx. 37 3/8" (94.9 cm) diam. Ten versions
Pp. 136, 142, 143

*Dark Wave.* 2006. Calcium carbonate and resin with graphite, 9' 11 11/16" × 12' 10 15/16" × 45' 1 5/16" (304 × 392 × 1,375 cm)
Essl Museum, Klosterneuberg/Vienna
Pp. 218–19

*Dépliage, White 4.* 2007. Oil on canvas, 26 × 26" (66 × 66 cm)
The Rachofsky Collection
P. 227

*Descending.* 2002. Chromogenic color print, 16 × 20" (40.6 × 50.8 cm), edition of 5; chromogenic color print mounted on Sintra board, 33 3/4 × 46 3/4" (85.7 × 118.7 cm), edition of 3
P. 173

*Dial Tone.* 1992. Cut-and-pasted phone book pages on Japanese paper, 11" × 10' 10" (27.9 × 330.2 cm). Artist's proof
Courtesy of Marian Goodman Gallery, New York
Pp. 68–69

* *Dial Tone.* 1992. Cut-and-pasted phone book pages on Japanese paper, 11" × 34' (27.9 × 1,036 cm). One of three versions
Collection of Carlos and Rosa de la Cruz
Pp. 68, 84

*Dog Circle.* 1995. Silver dye bleach print, 16 × 20" (40.6 × 50.8 cm). Edition of 5
P. 111

*Dog Urine in Snow.* 1993. Silver dye bleach print, 16 × 20" (40.6 × 50.8 cm). Edition of 5
P. 14

*Double Relief.* 1999. Silver dye bleach print, 16 × 20" (40.6 × 50.8 cm). Edition of 5
P. 148

*Double Tail.* 2002. Fired clay, 5 1/8 × 27 3/4 × 8 1/4" (13 × 70.5 × 20.9 cm)
Collection of the artist
P. 178

*Drawing.* 2007. Chromogenic color print, 16 × 20" (40.6 × 50.8 cm). Edition of 5
P. 224

*Drops on Trunk.* 2009. Graphite and plaster on mango tree trunk, 22 1/4 × 23 1/16 × 21 5/8" (56.5 × 58.5 × 55 cm)
Collection of Clarissa and Edgar Bronfman, Jr.
P. 238

**E**

* *Elevator.* 1994. Modified elevator cabin, 8' × 8' × 60" (243.8 × 243.8 × 152.4 cm)
The Dakis Joannou Collection
P. 100

* *Empty Shoe Box.* 1993. Shoe box, 4 7/8 × 13 × 8 1/2" (12.4 × 33 × 21.6 cm)
Courtesy of Marian Goodman Gallery, New York
P. 79

*Empty Shoe Box.* 1993. Silver dye bleach print, 16 × 20" (40.6 × 50.8 cm). Edition of 5
P. 80

*Eroded Suizekis 3.* 1998. Cut-and-pasted printed paper, 11 1/4 × 8 1/8" (28.6 × 20.6 cm)
Private collection; courtesy of Galeria Enrique Guerrero, Mexico City
P. 144

*Eroded Suizekis 5.* 1998. Cut-and-pasted printed paper, 11 1/4 × 8 1/8" (28.6 × 20.6 cm)
Collection of Martin and Rebecca Eisenberg, New York
P. 152

*Eroded Suizekis 25.* 2002. Cut-and-pasted printed paper, 11 1/4 × 8 1/8" (28.6 × 20.6 cm)
Collection of Cecilia and Ernesto Poma
P. 152

*Estela.* 2005. Graphite on wall, 59 1/16 × 66 15/16" (150 × 170 cm)
Courtesy of Marian Goodman Gallery, New York
P. 203

* *Extension of Reflection.* 1992. Chromogenic color print, 16 × 20" (40.6 × 50.8 cm). Edition of 5
P. 65

* *The Eye of Go.* 2005. Synthetic polymer paint on canvas, 47 1/4 × 47 1/4" (120 × 120 cm)
Collection of the artist
P. 201

*Eyes under Elephant Foot.* 2009. Beaucarnea trunk and glass eyes, 57 7/8 × 56 7/8 × 55 1/8" (147 × 144.5 × 140 cm)
Charpenel Collection, Guadalajara, Mexico
Pp. 43, 239

**F**

*Face Imprint.* 2007. Black makeup, 7 11/16 × 5 13/16" (19.6 × 14.7 cm). Edition of 3
P. 228

*Fear Not.* 2001. Synthetic polymer paint and felt-tip pen on paper, 11 × 8 1/2" (27.9 × 21.6 cm)
The Museum of Modern Art, New York. The Judith Rothschild Foundation Contemporary Drawings Collection Gift
P. 166

* *Fertile Structure.* 2008. Graphite and plaster on wood, 19 1/2 × 19 1/2" (49.5 × 49.5 cm)
Kunstmuseum Basel with funds from the Petzold-Müller Foundation

*Finger Ruler 1.* 1995. Graphite on paper, 11 × 8" (27.9 × 20.3 cm)
Private collection
P. 111

* *First Was the Spitting I.* 1993. Ink and graphite on graph paper, 16 1/2 × 12 3/4" (41.9 × 32.4 cm)
Collection of Catherine Orentreich, New York
P. 75

* *First Was the Spitting II.* 1993. Ink, graphite, and toothpaste spit on graph paper, 16 1/2 × 12 3/4" (41.9 × 32.4 cm)
Collection of Catherine Orentreich, New York
P. 75

* *First Was the Spitting III.* 1993. Ink, graphite, and toothpaste spit on graph paper, 16 1/2 × 12 3/4" (41.9 × 32.4 cm)
Collection of Catherine Orentreich, New York
P. 75

* *First Was the Spitting IV.* 1993. Ink, graphite, and toothpaste spit on graph paper, 16 1/2 × 12 3/4" (41.9 × 32.4 cm)
Collection of Catherine Orentreich, New York
P. 75

* *Five Problems.* 1992. Silver dye bleach print, 16 × 20" (40.6 × 50.8 cm). Edition of 5
P. 66

*Floating Sinking Shell 2.* 2004. Plaster and shell, 6 × 12 × 12" (15.3 × 30.5 × 30.5 cm)
Collection of Dean Valentine and Amy Adelson, Los Angeles
P. 197

*Fleuve.* 2003. Polyurethane foam, polystyrene foam balls, cotton, plaster, and wire, 7' 5" × 17" × 32" (226.1 × 43.2 × 81.3 cm)
François Pinault Collection
P. 190

*Foam.* 1992. Silver dye bleach print, 16 × 20" (40.6 × 50.8 cm). Edition of 5
P. 65

*Focos Philips.* 1997. Silver dye bleach print, 16 × 20" (40.6 × 50.8 cm). Edition of 5
P. 133

*Four and Two Fingers.* 2002. Fired clay, 5 1/8 × 15 3/8 × 7 1/2" (13 × 39 × 19 cm)
Private collection, New York
P. 179

* *Four Bicycles (There Is Always One Direction).* 1994. Bicycles, 6' 6" × 7' 4" × 7' 4" (198.1 × 223.5 × 223.5 cm)
Collection of Carlos and Rosa de la Cruz
Pp. 92, 94, 158–59

*Four Points Expanded.* 2005. Synthetic polymer paint on canvas, 6' 10 11/16" × 6' 10 11/16" (210 × 210 cm)
Collection of Luis Miguel Albores, Mexico City
P. 203

*From Cap in Car to Atlas.* 1997. Video (color, sound), 60 min. Edition of 3
P. 128

*From Flat Tire to Airplane.* 1997. Video (color, sound), 44 min., 40 sec. Edition of 3
P. 128

*From Green Glass to Federal Express.* 1997. Video (color, sound), 59 min. Edition of 3
P. 128

*From Roof to Roof.* 1993. Silver dye bleach print, 16 × 20" (40.6 × 50.8 cm). Edition of 5
P. 80

*Frozen Portable Puddle.* 1994. Silver dye bleach print, 16 × 20" (40.6 × 50.8 cm). Edition of 5
P. 90

*Futon Homeless.* 1992. Silver dye bleach print, 16 × 20" (40.6 × 50.8 cm). Edition of 2
P. 62

**G**

*Galaxy Pot.* 2002. Plaster and gouache, 5 1/2 × 10 1/2 × 10 1/2" (14 × 26.7 × 26.7 cm)
Private collection, Dallas
P. 201

*Study for Go 4 No Borders.* 2005. Digital rendering, dimensions variable
P. 200

*Go 4 No Borders.* 2005. Three hundred sixty concrete disks, dimensions variable
Courtesy of Marian Goodman Gallery, New York
P. 200

*Graphite Sequence.* 2008. Graphite and plaster on three canvases, each 15 3/4 × 15 3/4" (40 × 40 cm)
Collection of Charlotte and Bill Ford
P. 234

*Great Headlight.* 2009. Chromogenic color print, 16 × 20" (40.6 × 50.8 cm). Edition of 5
P. 241

*Green Paper.* 1991. Silver dye bleach print, 16 × 20" (40.6 × 50.8 cm). Edition of 5
P. 56

**H**

*Habemus Vespam.* 1995. Sarnico stone, 45 1/4 × 70 7/8 × 24 13/16" (115 × 180 × 63 cm)
Brae Art, New York
P. 106

*Half-Submerged Ferris Wheel.* 1997. Ferris wheel, dimensions variable. Temporary installation
P. 127

*Hammock Hanging Between Two Skyscrapers.* 1993. Cotton hammock, dimensions variable
Courtesy of Marian Goodman Gallery, New York
P. 84

*Hand Pressing Five Balls into a Mass, After a Drawing.* 2002. Graphite on clay, 3 1/2 × 6 1/2 × 5 1/4" (8.9 × 16.5 × 13.3 cm)
Fonds régional d'art contemporain, Picardie, France
P. 209

*Havre-Caumartin 1.* 1999. Graphite on Japanese paper, 6' 6 3/4" × 39 3/8" (200 × 100 cm)
Cesar Cervantes Collection
P. 150

*Havre-Caumartin 2.* 1999. Graphite on Japanese paper, 6' 6 3/4" × 39 3/8" (200 × 100 cm)
Cesar Cervantes Collection
P. 151

*Havre-Caumartin 3.* 1999. Graphite on Japanese paper, 6' 6 3/4" × 39 3/8" (200 × 100 cm)
Cesar Cervantes Collection
P. 151

*Head*. 2007. Bronze, 7 × 9 × 7" (17.8 × 22.9 × 17.8 cm). Edition of 7
P. 228

*Heart of the River*. 1991. Silver dye bleach print, 16 × 20" (40.6 × 50.8 cm). Edition of 5
P. 52

*Helicopter*. 2005. Chromogenic color print, 16 × 20" (40.6 × 50.8 cm). Edition of 6
P. 206

*The Hero of the Earthquake*. 1985 (printed 2005). Chromogenic color print, 16 × 20" (40.6 × 50.8 cm). Edition of 6
P. 52

*Home*. 2007. Chromogenic color print, 16 × 20" (40.6 × 50.8 cm). Edition of 5
P. 223

*Home Run*. 1993. Oranges, dimensions variable. Temporary installation
P. 83

*Horse*. 1992. Chromogenic color print, 20 × 16" (50.8 × 40.6 cm). Edition of 5
P. 71

* *Horses Running Endlessly*. 1995. Wood, 3 3/8 × 34 3/8 × 34 3/8" (8.7 × 87.5 × 87.5 cm). One of three versions
The Museum of Modern Art, New York. Gift of Agnes Gund and Lewis B. Cullman in honor of Chess in the Schools
P. 109

*Horseshit*. 1992. Silver dye bleach print, 16 × 20" (40.6 × 50.8 cm). Edition of 5
P. 70

**I**

*Inner Circles of the Wall*. 1999. Graphite on plaster, dimensions variable
The Rachofsky Collection, Collection of Deedie and Rusty Rose, and Dallas Museum of Art through the DMA/amfAR Benefit Auction Fund, 2007
P. 149

*Inner Tire Garden*. 2007. Chromogenic color print, 16 × 20" (40.6 × 50.8 cm). Edition of 5
P. 225

*Ironing Board*. 1994. Silver dye bleach print, 16 × 20" (40.6 × 50.8 cm). Edition of 5
P. 92

*Isadora's Necklace*. 2003. Chromogenic color print, 16 × 20" (40.6 × 50.8 cm). Edition of 5
P. 191

* *Island Within an Island*. 1993. Silver dye bleach print, 16 × 20" (40.6 × 50.8 cm). Edition of 5
P. 81

**J**

*Jaipur Kites*. 1998. Video (color, sound) transferred to Beta Cam and DVD, 29 min., 1 sec. Edition of 3
P. 168

**K**

*Kelly Kites 6*. 2001. Cut-and-pasted printed paper, 11 3/4 × 9 1/2" (29.8 × 24.1 cm)
Sir Evelyn and Lady Lynn Forester de Rothschild
P. 169

*Kelly Kites 8*. 2001. Cut-and-pasted printed paper, 11 3/4 × 9 1/2" (29.8 × 24.1 cm)
Collection of the artist
P. 169

*Kiss of the Egg*. 1997. Steel, cable, and egg, 28 1/2 × 47 1/4 × 22" (72.4 × 120 × 55.9 cm). Edition of 3
P. 137

*Korean Air*. 1997. Ink and colored pencil on cut-and-pasted printed paper on paper, 11 × 8 1/2" (28 × 21.6 cm)
The Museum of Modern Art, New York. Gift of Patricia and Morris Orden
P. 130

* *Kytes Tree*. 2005. Synthetic polymer paint on canvas, 6' 6 3/4" × 6' 6 3/4" (200 × 200 cm)
The Museum of Modern Art, New York. Purchase and gift of Anna Marie and Robert F. Shapiro and Donald B. Marron
P. 198

**L**

* *La DS*. 1993. Modified Citroën DS, 55 3/16" × 15' 9 15/16" × 45 5/16" (140.1 × 482.5 × 115.1 cm)
Fonds national d'art contemporain (Cnap), Ministère de la Culture et de la Communication, Paris, Fnac 94003
Pp. 40, 86, 89

*Landscape Flag*. 2004. Synthetic polymer paint on canvas, 31 7/8 × 23 5/8" (81 × 60 cm)
Collection of the artist
P. 193

*Lattice*. 1990. Mixed mediums, including vulcanized rubber, catcher's mask, and ball, 15 3/4 × 11 13/16 × 3 15/16" (40 × 30 × 10 cm)
Private collection, Mexico
P. 44

*Lemon Game*. 2001. Silver dye bleach print, 16 × 20" (40.6 × 50.8 cm). Edition of 5
P. 162

*Light Signs (Korea)*. 1995. Synthetic polymer paint on plastic sheet, and light box, 39 3/8 × 39 3/8 × 7 3/4" (100 × 100 × 19.7 cm). Two of ten versions
P. 109

*Light through Leaves* (for *Parkett*, no. 48). 1996. Ink-jet print, 20 × 32 3/16" (50.8 × 81.8 cm). Edition unknown
P. 119

*Lintels*. 2001. Dryer lint, dimensions variable
Courtesy of Marian Goodman Gallery, New York
Pp. 164–65, 166

*Long Yellow Hose*. 1996. Silver dye bleach print, 16 × 20" (40.6 × 50.8 cm). Edition of 5
P. 120

*Lost Line*. 1993. Plasticine and cotton string, approx. 19" (48.3 cm) diam. One of three versions
P. 74

**M**

*Maman*. 1998. Two pianos, slate roof, masonry tile, wood, metal, chair and mixed media, 10' × 8' 8" × 55" (304.8 × 264.2 × 139.7 cm)
Museum Moderner Kunst Stiftung Ludwig Wien, Leihgabe der Österreichischen Ludwigstiftung
P. 137

*Maria, Maria, Maria*. 1992. Phone book page with erasures, 11 × 9 1/8" (27.9 × 23.2 cm)
The Museum of Modern Art, New York. Gift of Patricia Phelps de Cisneros and the David Rockefeller Latin American Fund
P. 68

*Melon*. 1993. Silver dye bleach print, 16 × 20" (40.6 × 50.8 cm). Edition of 5
P. 82

*Mixiotes*. 2001. Maguey membrane, rubber balls, plastic bags, and cotton string, dimensions variable
Collection of Helen and Brice Marden, New York
P. 153

*Mobile Matrix*. 2006. Graphite on gray whale skeleton, 6' 5 3/16" × 35' 8 3/4" × 8' 8 3/4" (196 × 1,089 × 266 cm)
Biblioteca Vasconcelos, Mexico City
Pp. 39, 210, 214, 215, 216

*Moon Trees*. 1996. Wood, paper, and plastic, approx. 8' 4" × 66" × 66" (254 × 167.6 × 167.6 cm). Three of nine versions
P. 117

*Mop*. 2005. Chromogenic color print, 16 × 20" (40.6 × 50.8 cm). Edition of 5
P. 207

*Multiple Dropping on Copper Field*. 2003. Polyurethane foam on copper screen, 12 × 21 × 20 1/2" (30.5 × 53.3 × 52.1 cm)
Eugenio Lopez Collection
P. 187

*Mural Sol*. 2000. Synthetic polymer paint on wall, dimensions variable. Temporary installation
Pp. 258–59

* *My Hands Are My Heart*. 1991. Fired clay, 6 × 4 × 6" (15.2 × 10.2 × 15.2 cm)
Collection of the artist
P. 62

*My Hands Are My Heart*. 1991. Two silver dye bleach prints, each 9 1/8 × 12 1/2" (23.2 × 31.8 cm). Edition of 5
P. 41, 54

*My Hand Is the Memory of Space*. 1991. Wooden ice cream spoons, dimensions variable
Sammlung Goetz, Munich
P. 55

**N**

*Noodles in the Fence*. 2000. Silver dye bleach print, 16 × 20" (40.6 × 50.8 cm). Edition of 5
P. 156

*Notebook 1* (January 23, 1992–March 3, 1993). Mixed mediums, including felt-tip pen, cut-and-taped printed paper, and printed paper on notebook pages, pasted in notebook, 10 3/4 × 8 1/16" (27.3 × 20.5 cm)
Collection of the artist
Pp. 48, 64

*Notebook 2* (July 17, 1992–March 23, 1993). Mixed mediums, including ballpoint pen, graphite, printed paper, cut-and-taped printed paper, cut-and-pasted printed paper, photographs, cut phone book pages, toothpaste spit, and coffee stains, in notebook, 10 3/4 × 8 1/16" (27.3 × 20.5 cm)
Collection of the artist
Pp. 10, 22, 23, 25, 26, 33, 59, 60, 63, 67, 78, 85

*Notebook 4* (July 24, 1993–March 6, 1994). Mixed mediums, including ballpoint pen, graphite, gouache, printed paper, cut-and-taped printed paper, electrostatic prints, photographs, wood veneer, transfer letters, and leaves, in notebook, 10 3/4 × 8 1/16" (27.3 × 20.5 cm)
Collection of the artist
Pp. 30, 31, 77, 86, 87, 88, 91, 93, 101

*Notebook 5* (March 10, 1994–July 20, 1994). Mixed mediums, including ballpoint pen and photographs, in notebook, 10 3/4 × 8 1/16" (27.3 × 20.5 cm)
Collection of the artist
Pp. 15, 95

*Notebook 6* (July 21, 1994–November 5, 1994). Mixed mediums, including ballpoint pen, graphite, synthetic polymer paint, and photographs, in notebook, 10 3/4 × 8 1/16" (27.3 × 20.5 cm)
Collection of the artist
Cover and pp. 14, 32, 96, 101, 105

*Notebook 7* (November 1994–August 1995). Mixed mediums, including ballpoint pen, graphite, colored pencil, printed paper, photographs, postcards, and stickers, in notebook, 10 3/4 × 8 1/16" (27.3 × 20.5 cm)
Collection of the artist
Pp. 106, 108, 113, 119, 121

*Notebook 8* (September 3, 1995–September 10, 1996). Mixed mediums, including ballpoint pen, felt-tip pen, graphite, gouache, printed paper, photographs, Polaroids, and banknote, in notebook, 10 3/4 × 8 1/16" (27.3 × 20.5 cm)
Collection of the artist
Pp. 29, 110, 117, 129, 132

*Notebook 9* (September 12, 1996–February 5, 1999). Mixed mediums, including ballpoint pen, graphite, gouache, ink-jet print, printed paper, and postcard, in notebook, 10 3/4 × 8 1/16" (27.3 × 20.5 cm)
Collection of the artist
Pp. 21, 122, 126, 145

*Notebook 10* (March 1, 1999–March 29, 2000). Mixed mediums, including felt-tip pen, graphite, photographs, and napkin, in notebook, 10 3/4 × 8 1/16" (27.3 × 20.5 cm)
Collection of the artist
P. 157

*Notebook 12* (March 4, 2002–May 7, 2002). Mixed mediums, including ballpoint pen, graphite, notebook pages, and photographs, in notebook, 10 3/4 × 8 1/16" (27.3 × 20.5 cm)
Collection of the artist
Pp. 38, 170, 174, 175, 177

*Notebook 13* (August 18, 2002–September 5, 2003). Mixed mediums, including ballpoint pen, printed paper, photographs, and ink-jet prints, in notebook, 10 3/4 × 8 1/16" (27.3 × 20.5 cm)
Collection of the artist
Pp. 28, 180, 182, 192

Notebook 14 (September 7, 2003–February 28, 2006). Mixed mediums, including graphite and photographs, in notebook, 10 3/4 × 8 1/16" (27.3 × 20.5 cm)
Collection of the artist
Pp. 19, 21, 196, 202

Notebook 15 (February 3, 2006–December 20, 2007). Mixed mediums, including ballpoint pen, graphite, notebook pages, and photographs, in notebook, 10 3/4 × 8 1/16" (27.3 × 20.5 cm)
Collection of the artist
P. 217

Notebook 16 (January 2, 2008–May 3, 2009). Mixed mediums, including photograph and ballpoint pen on notebook pages, in notebook, 10 3/4 × 8 1/16" (27.3 × 20.5 cm)
Collection of the artist
P. 20

O

Obit: 'Bleak, Explosive Playwright'. 2008. Ink-jet print on Japanese paper, 6' 11" × 43 3/4" (210.8 × 111.1 cm) Edition of 3
P. 231

Observatory House. 2006. Oaxaca, Mexico
Pp. 211, 212

Oil Beetle. 2007. Chromogenic color print, 16 × 20" (40.6 × 50.8 cm). Edition of 5
P. 224

One Hundred Rupees. 1997. Gouache and graphite on banknote on paper, 11 × 8 1/2" (27.9 × 21.6 cm)
Collection of the artist
P. 128

Orange without Space. 1993. Plasticine and orange, approx. 12 3/4 × 15 1/2 × 15 1/2" (32.4 × 39.4 × 39.4 cm) One of three versions
P. 74

Orbit with Six Points of Gravity. 2005. Synthetic polymer paint on canvas, 14' 11 1/2" × 6' 11 1/16" (456 × 211 cm)
Courtesy of Marian Goodman Gallery, New York
P. 203

Organ Shell. 2003. Polyurethane foam, 8 1/2 × 39 × 22 1/2" (21.6 × 99 × 57.2 cm)
Courtesy of Marian Goodman Gallery, New York
P. 186

Study for Organic Composition. 1983. Graphite on paper, 3 15/16 × 6 11/16" (10 × 17 cm)
Collection of the artist
P. 47

Organic Composition II. 1982. Graphite on paper, 6 11/16 × 7 7/8" (17 × 20 cm)
Collection of the artist
P. 47

P

Paper Foam Waves. 1999. Cut-and-taped paper, five panels, each 22 3/8 × 67 3/4" (56.8 × 172.1 cm)
Private collection, Chicago
P. 118

Parachute in Iceland (East). 1996. Silver dye bleach print, 16 × 20" (40.6 × 50.8 cm). Edition of 5
P. 118

Parachute in Iceland (North). 1996. Silver dye bleach print, 16 × 20" (40.6 × 50.8 cm). Edition of 5
P. 118

Parachute in Iceland (South). 1996. Silver dye bleach print, 16 × 20" (40.6 × 50.8 cm). Edition of 5
P. 118

Parachute in Iceland (West). 1996. Silver dye bleach print, 16 × 20" (40.6 × 50.8 cm). Edition of 5
P. 118

PARIS010820071600. 2007. Oil on folded and unfolded paper, 9 13/16 × 9 13/16" (25 × 25 cm)
Private collection
P. 226

PARIS050820071800. 2007. Oil on folded and unfolded paper, 9 13/16 × 9 13/16" (25 × 25 cm)
Private collection, Paris
P. 226

Parking Lot. 1995. Temporary installation
P. 110

Path of Thought. 1997. Silver dye bleach print, 16 × 20" (40.6 × 50.8 cm). Edition of 5
P. 123

** Pelvis. 2007. Fired clay, 9 3/4 × 12 1/4 × 6 1/2" (24.8 × 31.1 × 16.5 cm). Artist's proof
Courtesy of Galerie Chantal Crousel, Paris

Pelvis. 2007. Bronze, 9 3/4 × 12 1/4 × 6 1/2" (24.8 × 31.1 × 16.5 cm). Edition of 7
P. 229

Penske Work Project: All In Between the Whites. 1998. Board and plasticine, 9 1/2 × 7 5/8 × 1 3/4" (24.1 × 19.4 × 4.4 cm)
Collection of Thomas H. Bjarnason, Toronto, Canada
P. 142

Penske Work Project: Blinds on Rubber Mat. 1998. Aluminum and rubber, 16 × 69 × 69" (40.6 × 175.3 × 175.3 cm)
Dimitris Daskalopoulos Collection, Greece
P. 143

Penske Work Project: Bucket Fractal. 1998. Three plastic buckets and garbage, 20 1/2 × 23 × 23" (52.1 × 58.4 × 58.4 cm)
Dimitris Daskalopoulos Collection, Greece
P. 144

Penske Work Project: End of the Octopus. 1998. Aluminum and printed board, 15" × 8' 2" × 46" (38.1 × 248.9 × 116.8 cm)
Dimitris Daskalopoulos Collection, Greece
P. 143

Penske Work Project: Fish Aquarium. 1998. Plastic and printed board, 13 3/4 × 11 1/2 × 11 1/2" (34.9 × 29.2 × 29.2 cm)
Dimitris Daskalopoulos Collection, Greece
P. 144

Penske Work Project: Folded Thread. 1998. Metal, plaster, and paint, 57" × 7' 11" × 38" (144.8 × 241.3 × 96.5 cm)
Dimitris Daskalopoulos Collection, Greece
P. 142

Penske Work Project: Open Door. 1998. Fiberboard and wood, 24" × 6' 4" × 23" (61 × 193 × 58.4 cm)
Collection of Steven Johnson and Walter Sudol, New York
P. 142

Photogravity. 1999. Ink-jet prints, foamcore, steel, rubber, and wood, twenty-eight parts, dimensions variable
Courtesy of Marian Goodman Gallery, New York
Pp. 154, 155

* Pi. 2002. Fired clay, 6 1/8 × 15 3/16" (15.5 × 38.5 cm)
Hoffmann Collection, Berlin
P. 176

* Pinched Ball. 1993. Silver dye bleach print, 16 × 20" (40.6 × 50.8 cm). Edition of 5
Pp. 35, 76

Pinched Stars I–VIII. 1997. Aluminum, dimensions variable. Each variation, edition of 3
Pp. 130–31, 136, 142, 143

Ping-Pond Table. 1998. Modified Ping-Pong table, water lilies, soil, stones, and water, 30" × 13' 11 3/4" × 13' 11 3/4" (76.2 × 426.1 × 426.1 cm). One of three versions
Pp. 137, 140

Plastic Bag with Water. 2009. Chromogenic color print, 16 × 20" (40.6 × 50.8 cm). Edition of 5
P. 240

Plato Solar. 2002. Silver dye bleach print, 16 × 20" (40.6 × 50.8 cm). Edition of 5
P. 173

* Polvo Impreso. 2002. Portfolio of twelve soft ground etchings with chine-collé, each 17 × 14 1/2" (43.1 × 36.8 cm). Loose portfolio edition of 25; bound portfolio edition of 25.
Tate Collection
Pp. 164, 165

Portable Puddle. 1994. Three silver dye bleach prints (one shown), each 16 × 20" (40.6 × 50.8 cm). Edition of 5
P. 90

Project for Shade Between Rings of Air. 2003. Gouache on four sheets of photographic paper, smallest to largest: 5 1/8 × 8 1/4" (13 × 21 cm); 5 5/8 × 8 1/4" (14.3 × 21 cm); 6 1/8 × 8 1/4" (15.6 × 21 cm); 6 1/4 × 8 1/4" (15.9 × 21 cm)
Courtesy of Marian Goodman Gallery, New York
P. 183

Prototype. 2004. Synthetic polymer paint on canvas, 19 11/16 × 19 11/16" (50 × 50 cm)
Collection of the artist
P. 193

Puddle 68. 1996. Synthetic polymer paint and graphite on ink-jet print, 11 × 8 1/2" (27.9 × 21.6 cm)
Marieluise Hessel Collection, Hessel Museum of Art, Center for Curatorial Studies, Bard College, Annandale-on-Hudson, New York
P. 118

R

* Recaptured Nature. 1990. Vulcanized rubber, approx. 29 1/2 × 41 5/16 × 33 7/16" (75 × 105 × 85 cm). One of three versions
Alma Colectiva, Guadalajara, Mexico
Pp. 34, 61, 84

Replaced Car Stoppers. 2001. Concrete, dimensions variable
Courtesy of Marian Goodman Gallery, New York
P. 163

Right Hand the Point. 1996. Color slide
Collection of the artist
P. 169

River of Trash. 1990. Silver dye bleach print, 16 × 20" (40.6 × 50.8 cm). Edition of 5
P. 53

Rolling Life's Hand Line. 2003. Chromogenic color print, 16 × 20" (40.6 × 50.8 cm). Edition of 5
P. 191

* Roto Spinal. 2005. Synthetic polymer paint on canvas, 6' 6 3/4" × 6' 6 3/4" (200 × 200 cm)
Private collection, Switzerland
P. 195

S

Salome's Dress. 1989. Synthetic polymer paint on wood, 12 3/16 × 17 15/16 × 1 9/16" (31 × 45.5 × 4 cm)
Collection of the artist
P. 49

Samurai Tree Invariants. 2006. Six hundred seventy-two digital prints with digital files, each print 21 7/16 × 21 7/16" (54.5 × 54.5 cm)
The Museum of Modern Art, New York. Acquired in honor of Lewis B. Cullman through the generosity of Agnes Gund, Jerry I. Speyer and Katherine G. Farley, Marie-Josée and Henry Kravis, Sue and Edgar Wachenheim III, Clarissa Alcock Bronfman, Robert B. Menschel, and also with the support of MoMA's Contemporary Arts Council
Pp. 220, 221

The Samurai's Tree. 2004. Synthetic polymer paint on canvas, 47 1/4 × 47 1/4" (120 × 120 cm)
Collection of the artist
P. 194

Sandball and Chair I. 1995. Silver dye bleach print, 16 × 20" (40.6 × 50.8 cm). Edition of 5
P. 146

Sandball and Chair II. 1995. Silver dye bleach print, 16 × 20" (40.6 × 50.8 cm). Edition of 5
P. 146

Sandball and Chair III. 1995. Silver dye bleach print, 16 × 20" (40.6 × 50.8 cm). Artist's proof
Courtesy of Galleria Monica De Cardenas, Milan
P. 146

Sandwich Steps. 2000. Silver dye bleach print, 16 × 20" (40.6 × 50.8 cm). Edition of 5
P. 161

Saturn. 1975. Pastel on paper, 13 3/16 × 18 11/16" (33.5 × 47.5 cm)
Collection of the artist
P. 49

*Scaffolding for Our Modern Ruins* (with Mauricio Maillé and Mauricio Rocha). 1987. Wood, dimensions variable. Temporary installation
Pp. 50–51

*Seed*. 2003. Galvanized steel mesh and polystyrene foam balls, 16 ¹⁵/₁₆ × 18 ¹/₈ × 7 ⁷/₈" (43 × 46 × 20 cm)
Collection of the artist
P. 199

*Shade Between Rings of Air*. 2003. Wood and metal, 9' 2 ¹/₄" × 26' 2 ¹⁵/₁₆" × 45' 11 ³/₁₆" (280 × 800 × 1,400 cm)
Courtesy of Marian Goodman Gallery, New York
P. 181

*Shoes*. 1993. Shoes, shoelaces, and metal, 6 ¹¹/₁₆ × 11 × 4 ³/₄" (17 × 28 × 12 cm)
Yves and Jeanine Le Goff Collection
P. 104

*Shower Head*. 2008. Chromogenic color print, 16 × 20" (40.6 × 50.8 cm). Edition of 5
P. 235

*Simon's Island*. 2005. Chromogenic color print, 16 × 20" (40.6 × 50.8 cm). Edition of 6
P. 197

*Sleeping Dog*. 1990. Silver dye bleach print, 20 × 16" (50.8 × 40.6 cm). Edition of 5
P. 57

*Soft Blue*. 1993. Plasticine and Letraset, approx. 4 ¹/₂" (11.4 cm) diam. One of three versions
P. 74

*Solar Graphite*. 2006. Graphite and plaster on wood, 21 ⁷/₈ × 21 ⁷/₈" (55.5 × 55.5 cm)
Collection of Mandy and Cliff Einstein
P. 221

*Spider House*. 2001. Silver dye bleach print, 16 × 20" (40.6 × 50.8 cm). Edition of 5
P. 167

*Spume 2*. 2003. Polyurethane foam, 11" × 6' 1" × 38" (27.9 × 183.4 × 96.5 cm)
Charpenel Collection, Guadalajara, Mexico
P. 186

*Spume after Trace 2*. 2003. Transfer print on polyurethane foam, 51 × 38 × 1" (129.5 × 96.5 × 2.5 cm)
Sir Evelyn and Lady Lynn Forester de Rothschild
P. 188

* *Spume Stream*. 2003. Polyurethane foam, 10 × 68 × 41" (25.4 × 172.7 × 104.1 cm)
Collection of Nancy and Stanley Singer
P. 186

*Stones in the Fence*. 1989. Silver dye bleach print, 16 × 20" (40.6 × 50.8 cm). Edition of 5
P. 53

*Storm*. 1989. Synthetic polymer paint on wood, 15 ³/₄ × 11 ¹³/₁₆ × 5 ⁷/₈" (40 × 30 × 15 cm)
Private collection
P. 48

*Stuck Stones*. 2005. Chromogenic color print, 16 × 20" (40.6 × 50.8 cm). Edition of 6
P. 207

*Suspended Leaf*. 2001. Silver dye bleach print, 16 × 20" (40.6 × 50.8 cm). Edition of 5
P. 167

**T**

*Total Perception*. 2002. Chromogenic color print, 16 × 20" (40.6 × 50.8 cm), edition of 5; chromogenic color print mounted on Sintra board, 33 ³/₄ × 46 ³/₄" (85.7 × 118.7 cm), Edition of 3
P. 172

* *Traffic Worm*. 1993. Silver dye bleach print, 16 × 20" (40.6 × 50.8 cm). Edition of 5
P. 73

*Tree through Leaves*. 2001. Silver dye bleach print, 16 × 20" (40.6 × 50.8 cm). Edition of 5
P. 161

* *Tronco 2*. 2008. Tempera and gold leaf on wood, 35 × 11 × 5 ⁷/₈" (88.9 × 27.9 × 14.9 cm)
Courtesy of Marian Goodman Gallery, New York
P. 233

*Tronco 3*. 2008. Tempera and gold leaf on wood, 35 ⁷/₈ × 11 ⁵/₈ × 5 ⁷/₈" (90 × 29.5 × 15 cm)
Collection of Rachel and Jean-Pierre Lehmann
P. 233

* *Tronco Verde*. 2008. Tempera and gold leaf on wood, 35 ⁷/₈ × 8 ¹/₄ × 5 ¹/₂" (91.1 X 21 X 14 cm)
Miguel Angel Pérez Santander Collection
P. 233

*Tuttifruti*. 2008. Tempera and gold leaf on canvas, 6' 6 ³/₄" × 6' 6 ³/₄" (200 × 200 cm)
Private collection, New York
P. 232

*Twelve Korean Notebook Pages*. 1995. Gouache and graphite on twelve sheets of notebook paper, each sheet 7 × 5" (17.8 × 12.7 cm)
Private collection, New York
P. 108

* *Two Socks*. 1995. Papier-mâché, 6 ¹¹/₁₆ × 11 × 4 ³/₄" (17 × 28 × 12 cm)
Collection of Didier Grumbach, Paris
P. 104

**U**

* *Until You Find Another Yellow Schwalbe*. 1995. Forty chromogenic color prints, each 12 ⁷/₁₆ × 18 ⁵/₈" (31.6 × 47.3 cm)
Tate presented by George and Angie Loudon
P. 107

Untitled. 1992. Graphite and ink on paper, 10 ¹/₂ × 8 ¹/₄" (26.7 × 20.9 cm)
Private collection
P. 70

Untitled. 1992. Ink, graphite, toothpaste spit, and tape on paper, 11 × 8" (27.9 × 20.3 cm)
Collection of Carlos and Rosa de la Cruz
P. 70

Untitled. 1993. Synthetic polymer paint, graphite, and marker on three sheets of paper, each sheet 10 ¹/₂ × 8" (26.7 × 20.3 cm)
Agnes Gund Collection, New York
P. 103

Untitled. 1994. Bottle cap rubbing on paper, 10 ¹/₂ × 8 ³/₄" (26.7 × 22.2 cm)
Collection of Denise and Eli Kam, Mexico City
P. 102

Untitled. 1994. Graphite and paint on printed paper on paper, 10 ¹/₂ × 8 ¹/₄" (26.7 × 20.9 cm)
Courtesy of Marian Goodman Gallery, New York
P. 103

Untitled. 2000. Graphite and ink on paper, 11 ³/₈ × 8 ¹/₄" (28.9 × 20.9 cm)
Collection of Patricia and Morris Orden, New York
P. 160

Untitled. 2000. Graphite and ink on paper, 11 ¹/₂ × 8 ¹/₄" (29.2 × 20.9 cm)
The Museum of Modern Art, New York. Fractional and promised gift of Martina Yamin
P. 160

Untitled. 2001. Graphite, powdered pigments, gouache, and charcoal on three sheets of paper, each sheet 5 ¹/₈ × 4 ³/₈" (13 × 11 cm)
Collection of Patricia and Morris Orden, New York
P. 176

Untitled. 2003. Charcoal on paper, 11 × 8 ¹/₄" (27.9 × 20.9 cm)
Private collection
P. 189

Untitled. 2003. Charcoal on paper, 11 × 8 ¹/₄" (27.9 × 20.9 cm)
Private collection
P. 189

Untitled. 2003. Charcoal on paper, 11 × 8 ¹/₄" (27.9 × 20.9 cm)
Private collection
P. 189

Untitled. 2007. Ink on paper with pottery shards, sixty sheets, each 5 ¹/₂ × 3 ³/₈" (14 × 8.6 cm)
Instituto Inhotim, Minas Gerais, Brazil
P. 222

*Untitled (hand prints)*. 2000. Ink and gouache on paper, 12 × 9" (30.5 × 22.9 cm)
The Museum of Modern Art, New York. Fractional and promised gift of Martina Yamin
P. 160

*Untitled (Yokohama)*. 2001. Luggage, 29 × 22 × 12" (73.7 × 55.9 × 30.5 cm)
Courtesy of Marian Goodman Gallery, New York
P. 162

**V**

*Ventilator*. 1997. Ceiling fan and toilet paper, dimensions variable. One of four multipart versions
P. 136

*Vitral*. 1998. Silver dye bleach print, 16 × 20" (40.6 × 50.8 cm). Edition of 5
P. 168

**W**

*The Weight of the Sun*. 2003. Mixed mediums, dimensions variable
Colección de Arte CORPUS, Mexico City
Pp. 184, 185

*Well*. 2002. Chromogenic color print, 16 × 20" (40.6 × 50.8 cm), edition of 5; chromogenic color print mounted on Sintra board, 33 ³/₄ × 46 ³/₄" (85.7 × 118.7 cm), edition of 3
P. 178

*Wet Watch*. 1993. Silver dye bleach print, 20 × 16" (50.8 × 40.6 cm). Edition of 5
P. 36

*Whale in the Sand*. 2006. Chromogenic color print, 16 × 20" (40.6 × 50.8 cm). Edition of 5
P. 213

*Whale Skull*. 2006. Chromogenic color print, 20 × 16" (50.8 × 40.6 cm). Edition of 5
P. 213

*Windshield Altar with Bullet Hole*. 2009. Chromogenic color print, 16 × 20" (40.6 × 50.8 cm). Edition of 5
P. 241

*Winter Hoop*. 2009. Chromogenic color print, 16 × 20" (40.6 × 50.8 cm). Edition of 5
P. 240

*Working Tables, 1991–2006, Mexico*. 2006. Mixed mediums, dimensions variable
Kunstmuseum Basel with Funds from the Karl and Margrith Schaub-Tschudin Foundation
P. 221

*Working Tables, 1993–1996*. 1996. Mixed mediums, dimensions variable. Elements dispersed
P. 114

*Working Tables, 1993–2000*. 2000. Mixed mediums, dimensions variable. Elements dispersed
P. 157

*Working Tables, 2000–2005*. 2005. Mixed mediums, including unfired clay, straw, egg container, bottle caps, wire mesh screen, string, stones, shells, plaster, bark, polystyrene foam, painted wood elements, and pizza dough, dimensions variable
The Museum of Modern Art, New York. Purchase and gift of Anna Marie and Robert F. Shapiro and Donald B. Marron
P. 208

**Y**

* *Yielding Stone*. 1992. Plasticine, approx. 14 × 17 × 17" (35.6 × 43.2 × 43.2 cm). One of three versions
Collection of the artist
Pp. 14, 35, 72

* *Yogurt Caps*. 1994. Four yogurt lids, each lid 3 ¹/₈" (7.9 cm) diam.
Courtesy of Marian Goodman Gallery, New York
Pp. 96, 98–99, 142, 143

## Works by Other Artists

Manuel Álvarez Bravo. *Optical Parable*. 1931. Gelatin silver print, 9 1/2 × 7 3/16" (24.1 × 18.2 cm)
The Museum of Modern Art, New York. The Photography Council Fund
P. 43

Arman. *La vie à pleines dents*. 1960. Resin, metal, and wood, 7 1/16 × 13 3/4 × 2 3/8" (18 × 35 × 6 cm)
Musée national d'art moderne, Centre Georges Pompidou, Paris. Museum purchase from Daniel Cordier (Juan-les-Pins) in 1968
P. 37

Joseph Beuys. *Eurasia Siberian Symphony 1963*. 1966. Panel with chalk drawing, felt, fat, hare, and painted poles, 6" × 7' 6 3/4" × 20" (183 × 230 × 50 cm)
The Museum of Modern Art, New York. Gift of Frederic Clay Bartlett (by exchange)
P. 40

Constantin Brancusi. View of the studio with *Blond Negress I*. c. 1923. Gelatin silver glass plate negative, 9 7/16 × 7 1/16" (24 × 18 cm)
Musée national d'art moderne, Centre Georges Pompidou, Paris
P. 12

Constantin Brancusi. *Princess X*. 1915–16. Polished bronze and limestone block, 24 5/16 × 15 15/16 × 8 3/4" (61.7 × 40.5 × 22.2 cm); base, 7 1/4 × 7 1/4 × 7 1/4" (18.4 × 18.4 × 18.4 cm)
The Louise and Walter Arensberg Collection, 1950. Philadelphia Museum of Art
P. 34

Charles Darwin. *Tree of Life*. c. 1837. Ink on paper, 6 9/16 × 3 11/16" (16.6 × 9.3 cm)
Charles Darwin Papers, Notebook 'B,' p. 36, MS.DAR 121. Cambridge University Library
P. 24

Marcel Duchamp. *Belle haleine – Eau de voilette*. 1921. Glass and paperboard, 6 1/2 × 4 3/8" (16.5 × 11.2 cm)
Private collection
P. 35

Alberto Giacometti. *Bust of Diego*. 1954. Bronze, 15 3/4 × 13 1/4 × 7 1/2" (40 × 33.7 × 19 cm)
Musée national d'art moderne, Centre Georges Pompidou, Paris. Museum purchase from the artist in 1961
P. 40

Hans Haacke. *Condensation Cube*. 1963–65. Clear plexiglass and distilled water, 30 × 30 × 30" (76.2 × 76.2 × 76.2 cm). Edition of 5
P. 36

Marcellus Hall. Illustration originally published in the *New Yorker*, January 11, 1999, p. 10, with the caption "Free-form Ping-Pong courtesy of Gabriel Orozco, at Marian Goodman"
P. 140

Eva Hesse. *Repetition Nineteen III*. 1968. Fiberglass and polyester resin, nineteen units, each 19 to 20 1/4 × 11 to 12 3/4" (48 to 51 × 27.8 to 32.2 cm) diam.
The Museum of Modern Art, New York. Gift of Charles and Anita Blatt
P. 38

Mauricio Maillé. See *Scaffolding for Our Modern Ruins* in "Works by Gabriel Orozco"

Piero Manzoni. *Artist's Shit no. 31*. 1961. Metal and paper, 1 15/16 × 2 9/16" (5 × 6.5 cm)
Musée national d'art moderne, Centre Georges Pompidou, Paris. Donated by Liliane and Michel Durand-Dessert (Paris) in 1994
P. 35

Stéphane Mallarmé. *Jamais un coup de dés n'abolira le hasard: poème*. Paris : A. Vollard, 1897. Proofs with corrections and annotations by the author, pp. 6–7
Bibliothèque nationale de France, Paris
P. 33

Juan Carlos Martín. Stills from *Gabriel Orozco*. 2002. Film, 80 min.
Pp. 141, 147

László Moholy-Nagy. *EM2*. 1922. Porcelain enamel on steel, 18 3/4 × 11 7/8" (47.5 × 30.1 cm)
The Museum of Modern Art, New York. Gift of Philip Johnson in memory of Sibyl Moholy-Nagy
P. 19

Damián Ortega. Detail from "El pájaro: Para principiantes." Originally published in Alma Ruiz, ed., *Gabriel Orozco* (Los Angeles: The Museum of Contemporary Art; and Mexico City: Museo Internacional Rufino Tamayo, 2000)
P. 158

Pablo Picasso. *Sketchbook No. 92*. 1926. Cardboard-covered notebook; p. 14, colored pencil on paper, 12 3/16 × 19 5/16" (32.5 × 49 cm)
Private collection
P. 27

Pablo Picasso. *Sketchbook No. 92*. 1926. Cardboard-covered notebook; p. 17, leaf collage, 12 3/16 × 19 5/16" (32.5 × 49 cm)
Private collection
P. 28

José Guadalupe Posada. *Calavera huertista (Death of the Dictator Huerta)*. 1911. Engraving, 8 11/16 × 8 11/16" (22 × 22 cm)
P. 42

Robert Rauschenberg. *Seven Untitled Hanging Assemblages, Rome*. 1953. Gelatin silver print, 13 × 15" (33 × 38.1 cm). Arranged and photographed by the artist, Pincio Gardens, Villa Borghese, Rome, 1953
P. 12

Bridget Riley. *Fission*. 1963. Tempera on composition board, 35 × 34" (88.8 × 86.2 cm)
The Museum of Modern Art, New York. Gift of Philip Johnson
P. 42

Mauricio Rocha. See *Scaffolding for Our Modern Ruins* in "Works by Gabriel Orozco"

Aleksandr Rodchenko. *Spatial Construction no. 12*. c. 1920. Plywood, open construction partially painted with aluminum paint, and wire, 24 × 33 × 18 1/2" (61 × 83.7 × 47 cm)
The Museum of Modern Art, New York. Acquisition made possible through the extraordinary efforts of George and Zinaida Costakis, and through the Nate B. and Frances Spingold, Matthew H. and Erna Futter, and Enid A. Haupt Funds
P. 39

Richard Serra. *One Ton Prop (House of Cards)*. 1969 (refabricated 1986). Lead antimony, four plates, each 48 × 48 × 1" (122 × 122 × 2.5 cm)
The Museum of Modern Art, New York. Gift of the Grinstein Family
P. 34

# Selected Exhibition History Compiled by Paulina Pobocha

## One-Person Exhibitions

**1991**  *Cuerpos Encontrados*, part of the Festival Internacional Cervantino. Museo de la Alhóndiga de Granaditas, Guanajuato, Mexico.

**1993**  Kanaal Art Foundation, Kortrijk, Belgium. April 24–June 26.

*Projects 41: Gabriel Orozco*. The Museum of Modern Art, New York. September 3–October 19.

Galerie Chantal Crousel, Paris. December 4, 1993–January 29, 1994.

**1994**  *Options 47: Gabriel Orozco*. Museum of Contemporary Art, Chicago. September 3–October 30.

Marian Goodman Gallery, New York. September 12–October 15.

**1995**  *Migrateurs: Gabriel Orozco*. Musée d'Art Moderne de la Ville de Paris. February 8–March 19.

Galleria Monica De Cardenas, Milan. March 15–May 12.

*Gabriel Orozco: Projekt 'Gelbe Schwalbe'* (*Until You Find Another Yellow Schwalbe*). daadgalerie, Berlin. October 17–November 26.

Galerie Micheline Szwajcer, Antwerp. October 20–December 2.

**1996**  Kunsthalle Zürich. May 5–June 23. Traveled to: Institute of Contemporary Arts, London, July 25–September 22; Deutscher Akademischer Austauschdienst, Berliner Künstlerprogramm, Berlin, January 11–March 2, 1997.

*Gabriel Orozco: Empty Club*. 50 St. James's Street, London (organized by Artangel, London). June 25–July 28.

Marian Goodman Gallery, New York. September 10–October 12.

*Present Tense: Gabriel Orozco (Placement/ Displacement)*. Art Gallery of Ontario, Toronto. December 4, 1996–March 9, 1997.

*Gabriel Orozco: Atomists*. Galleria Monica De Cardenas, Milan. December 11, 1996–January 29, 1997.

**1997**  Staatliche Museen zu Berlin, Kulturforum, Berlin. January 11–March 2.

Chapelle – Centre de la Vieille Charité, Marseille, France. January 14–March 9.

*Gabriel Orozco: Recordings and Drawings*. Stedelijk Museum, Amsterdam. November 1–December 14.

Anthony d'Offay Gallery, London. December 5, 1997–January 17, 1998.

**1998**  *Gabriel Orozco: Que triunfen los estranjeros*. Centro Fotográfico Manuel Álvarez Bravo, Oaxaca, Mexico.

*Gabriel Orozco: Clinton Is Innocent*. Musée d'Art Moderne de la Ville de Paris. May 28–September 13.

*Gabriel Orozco: Free Market Is Anti-Democratic*. Marian Goodman Gallery, New York. November 24, 1998–January 9, 1999.

*Currents 76: Gabriel Orozco*. Saint Louis Art Museum, Missouri. December 11, 1998–February 7, 1999.

**1999**  *Exhibition 91: Gabriel Orozco*. Portikus Gallery, Frankfurt am Main. January 23–March 7.

*Gabriel Orozco: Photographies et Vidéos*. Centre pour l'image contemporaine and Centre de la photographie Genève. April 15–June 20.

*Gabriel Orozco: The Inner Circles of the Wall*. Galerie Chantal Crousel, Paris. May 20–July 31.

*Gabriel Orozco: Photogravity*. Philadelphia Museum of Art. October 27–December 12.

**2000**  The Museum of Contemporary Art, Los Angeles. June 4–September 3. Traveled to: Museo Internacional Rufino Tamayo, Mexico City, September 28, 2000–February 4, 2001; Museo de Arte Contemporáneo de Monterrey (MARCO), Mexico, February 22–May 27, 2001.

*Blue Memory/Gabriel Orozco*. Shima/Islands, Mirei Shigemori Residence, Kyoto. September 16–October 14.

*Gabriel Orozco: Immediately Past*. MK2 project café, Paris. December 1–22.

**2001**  *Gabriel Orozco: Fear Not*. Marian Goodman Gallery, New York. November 7–December 29.

**2002**  Galerie Chantal Crousel, Paris. November 7, 2002–January 11, 2003.

*Gabriel Orozco: New Photographs*. Marian Goodman Gallery, New York. November 14, 2002–January 4, 2003.

*Gabriel Orozco: Nuevas Fotografías/ New Photographs*. kurimanzutto, Mexico City. November 27, 2002–January 25, 2003.

**2003**  Centro de Artes Visuais – Encontros de Fotografia, Coimbra, Portugal. May 3–June 15.

*Gabriel Orozco: The Weight of the Sun*. The Douglas Hyde Gallery, Trinity College, Dublin. August 15–September 25.

Marian Goodman Gallery, New York. October 22–November 22.

**2004**  *Directions: Gabriel Orozco. Extension of Reflection*. Hirshhorn Museum and Sculpture Garden, Smithsonian Institution, Washington, D.C. June 10–September 6.

Serpentine Gallery, London. July 1–August 30.

**2005**  Museo Nacional Centro de Arte Reina Sofía, Palacio de Cristal, Madrid. February 8–April 18.

Fundación Marcelino Botín, Villa Iris, Santander, Spain. July.

Marian Goodman Gallery, New York. October 6–November 12.

**2006**  *Gabriel Orozco: Mátrix Móvil*. Biblioteca Vasconcelos, Mexico City. May 16–present.

*Gabriel Orozco: Twelve Paintings and a Drawing*. White Cube, London. September 29–November 11.

*Gabriel Orozco: Samurai's Tree Invariant*. Museum Ludwig, Cologne. November 3, 2006–January 28, 2007.

Museo del Palacio de Bellas Artes, Mexico City. November 29, 2006–February 25, 2007.

**2007**  Fonds régional d'art contemporain de Picardie, Amiens, France. January 26–April 4.

*Gabriel Orozco: Dépliages*. Galerie Chantal Crousel, Paris. September 15–October 20.

*Gabriel Orozco: Inner Circles of the Wall*. Dallas Museum of Art. November 29, 2007–March 30, 2008.

**2008**  Marian Goodman Gallery, New York. May 6–June 14.

**2009**  kurimanzutto, Mexico City. April 29–June 13.

The Museum of Modern Art, New York. December 13, 2009–March 1, 2010. Travels to: Kunstmuseum Basel, April 18–August 10, 2010; Musée national d'art moderne, Centre Georges Pompidou, Paris, September 15, 2010–January 3, 2011; Tate Modern, London, February 16–May 22, 2011.

## Group Exhibitions

**1983**  Salón Nacional de Artes Plásticas (drawing section). Instituto Nacional de Bellas Artes, Mexico City.

3rd Encuentro Nacional de Arte Joven. Instituto Nacional de Bellas Artes, Mexico City.

**1984**  *Neográfica*. Museo Universitario del Chopo, Mexico City.

**1985**  *Sin motivos aparentes*. Museo Carrillo Gil, Mexico City.

**1987**  Salón Nacional de Artes Plásticas, Secció Espacios Alternativos. Museo de Arte Moderno, Mexico City.

*Six Nouveaux Regards Mexicains*. Centre culturel du Méxique, Paris.

**1989**  *Artistas mexicanos contemporáneos*. Segundo Festival Latino Americano de Arte y Cultura, Brasilia.

*A propósito*. Museo del Ex-Convento del Desierto de los Leones, Mexico City. April 15–May 25.

**1990**  *Installations: Current Directions*. The Museum of Contemporary Hispanic Art, New York.

*Sculpture of the Americas in the Nineties*. Museum of Modern Art of Latin America, Washington, D.C. June 7–September 8.

*Mexican Video*. The Bronx Museum of the Arts, New York. Fall/Winter.

**1991**  *D.F.: Art from Mexico City*. Blue Star Art Space, San Antonio. September 6–October 13.

*The Perennial Illusion of a Vulnerable Principle: Another Mexican Art*. Art Center College of Design, Pasadena. September 15–October 27.

**1992**  *America: Bride of the Sun*. Royal Museum of Fine Arts, Antwerp. February 1–May 31.

*Si colón supiera! . . . /If Columbus Only Knew! . . .* Museo de Monterrey, Mexico. October.

**1993**  *In Transit*. The New Museum of Contemporary Art, New York. January 15–April 11.

*Lesa natura: Reflexiones sobre ecología*. Museo de Arte Moderno, Mexico City. June 3–August 17.

*45th International Art Exhibition: The Cardinal Points of Art*. Venice Biennale. June 13–October 10.

*Real Time*. Institute of Contemporary Arts, London. June 19–July 18.

*Summer Group Show*. Marian Goodman Gallery, New York. June 25–August.

*Briques*. Galerie Chantal Crousel, Paris. October 30–November 27.

*Eros c'est la vie*. Le Confort Moderne, Poitiers, France. December 9, 1993–March 9, 1994.

**1994** *WATT*. Witte de With Center for Contemporary Art, Rotterdam, The Netherlands. February 5–March 20.

*The Epic and the Everyday: Contemporary Photographic Art*. Hayward Gallery, Southbank Centre, London. June 23–August 29.

*Endstation Sehnsucht*. Kunsthaus Zürich. July 2–August 28.

*A Sculpture Show*. Marian Goodman Gallery, New York. August.

*Cocido y crudo*. Museo Nacional Centro de Arte Reina Sofía, Madrid. December 14, 1994–March 6, 1995.

**1995** 1995 Biennial Exhibition. Whitney Museum of American Art, New York. March 23–June 4.

*Where Is Abel, Thy Brother?* The Zachęta Gallery Contemporary of Art, Warsaw. May 7–July 2.

*Currents 95: Familiar Places*. The Institute of Contemporary Art, Boston. July 26–October 1.

*Beyond the Borders*. Kwangju Biennale, South Korea. September 20–November 20.

*Morceaux choisis du Fonds national d'art contemporain*. Centre National d'Art Contemporain de Grenoble, France. October 14, 1995–January 7, 1996.

*Glaube Hoffnung Liebe Tod*. Kunsthalle Wien, Vienna. December 15, 1995–January 31, 1996.

**1996** *Traffic*. CAPC Musée d'art contemporain, Bordeaux. January 26–March 24.

*Defining the Nineties: Consensus Making in New York, Miami and Los Angeles*. Museum of Contemporary Art, Miami. February 24–April 6.

*Inside-out: Inaugural Exhibition*. Museum of Contemporary Art San Diego. March 10, 1996–January 29, 1997.

*Inklusion/Exklusion Kunst im Zeitalter von Postkolonialismus und globaler Migration*. Streirischer Herbst 96, Graz, Austria. September 22–October 26.

*Campo 6: Il villaggio a spirale/Campo 6: The Spiral Village*. Galleria Civica d'Arte Moderna e Contemporanea, Torino, Italy. September 28–November 3. Traveled to: Bonnefanten Museum, Maastricht, The Netherlands, January 19–May 25, 1997.

*Gabriel Orozco, Rirkrit Tiravanija*. The Living Art Museum, Reykjavik. October 12–27.

**1997** *L'Empreinte*. Musée national d'art moderne, Centre Georges Pompidou, Paris. February 19–May 12.

1997 Biennial Exhibition. Whitney Museum of American Art, New York. March 20–June 15.

*Gabriel Orozco, Sigmar Polke: Voyages*. Galerie Chantal Crousel, Paris. May 24–July 30.

Documenta 10. Kassel, Germany. June 21–September 28.

*Skulpture. Projekte in Münster*. Münster, Germany. June 22–September 28.

*L'Autre: The 4th Biennial of Contemporary Art*. Lyon, France. July 9–September 24.

*Asi esta la cosa: Instalación y arte objeto en América Latina*. Centro Cultural Arte Contemporáneo, Mexico City. July 25–October 2.

*Mona Hatoum, Ann Veronica Janssens, Gabriel Orozco*. Galerie Micheline Szwajcer, Antwerp. September 12–October 18.

*Present Tense: Nine Artists in the Nineties*. San Francisco Museum of Modern Art. September 13, 1997–January 13, 1998.

*Lines of Loss* (organized by Gabriel Orozco). Artists Space, New York. November 14, 1997–January 10, 1998.

**1998** 1st Berlin Biennial. September 30–December 30.

24th São Paulo Bienal. October 3–December 13.

*Unfinished History*. Walker Art Center, Minneapolis. October 18, 1998–January 10, 1999. Traveled to: Museum of Contemporary Art, Chicago, January 30–April 4, 1999.

*Auf der Spur: Kunst der 90er Jahre im Spiegel von Schweizer Sammlungen*. Kunsthalle Zürich. October 31–December 27.

**1999** *. . . om det sublima/ . . . on the sublime*. Rooseum Center for Contemporary Art, Malmö, Sweden. January 23–March 21.

*Infra-slim Space: The Physical and Spiritual in the Art of Today*. Birmingham Museum of Art, Alabama. February 12–April 4.

*La Ville, le jardin, la mémoire*. Villa Medici, Rome. May 29–August 30.

*La casa, il corpo, il cuore: Konstruktion der Identitaten*. Museum Moderner Kunst Stiftung Ludwig, Vienna. June 24–October 10. Traveled to: National Gallery, Prague.

*The Hand*. The Power Plant, Toronto. June 25–September 6.

*Laboratorium*. Antwerpen Open and FotoMuseum, Antwerp. June 27–October 3.

*Third International Biennial Exhibition: Looking for a Place*. SITE Santa Fe. July 10–December 31.

*Economía de mercado/Market Economics*. Mercado de Medellín, Mexico City (organized by kurimanzutto, Mexico City). August 21.

1999 Carnegie International. Carnegie Museum of Art, Pittsburgh. November 6, 1999–March 26, 2000.

**2000** *Sabrosa*. El Instituto de Cultura de Morelos, Cuernavaca, Mexico.

*Diary: Different Approaches to Diary-Making*. Cornerhouse, Manchester. January 15–March 12.

*Aprendiendo menos/Learning Less*. Centro de la Imagen, Mexico City. January 27–March 6.

*Let's Entertain: Life's Guilty Pleasures*. Walker Art Center, Minneapolis. February 12–April 30. Traveled to: Portland Museum of Art, Oregon, July 7–September 17; presented as *Sons et lumières*, Musée national d'art moderne, Centre Georges Pompidou, Paris, November 15–December 18; Kunstmuseum Wolfsburg, Germany, March 16–July 15, 2001; Miami Art Museum, September 14–November 18, 2001.

*Vanitas: Meditations on Life and Death in Contemporary Art*. Virginia Museum of Fine Arts, Richmond. April 4–June 18.

*Soleils mexicains*. Petit Palais, Musée des Beaux-Arts de la Ville de Paris. April 29–August 13.

*Continental Shift: A Voyage Between Cultures*. Ludwig Forum, Aachen, Germany; Bonnefantenmuseum, Maastricht, The Netherlands; Stadsgalerij, Heerlen, The Netherlands; Musée d'Art moderne de Liège, France. May–September.

*Between Cinema and a Hard Place*. Tate Modern, London. May 12–December 3.

*Gabriel Orozco Invite à la Galerie Chantal Crousel la Galeria kurimanzutto, Mexico*. Galerie Chantal Crousel, Paris. May 13–July 29.

*In Between*. Expo 2000, Hannover. June 1–October 31.

*Orbis Terrarum: Ways of Worldmaking*. Museum Plantin-Moretus, Antwerp. June 22–September 24.

*Versiones del sur: Cinco propuestas en torno al arte en América*. Museo Nacional Centro de Arte Reina Sofía, Madrid. December 12, 2000–March 26, 2001.

**2001** *The Beauty of Intimacy: Lens and Paper*. Gemeentemuseum Den Haag, The Hague. January 20–May 6. Traveled to: Staatliche Kunsthalle, Baden-Baden, Germany, September 14–November 4; Kunstraum, Innsbruck, Austria, November 24, 2001–January 12, 2002.

*Nothing in the Main Hall*. Northern Gallery for Contemporary Art, Sunderland, England. April 12–June 3. Traveled to: Contemporary Art Centre, Vilnius, Lithuania, June 29–August 19; Rooseum Center for Contemporary Art, Malmö, Sweden, November 3–December 16.

*Mega-Wave: Towards a New Synthesis. Yokohama 2001: International Triennial of Contemporary Art*. September 2–November 11.

*Egofugal: 7th International Istanbul Biennial*. September 22–November 17.

*ARS 01*. Museum of Contemporary Art Kiasma, Helsinki. September 30, 2001–January 20, 2002.

*Forma e finzione nell'arte di oggi/Form Follows Fiction*. Castello di Rivoli Museo d'Arte Contemporanea, Rivoli-Torino, Italy. October 17, 2001–January 27, 2002.

**2002** *Dialogos entre dos momentos del arte Mexicano*. Museo de Arte Moderno, Mexico City.

*Passenger: The Viewer As Participant*. Astrup Fearnley Museum of Modern Art, Oslo. January 19–April 21.

Documenta 11. Kassel, Germany. June 8–September 15.

*Tempo*. The Museum of Modern Art, New York. June 29–September 9.

*Public Affairs*. Kunsthaus Zürich. September 13–December 1.

*En Route*. Serpentine Gallery, London. September 18–October 27.

*Sonic Process: A New Geography of Sounds*. Musée national d'art moderne, Centre Georges Pompidou, Paris. October 16, 2002–January 6, 2003. Traveled to: Museu d'art contemporani de Barcelona, Spain, May 3–July 1, 2003.

**2003** *Le Cabinet de Gabriel Orozco*. Fonds régional d'art contemporain de Picardie, Amiens, France. January 24–February 22.

*Orozco, Wentworth, Wurm. La luna nel rigagnolo.* Museo Hendrik Christian Andersen, Festival Internazionale FotoGrafia di Roma, Rome. April 24–June 20.

*Looking in, Looking out: Positionen zeitgenössischer Fotografie.* Kunstmuseum Basel. April 26–June 29.

*Les 20 ans des FRAC.* Fonds régional d'art contemporain, France. Traveled to various venues throughout France, June–December.

*The Everyday Altered* (organized by Gabriel Orozco), part of the *50th International Art Exhibition: Dreams and Conflicts. The Dictatorship of the Viewer.* Venice Biennale. June 15–November 2.

*50th International Art Exhibition: Dreams and Conflicts. The Dictatorship of the Viewer.* Venice Biennale. June 15–November 2.

*Plunder: Culture As Material.* Dundee Contemporary Arts, Scotland. November 2, 2003–January 11, 2004.

*Sitings: Installation Art, 1969–2002.* The Geffen Contemporary at MOCA, Los Angeles. October 12, 2003–June 7, 2004.

*Work Ethic.* The Baltimore Museum of Art. October 12, 2003–January 4, 2004. Traveled to: Des Moines Art Center, Iowa, May 15–August 1, 2005; Wexner Center for the Arts, Columbus, Ohio, September 17, 2005–January 2, 2006.

*Common Wealth.* Tate Modern, London. October 22–December 28.

*Drawing Modern: Works from the Agnes Gund Collection.* The Cleveland Museum of Art. October 26, 2003–January 11, 2004.

**2004** *Made in Mexico.* The Institute of Contemporary Art, Boston. January 21–May 9. Traveled to: UCLA Hammer Museum, Los Angeles, June 6–September 12.

*MoMA at El Museo: Latin American and Caribbean Art from the Collection of The Museum of Modern Art.* El Museo del Barrio, New York. March 4–July 25.

*Paisaje y Memoria/Landscape and Memory.* La Casa Encendida, Madrid. March 30–June 13. Traveled to: Centro Atlántico de Arte Moderno – CAAM, Las Palmas de Gran Canaria, Spain, June 30–August 22.

*"The personal is political" und peinlich.* Kunsthalle Exnergasse, Vienna. April 22–May 29.

*The Big Nothing.* Institute of Contemporary Art, Philadelphia. May 1–August 1.

*Contre-images.* Carré d'Art, Musée d'art contemporain, Nîmes, France. June 3–September 26.

*Monument to Now: The Dakis Joannou Collection,* part of *Athens 2004, Culture.* Deste Foundation for Contemporary Art, Athens. June 22–December 31.

*Stalemate.* Museum of Contemporary Art, Chicago. July 24, 2004–January 2, 2005.

*Los usos de la imagen: Fotografía, film y video en La Colección Jumex/Uses of the Image: Photography, Film and Video in the Jumex Collection.* Museo de Arte Latinoamericano de Buenos Aires, Argentina. September 29–November 22.

*Encounters in the 21st Century: Polyphony— Emerging Resonances.* 21st Century Museum of Contemporary Art, Kanazawa, Japan. October 9, 2004–March 21, 2005.

*2004 Taipei Biennial: Do You Believe in Reality?* October 23, 2004–January 23, 2005.

**2005** *Universal Experience: Art, Life, and the Tourist's Eye.* Museum of Contemporary Art, Chicago. February 12–June 5. Traveled to: Hayward Gallery, Southbank Centre, London, October 6–December 11; Museo Arte Moderna Contemporanea, Rovereto, Italy, February 11–May 14, 2006.

*El mito de dos volcanes: Popocatépetl Iztaccíhuatl.* Museo del Palacio de Bellas Artes, Mexico City. February 23–June 19.

*Covering the Real: Arts and the Press Picture, from Warhol to Tillmans.* Kunstmuseum Basel. April 30–August 20.

*Luna Park. Fantastic Art.* Villa Manin Center for Contemporary Art, Udine, Italy. June 8–November 6.

*51st International Art Exhibition: The Experience of Art.* Venice Biennale. June 12–November 6.

*Translation.* Palais de Tokyo, Paris. June 23–September 18.

*Farsites: Urban Crisis and Domestic Symptoms in Recent Contemporary Art.* San Diego Museum of Art. August 27–November 13.

*Carlos Amorales, Gabriel Orozco, Damián Ortega.* Museo Experimental El Eco, Mexico City. September.

*General Ideas: Rethinking Conceptual Art, 1987–2005.* CCA Wattis Institute for Contemporary Arts, San Francisco. September 15–November 13.

*Part Object, Part Sculpture.* Wexner Center for the Arts, Columbus, Ohio. October 30, 2005–February 26, 2006.

*Beyond: An Extraordinary Space of Experimentation for Modernization.* 2nd Guangzhou Triennial, Guangdong Museum of Art, Guangzhou, China. November 18, 2005–January 15, 2006.

**2006** *Biella Prize for Engraving 2006.* Museo del Territorio Biellese, Biella, Italy. March 19–June 4.

*Infinite Painting: Contemporary Painting and Global Realism.* Villa Manin Centre for Contemporary Art, Codroipo, Italy. April 9–September 24.

*Grey Flags.* Sculpture Center, Long Island City, New York. May 7–July 30. Traveled to: CAPC Musée d'art contemporain, Bordeaux, December 20, 2006–March 18, 2007.

*The Exotic Journey Ends.* Foksal Gallery Foundation, Warsaw. October 21–November 21

*Wrestle.* Hessel Museum of Art, Center for Curatorial Studies, Bard College, Annandale-on-Hudson, New York. November 12, 2006–May 27, 2007.

*Super Vision.* Institute of Contemporary Art, Boston. December 10, 2006–April 29, 2007.

**2007** *Merce Cunningham: Dancing on the Cutting Edge, Part I.* Museum of Contemporary Art, Miami. January 26–April 29.

*Mapas, cosmogonías e puntos de referencia.* Centro Galego de Arte Contemporánea, Santiago de Compostela, Spain. February 8–June 3.

*Speed 1.* IVAM, Institut Valencià d'Art Modern, Spain. February 22–July 8.

*Passion for Art.* Essl Museum, Klosterneuburg, Austria. March 15–August 26.

*The Shapes of Space.* Solomon R. Guggenheim Museum, New York. April 14–September 5.

*Airs de Paris.* Musée national d'art moderne, Centre Georges Pompidou, Paris. April 25–August 15.

*30/40.* Marian Goodman Gallery, New York. September 10–November 24.

*Reflection.* PinchukArtCentre, Kiev, Ukraine. October 6–December 30.

*Le Plaisir au dessin.* Musée des Beaux-Arts de Lyon, Palais Saint-Pierre, Lyon, France. October 12, 2007–January 14, 2008.

*Viva la Muerte!* Kunsthalle Wien, Vienna. October 17, 2007–February 17, 2008.

*La Planta.* Arte Contemporáneo Omnilife, Guadalajara, Mexico. November 10, 2007–February 3, 2008.

**2008** *Re-Imagining Asia.* Haus der Kulturen der Welt, Berlin. March 13–May 18.

*MMKK Länderspiel.* Museum Moderner Kunst Kärnten, Klagenfurt, Austria. May 8–June 29.

*Art Stations: It from Bit.* Art Stations Foundation, Poznan, Poland. May 31–September 30.

*Sand: Memory, Meaning and Metaphor.* The Parrish Art Museum, Southampton, New York. June 29–September 14.

*An Unruly History of the Readymade.* Colección Jumex, Ecatepec, Mexico. September 6, 2008–March 5, 2009.

*Held Together with Water: Art from the Sammlung Verbund.* Istanbul Museum of Modern Art. September 10, 2008–January 11, 2009.

*Knockin' on Heaven's Door.* Kunstmuseum Liechtenstein, Vaduz. September 26, 2008–January 18, 2009.

*Betwixt.* Magasin 3 Stockholm Konsthall. September 27–December 14.

*Mexico: Expected/Unexpected. Collection Isabel & Agustín Coppel.* La Maison Rouge, Paris. October 26, 2008–January 18, 2009. Traveled to: Tenerife Arts Space, Santa Cruz de Tenerife, Canary Islands, Spain. July 10–October 12, 2009.

*Exposición inaugural del nuevo espacio.* kurimanzutto, Mexico City. November 29, 2008–March 21, 2009.

**2009** *Collected Visions, Modern and Contemporary Works from the JP Morgan Chase Art Collection.* The Bronx Museum of the Arts, New York. March 5–May 10.

*The Human Stain.* Centro Galego de Arte Contemporánea, Santiago de Compostela, Spain. March 12–May 3.

*Compass in Hand: Selections from The Judith Rothschild Foundation Contemporary Drawings Collection.* The Museum of Modern Art, New York. April 22, 2009–January 4, 2010.

*Universal Code.* The Power Plant, Toronto. June 12–August 30.

# Selected Bibliography Compiled by Paulina Pobocha

## Artists' Books

*Gabriel Orozco: The Samurai Tree Invariants*. Cologne: Verlag der Buchhandlung Walther König, 2006.

Obrist, Hans Ulrich, ed. *Triunfo de la libertad No. 18, Tlalpan, C.P. 14000*. Stuttgart, Germany: Oktagon Verlag, 1995.

## Books and Exhibition Catalogues

Birnbaum, Daniel. *Chacahua*. Translated by Barbara Hess and Karl Hoffmann. Frankfurt am Main: Portikus, 2000.

Bonami, Francesco, ed. *Supercontemporary: Gabriel Orozco*. Text by Sarah Cosulich Canarutto. Translated by Richard Sadlier. Milan: Mondadori Electa, 2008.

Brown, Gavin. *Real Time: Gabriel Orozco, Rirkrit Tiravanija, Lincoln Tobier, Andrea Zittel*. London: Institute of Contemporary Arts, 1993.

Buchloh, Benjamin H. D. *30/40: A Selection of Forty Artists from the Thirty Years at Marian Goodman Gallery*. Interviews with Marian Goodman by Jean-François Chevrier and Lynne Cooke. New York: Marian Goodman Gallery, 2007.

Debroise, Olivier, ed. *La era de la discrepancia: Arte y cultura visual en México, 1968–1997 The Age of Discrepancies: Art and Visual Culture in Mexico, 1968–1997*. Texts by Olivier Debroise, Tatiana Falcón, Pilar García de Germenos, Vania Macías, Cuauhtémoc Medina, Lourdes Morales, Alejandro Navarrete Cortés, and Álvaro Vázquez Mantecón. Translated by Joëlle Rorive, Ricardo Vinós, and James Oles. Mexico City: Universidad Nacional Autónoma de México/Turner, 2006.

de Zegher, M. Catherine, ed. *Gabriel Orozco*. Texts by Benjamin H. D. Buchloh and Jean Fisher. Translated by Jaime Floréz and Catherine Thys. Kortrijk, The Netherlands: Kanaal Art Foundation, in association with La Vaca Independiente Promoción de Arte y Cultura, Mexico City, and Les Éditions la Chambre, Ghent, Belgium, 1993.

*Gabriel Orozco*. Texts by Benjamin H. D. Buchloh and Bernhard Bürgi. Translated by Benjamin H. D. Buchloh and Catherine Schelbert. Zurich: Kunsthalle Zürich, 1996.

*Gabriel Orozco*. Texts by Benjamin H. D. Buchloh, Abraham Cruzvillegas, Gabriel Kuri, Molly Nesbit, Damián Ortega, and Alma Ruiz. Translated by Chelo Alvarez, Isabelle Marmasse, and Richard Moszka. Los Angeles: The Museum of Contemporary Art; Mexico City: Museo Internacional Rufino Tamayo; Monterrey, Mexico: Museo de Arte Contemporáneo de Monterrey (MARCO), 2000.

*Gabriel Orozco*. Text by João Miguel Fernandes Jorge. Coimbra, Portugal: Centro de Artes Visuais–Encontros de Fotografia, 2003.

*Gabriel Orozco*. Texts by Briony Fer, Benjamin H. D. Buchloh, and Rochelle Steiner. London: Serpentine Gallery; Cologne: Verlag der Buchhandlung Walther König, 2004.

*Gabriel Orozco*. Interview by Guillermo Santamarina. Translated by Laura Suffield. Madrid: Museo Nacional Centro de Arte Reina Sofia, 2005.

*Gabriel Orozco*. Texts by Mercedes Iturbe, Patrick Charpenal, Benjamin H. D. Buchloh, and Yve-Alain Bois. Interview by Briony Fer. Mexico City: Museo del Palacio de Bellas Artes/Turner, 2006.

*Gabriel Orozco*. Texts by Mark Godfrey and Philip Hoare. London: White Cube, 2006.

*Gabriel Orozco: Clinton Is Innocent*. Text by Francesco Bonami and interview by Benjamin H. D. Buchloh. Translated by Dennis Collins. Paris: Musée d'Art Moderne de la Ville de Paris, 1998.

*Gabriel Orozco: Empty Club*. Texts by James Lingwood, Jean Fisher, Mark Haworth-Booth, and Guy Brett. London: Artangel, 1998.

*Gabriel Orozco: Photographs*. Texts by Phyllis D. Rosenzweig and Mia Fineman. Washington, D.C.: Hirshhorn Museum and Sculpture Garden, Smithsonian Institution; Göttingen, Germany: Steidl Publishers, 2004.

*Gabriel Orozco: Photogravity*. Afterword by Ann Temkin. Translations by Jill Corner. Philadelphia: Philadelphia Museum of Art, 1999.

*Gabriel Orozco: Samurai's Tree Invariant*. Texts by Lumita Sabau, Paola Malavassi, and Hubert Beck. Cologne: Verlag der Buchhandlung Walther König, 2006.

*Gabriel Orozco: Trabajo*. Texts by Jean-Pierre Criqui, Angéline Scherf, and Molly Nesbit. Translated by Deke Dusinberre and Jeanne Bouniort. Cologne: Verlag der Buchhandlung Walther König; Paris: Galerie Chantal Crousel, 2003.

González Virgen, Miguel. *Of Games, the Infinite and Worlds: The Work of Gabriel Orozco*. Dublin: The Douglas Hyde Gallery, Trinity College, 2003.

Hoptman, Laura J. "Options 47: Gabriel Orozco." Exhibition brochure. Chicago: Museum of Contemporary Art, 1994.

Macel, Christine. *Time Taken: Time at Work in the Work of Art*. Paris: Monografik Éditions/Musée national d'art moderne, Centre Georges Pompidou, 2008.

*Migrateurs: Gabriel Orozco*. Paris: Musée d'Art Moderne de la Ville de Paris, 1995.

Molesworth, Helen, ed. *Part Object, Part Sculpture*. Texts by Helen Molesworth, Briony Fer, Rosalind E. Krauss, Rachel Haidu, David Joselit, Molly Nesbit, and Lisa Florman. Columbus: Wexner Center for the Arts, The Ohio State University; University Park: The Pennsylvania State University Press, 2005.

Orozco, Gabriel. *Gabriel Orozco en Villa Iris*. Text by Juan Botella. Interviews by Gloria Moure, Ángel Ramos, and Sergio Rubira. Santander, Spain: Fundación Marcelino Botín, 2005.

Sollins, Susan. *Art:21: Art in the Twenty-First Century 2*. New York: Harry N. Abrams, 2003.

Steiner, Rochelle. *Currents 76: Gabriel Orozco*. Saint Louis, Missouri: Saint Louis Art Museum, 1998.

*Textos sobre la obra de Gabriel Orozco*. Prologue by Pablo Soler Frost. Texts by Daniel Birnbaum, Francesco Bonami, Guy Brett, Benjamin H. D. Buchloh, Jean Fisher, Mark Haworth-Booth, James Lingwood, Molly Nesbit, Hans Ulrich Obrist, and Ann Temkin. Translated by Francisco Fenton, Jaime Flórez, Pura López Colomé, Isabelle Marmasse, and Elisa Ramírez. Mexico City: Conaculta; Madrid: Turner, 2005.

van Nieuwenhuyzen, Martijn. *Gabriel Orozco: From Green Glass to Airplane. Recordings*. Amsterdam: Stedelijk Museum/Artimo Foundation, 2001.

Zelevansky, Lynn. *Gabriel Orozco: Projects 41*. New York: The Museum of Modern Art, 1993.

## Articles and Reviews

Amor, Monica. "Gabriel Orozco." *Art Nexus*, no. 23 (January–March 1997): 140–41.

Attias, Laurie. "Gabriel Orozco: Galerie Chantal Crousel." *Artnews* 98, no. 9 (October 1999): 200–01.

Baker, Kenneth. "Gabriel Orozco." *Artnews* 99, no. 8 (September 2000): 176.

Basualdo, Carlos. "Gabriel Orozco: Marian Goodman Gallery." *Artforum* 36, no. 6 (February 1997): 88–89.

Bello, Milagros M. "Gabriel Orozco: Transgressions of Time and Matter"/ "Gabriel Orozco: Transgresiones del tiempo y de la materia." *Arte al Día*, no. 102 (April 2004).

Birnbaum, Daniel. "Gabriel Orozco." *Artforum* 38, no. 9 (May 2000): 41.

———. "Impact and Satori: Instruments of Comprehension—Gabriel Orozco." *Artforum* 40, no. 3 (November 2001): 118–19.

Birnbaum, Daniel, and Gabriel Orozco. "A Thousand Words: Gabriel Orozco Talks about His Recent Films." *Artforum* 36, no. 10 (Summer 1998): 114–15.

Bonami, Francesco. "Gabriel Orozco." *Flash Art* 26, no. 171 (Summer 1993): 93.

———. "Gabriel Orozco: Back in Five Minutes." *Parkett*, no. 48 (December 1996): 40–53.

———. "Gabriel Orozco: La DS." *Flash Art* 27, no. 175 (March–April 1994): 95.

———. "Now Is for Ever, Again." *Tate Etc.*, no. 15 (Spring 2009): 30–37.

———. "Sudden Death: Roughs, Fairways and the Game of Awareness—Gabriel Orozco." *Parachute*, no. 90 (April–June 1998): 26–32.

Boullosa, Carmen. "Gabriel Orozco." *Bomb Magazine*, no. 98 (Winter 2007): 66–73.

Cameron, Dan. "Gabriel Orozco: Marian Goodman Gallery." *Artforum* 33, no. 3 (November 1994): 84.

Carrion Parga, A. "Exposición inaugural." *Arte y Parte*, no. 78 (December 2008–January 2009): 159.

———. "Gabriel Orozco." *Arte y Parte*, no. 66 (December 2006–January 2007): 128.

Chattopadhyay, Collette. "Gabriel Orozco: Museum of Contemporary Art." *Sculpture* 20, no. 1 (January–February 2001): 53.

Cid de León, Oscar. "Llega Orozco a kurimanzutto." *Reforma*, April 24, 2009.

Clothier, Peter. "Gabriel Orozco: Museum of Contemporary Art, Los Angeles." *Artnews* 99, no. 8 (September 2000): 176.

Coles, Alex. "Gabriel Orozco: White Cube Mason's Yard, London." *Art Monthly*, no. 301 (November 2006): 22–23.

Conley, Kevin. "Art of Darkness." *Men's Vogue* (September 2007) pp. 243–49, 262–63.

Cotter, Holland. "Gabriel Orozco: Marian Goodman." *New York Times*, November 11, 2005.

———. "Lines of Loss: Artists Space." *New York Times*, December 12, 1997.

———. "Projects: Gabriel Orozco." *New York Times*, September 10, 1993.

Criqui, Jean-Pierre. "Gabriel Orozco: Galerie Crousel-Robelin/BAMA." *Artforum* 32, no. 7 (March 1994): 95–96.

———. "Like a Rolling Stone: Gabriel Orozco." *Artforum* 34, no. 8 (April 1996): 88–93.

Debroise, Olivier. "Gabriel Orozco en el MoMA." *La Jornada*, September 21, 1993.

Delgado, Monica. "Ve Orozco en Mexico una 'Incultura politica.' " *Reforma*, June 30, 2004, 2.

Dezeuze, Anna. "Gabriel Orozco." *Art Monthly*, no. 279 (September 2004): 35–36.

Dixon, Glenn. "Moments of Insight." *Art on Paper* 9, no. 1 (September–October 2004): 50–53.

Ebony, David. "Improbable Games." *Art in America* 84,

no. 1 (November 1996): 104–05.

"Edition for Parkett: Gabriel Orozco." *Parkett*, no. 48 (December 1996): 80–81.

Fer, Briony. "Sculpture's Orbit: The Art of Gabriel Orozco." *Artforum* 45, no. 3 (November 2006): 262–69.

Fernández-Santos, Elsa. "Gabriel Orozco: Artista." *El País*, February 6, 2005.

Fisher, Jean. "The 'Bride' Stripped Bare. Even so. . . " *Artforum* 31, no. 3 (November 1992): 98–101.

Frerot, Christine. "Gabriel Orozco: Museum of Modern Art of the City of Paris." *Art Nexus*, no. 31 (February–April 1999): 111–12.

Galloway, David. "Berlin/Berlin: Akademie der Künste, Postfuhramt, Kunst-Werk, Berlin." *Artnews* 91, no. 1 (January 1999): 135.

García Canclini, Néstor. "Nacionalismo y arte en la era global." *Reforma*, April 17, 2005.

Gayford, Martin. "New Master of the Mind Game." *Daily Telegraph* (London), June 21, 2004.

Gee, Maggie. "Sculpture." *New Statesman* 125, no. 4293 (July 19, 1996): 40.

Gili, Jaime. "En las calles." *Lapiz* 18, no. 153 (May 1999): 58–61.

Gintz, Claude. "Orozco in Paris." *Parkett*, no. 39 (1994): 10–12.

Goodman, Jonathan. "Gabriel Orozco: Marian Goodman." *Sculpture* 18, no. 6 (July–August 1999): 71–72.

Grant, Simon. "Gabriel Orozco: 50 St. James's Street, London; ICA, London." *Art Monthly*, no. 199 (September 1996): 33–34.

Griffin, Tim. "Gabriel Orozco's Game Gets Real." *Art on Paper* 4, no. 3 (January–February 2000): 51–55.

Grundberg, Andy. "Present Tense: Nine Artists in the Nineties." *Artforum* 36, no. 6 (February 1998): 87.

Gutiérrez, Natalia. "Aprendiendo menos: Biblioteca Luis Angel Arango." *Art Nexus*, no. 41 (August–October 2001): 138–39.

Heartney, Eleanor. "Review of Exhibitions: Gabriel Orozco." *Art in America* 82, no. 11 (November 1994): 122.

Hoare, Philip. "Tattooed Leviathan: Gabriel Orozco's Inscribed Andalusian Whale." *Modern Painters* (October 2006): 68–75.

Hollander, Kurt. "Gabriel Orozco." *Poliester* 5, no. 17 (Winter 1996/1997): 10–15.

Hubbard, Sue. "Where There's Waste, There's Art." *Independent* (London), July 6, 2004.

Hurwitz, Laurie. "Gabriel Orozco." *Art + Auction* (July 2004): 38–42.

Iversen, Margaret. "Readymade, Found Object, Photograph." *Art Journal* 63, no. 2 (Summer 2004): 44–57.

Johnson, Ken. "Gabriel Orozco 'Fear Not.'" *New York Times*, December 21, 2001.

Jones, Kristin M. "Gabriel Orozco: Marian Goodman Gallery, New York." *Frieze*, no. 66 (March 2002).

Joselit, David. "Gabriel Orozco: Museum of Contemporary Art, Los Angeles." *Artforum* 39, no. 1 (September 2000): 173–74.

Kerr, Merrily. "Gabriel Orozco: Marian Goodman." *Flash Art* 37, no. 234 (January–February 2004): 109.

Kimmelman, Michael. "When Meaning Emerges Slowly from Missing Parts." *New York Times*, December 11, 1998.

King, Elaine A. "Washington DC: Gabriel Orozco: Hirshhorn Museum and Sculpture Garden." *Sculpture* 24, no. 5 (June 2005): 67–68.

Knight, Christopher. "Conceptually, It's Not Exactly New." *Los Angeles Times*, June 7, 2000.

Kwon, Miwon. "The Fullness of Empty Containers." *Frieze*, no. 24 (September–October 1995): 54–57.

Lafuente, Pablo. "Gabriel Orozco: Serpentine Gallery." *Flash Art* 37, no. 238 (October 2004): 83.

Lambert-Beatty, Carrie. "Part Object Part Sculpture." *Artforum* 44, no. 6 (February 2006): 203–04.

Lerner, Jesse. "He Ain't Heavy, He's My Heritage: Gabriel Orozco's Photography." *Afterimage* 28, no. 5 (March–April 2001): 13–15.

Levin, Kim. "Trans-Europe Express." *Village Voice*, September 27, 1994.

Maldonado, Guitemie. "Gabriel Orozco: Galerie Chantal Crousel." Translated by Jeanine Herman. *Artforum* 41, no. 9 (May 2003): 178.

Medina, Cuauhtémoc. "Dos clases de eco." *Reforma*, September 28, 2005.

———. "El caso Orozco." *Reforma*, October 25, 2000.

Meyer, James. "Nomads." *Parkett*, no. 49 (May 1997): 205–09.

Miles, Christopher. "Gabriel Orozco." *Art Nexus*, no. 38 (November 2000–January 2001): 44–48.

Molesworth, Helen. "From Dada to Neo-Dada and Back Again." *October*, no. 105 (Summer 2003): 177–81.

Morgan, Jessica. "Circles in the Sand." *Art Review*, no. 54 (December 2003–January 2004): 76–79.

Müggenburg, Norma. "Deja de ser un simple Eco." *Reforma*, September 9, 2005.

Muller, Markus. "Gabriel Orozco." *Art Papers* 23, no. 3 (May–June 1999): 60.

Myers, Terry R. "Gabriel Orozco: Musée d'Art Moderne de la Ville de Paris." *Art/Text*, no. 63 (November 1998–January 1999): 92–93.

Nichols, Matthew Guy. "Gabriel Orozco at Marian Goodman." *Art in America* 92, no. 2 (February 2004): 121.

Obrist, Hans Ulrich. "Interview: Gabriel Orozco." Reprinted in Obrist, *Interviews*. Milan: Charta, 2003, 640–57.

"October Portfolio Three." *October*, no. 119 (Winter 2007): 46–59.

Olmo, Santiago. "Gabriel Orozco: Palacio de Cristal/Museo Nacional Centro de Arte Reina Sofía." *Art Nexus* 3, no. 57 (June–August 2005): 135–36.

"Orozco at the Stedelijk." *Flash Art* 31, no. 198 (January–February 1998): 51.

Orozco, Gabriel, and Molly Nesbit. "Location! Location! Location!" *Trans*, no. 7 (2000): 25–50.

Pérez Soler, Eduardo. "Reflexivo, ironico, posrelacional (Reflective, Ironic, and Post-Relational)." *Lapiz* 20, no. 173 (May 2001): 24–33.

Pollack, Barbara. "Thinking Outside the Box: Gabriel Orozco." *Art News* 100, no. 7 (Summer 2001): 164–67.

Princenthal, Nancy. "Gabriel Orozco at Marian Goodman." *Art in America* 87, no. 7 (July 1999): 88–90.

Ratnam, Niru. "Gabriel Orozco." *Contemporary*, no. 64 (2004): 78–81.

Rehberg, Vivian. "Gabriel Orozco: Galerie Chantal Crousel." *Modern Painters* 19, no. 10 (December 2007–January 2008): 99.

Reindl, Uta M. "Gabriel Orozco." *Kunstforum International*, no. 176 (June–August 2005): 384–86.

Reineck, Ryan. "Gabriel Orozco: New York." *Art Papers* 32, no. 5 (September–October 2008): 66.

Renton, Andrew. "Here Today, Gone Tomorrow." *Evening Standard* (London), June 29, 2004.

Richard, Frances. "Gabriel Orozco: Marian Goodman Gallery." *Artforum* 42, no. 5 (January 2004): 152.

Ritchie, Matthew. "Gabriel Orozco." *Flash Art* 28, no. 180 (January–February 1995): 96.

Roth, Charlene. "Gabriel Orozco: The Museum of Contemporary Art." *New Art Examiner* 28, no. 2 (October 2000): 61.

Saltz, Jerry. "Here and Gone." *Village Voice*, January 5, 1999.

Santamarina, Guillermo. "Gabriel Orozco: Inventar el Enigma." *La Jornada*, July 5, 1990.

Schimmel, Paul. "Unrealized." *Modern Painters* 19, no. 5 (June 2007): 88–99.

Schjeldahl, Peter. "Exquisite Debris: The Transforming Eye of Gabriel Orozco." *New Yorker*, December 3, 2001, pp. 102–04.

———. "The Global Salon: European Extravaganzas." *New Yorker*, July 1, 2002, pp. 94–95.

Schuster, Aaron. "Gabriel Orozco." *Frieze*, no. 113 (March 2008): 194–95

Searle, Adrian. "The Long and the Short of It: Gabriel Orozco Is Hot Property." *Guardian* (London), July 30, 1996.

———. "Lovely Bones." *Guardian* (London), September 28, 2006.

———. "The Player of Games." *Guardian* (London), July 6, 2004.

Seidel, Martin. "Gabriel Orozco: Samurai's Tree Invariant." *Kunstforum International*, no. 183 (December 2006): 334–35.

Siegel, Katy. "Gabriel Orozco: Marian Goodman Gallery." *Artforum* 37, no. 8 (April 1999): 121.

Smith, Roberta. "Gabriel Orozco: Marian Goodman." *New York Times*, November 6, 2003.

Springer, José Manuel. "Gabriel Orozco: Placement, Displacement." *Art Nexus*, no. 25 (July–September 1997): 90–91.

———. "Garbage and Art in Mexico." *Poliester*, no. 3 (Fall 1992): 8–19.

Storr, Robert. "Gabriel Orozco: The Power to Transform." *Art Press*, no. 225 (June 1997): 20–27.

Tibol, Raquel. "Gabriel Orozco se internacionaliza." *Proceso*, September 18, 1993.

Urbach, Marina. "Gabriel Orozco at the MoMA." *Art Nexus*, no. 12 (April–June 1994): 192.

———. "Gabriel Orozco: Marian Goodman." *Art Nexus*, no. 15 (January–March 1995): 140.

Verhagen, Erik. "Gabriel Orozco: Galerie Chantal Crousel." *Art Press*, no. 339 (November 2007): 86.

Ward, David. "Gabriel Orozco New Work: Memos from the Present Moment." *Portfolio Magazine*, no. 24 (1996): 10–15.

Weissman, Terri. "Gabriel Orozco." *Art Nexus* 3, no. 55 (January–March 2005): 166–67.

Zamudio, Raúl. "Gabriel Orozco." *Art Nexus* 4, no. 59 (December 2005–February 2006): 170–71.

———. "Nature Denatured on Gabriel Orozco's 'Recuperated Nature.' " *NY Arts Magazine* 6, no. 7 (July–August 2001): 46–48.

de Zegher, M. Catherine. "The Os of Orozco." *Parkett*, no. 48 (December 1996): 55–67.

# Credits